To you —
a true feminist and sister!
"Enjoy, my friend!"
With love always —
Barb

— April 30, 2001 —

In the
Company
of
Women

To Jan,
a new-found
feminist
and future
L.O.T.T. alum —
with all good wishes,
Rosalie Wahl

August 24, 2000

In the Company of Women

VOICES FROM THE WOMEN'S MOVEMENT

Bonnie Watkins & Nina Rothchild
Foreword by Gloria Steinem

MINNESOTA HISTORICAL SOCIETY PRESS
ST. PAUL

Publication of this book was supported, in part, with funds provided by the
June D. Holmquist Publication Endowment Fund of the Minnesota Historical Society.

Minnesota Historical Society Press
St. Paul Minnesota 55102

Manufactured in the United States of America
10 9 8 7 6 5 4 3 2 1

International Standard Book Number 0-87351-328-2 (cloth)
0-87351-329-0 (paper)

♾ The paper in this publication meets the minimum requirements of the American
National Standard for Information Sciences—Permanence for Printed Library Materials,
ANSI A39.48-1984

Library of Congress Cataloging-in-Publication Data

In the company of women : voices from the women's movement /
Bonnie Watkins and Nina Rothchild.
 p. cm.
 ISBN 0-87351-328-2 (cloth).—ISBN 0-87351-329-0 (paper)
 1. Women—United States—Biography. 2. Women—United States—
History—20th century. 3. Feminism—United States—History—
20th century. I. Watkins, Bonnie, 1950– . II. Rothchild,
Nina, 1930– .
 HQ1412.I47 1966
 305.42'092'273—dc20   96-12276

CONTENTS

PART ONE: BEGINNINGS

PART TWO: SISTERHOODS

FOREWORD

by Gloria Steinem

"The universe is made of stories, not of atoms."
—Muriel Rukeyser

Telling stories is a very old way of birthing and sustaining a movement. It is populist in the true sense of being in the control of the people, being a force that cannot be stopped or dictated from above. It was oral traditions that preserved the cultures of indigenous peoples through centuries of annihilation, "speaking bitterness" that planted the seed of revolution in China after millennia of feudalism, and "testifying" in the African-American churches of the South that began the civil rights movement.

For girls and women, storytelling has a double and triple importance. Because the stories of our lives have been marginalized and ignored by history, and often dismissed and treated as "gossip" within our own cultures and families, female human beings are more likely to be discouraged from telling our stories and from listening to each other with seriousness. We are also the one oppressed group that has no country or physical territory of our own, and thus we have an even greater need for the psychic territory that is created by listening to each other's stories, finding an organic politics in their shared themes, and pursuing a feminist vision of a world *as if everybody mattered.*

I remember going to cover a local abortion hearing as a reporter for *New York* magazine. It was 1969, and New York State was considering liberalizing anti-abortion laws that were still unchallenged by the U.S. Supreme Court. Fourteen men and one nun had been invited to testify on this question in the state legislature, so in protest, a group of feminists convened a public hearing in a church basement in Manhattan. It was the first time in my life that I heard women telling the truth in public about what it was like to risk health, life, and safety in the search for an abortion. Listening to those emotional, rock-bottom, personal truths, I wasn't learning intellectually about the dangers and humiliations of criminalized abortion. Suddenly, I *knew,* for I, too, had had an abortion and told no one. One in three or four American women has had an abortion at some time in her life, even when it was illegal, yet we were supposed to blame ourselves and remain silent. Society needed this shame and silence for the same reason we needed to share our stories with honesty: to create the choice between enshrining or overturning the status quo.

In later years, I thought of that abortion hearing as a light coming on in a dark room. Indeed, it was the beginning of my realization that the position of females was political, not "natural," and that it could be—must be—changed. But looking back, I now realize that I'd heard and even written many feminist insights in the years before that. The problem was that I had listened and written *without consciousness;* that is, without understanding the political importance of such insights or admitting their relevance to my own life. What was different at that abortion hearing was stories told *with consciousness:* with faith in their importance, personally and politically.

As Doris Lessing wrote, "That's what learning is. You suddenly understand something you've understood all your life, but in a new way." To put it another way, learning must travel the distance from head to heart.

In reading the stories in this book, I am reminded once again that the source of the women's movement—like that of all social justice movements—is intensely personal. The rise of feminism was not the result of a think-tank study, a public-opinion poll, or a membership drive; it was not a function of industrialization, poverty, prosperity, or even contraception—all of which may work in favor of or against women, depending on who controls them. Feminism began (and continues) as a movement of individual women, where they live and work, one by one and in twos and threes.

Linda Miller didn't decide to become the first policewoman in her town because of a theory about women's rights to equal representation, or about women's presence as an inhibitor of violence—both of which were strengthened by her action—but because she needed the job and the money. Charlotte Striebel didn't fight for girls' access to athletics because of an academic study on the importance of sports, but because her daughter wanted to be on the swim team. Lurline Baker-Kent didn't want to become a probation officer because she had read about the gendered nature of violence, but because she herself had been at risk. It was not a theoretical premise that led Diane Fass to walk through the front door of a male-only club; it was the irritation of going all the way around to the back.

The work of feminism has always been undertaken by women like these: mostly unknown on the national scene, but active in their neighborhoods, towns, and states. Many of them would not be considered "political" in the narrow, electoral sense of that word, but all are political in the deep sense of relating to power relationships in their daily lives, the reason why the personal *is* political. This modern women's movement has shaped (and been shaped by) shoe-repair workers, nuns, poets, homemakers, bankers, athletes—of every race, class, ethnicity, sexuality, and physical ability—and countless others who have taken action on behalf of women.

Feminists have often been characterized by the media as white, middle class, and privileged. But the first feminists I heard of in the 1960s were working-class women who protested the sex barrier in factory assembly lines in my hometown of Toledo; the first I actually met and worked with were black women on welfare who had analyzed the welfare system as a gigantic husband who kept women at subsistence level, and jealously looked under their beds to make sure there were no other men in their lives. *In the Company of Women* also helps to break this media stereotype by showing us the full range of feminists—young and old, rich and poor, city and country, women of all races and ways of living. One of my favorite lines comes from Toni McNaron: "We've stopped believing that there's any such thing as one kind of woman, one kind of feminism." *What* we choose is less important than *the power to make a choice.* Supporting each other in gaining that power is what feminists do.

I'm also glad to have this book as concrete evidence that the women's movement didn't begin and end in New York or Los Angeles, Washington or San Francisco, just because the nation's media are centered there. Having traveled as an organizer almost every week for the last 25 years, I know that feminist stories are everywhere. Through my long friendship with Koryne Horbal, one of the country's most creative activists, and through my many trips to every part of the state, I've known from the beginning that Minnesota is a special place. Its progressive social climate, openness of political process, and commonsense people have nurtured a strong feminist community.

Like all good art, however, these stories start from a particular place and become universal. The newspaper editor who remembers changing the "society" pages, the factory worker who invents lethal comebacks for the men who harass her, the political candidate who has to prove herself in ways a male equivalent would not—these are stories that could happen anywhere. Indeed, they are continuing to happen as you read this. Women in all parts of the country—and in many other countries—will find themselves in this book.

In the 30 years or so since the beginning of the modern women's movement, new generations have come of age. Young women may have heard of the *Roe v. Wade* decision that finally de-criminalized abortion, yet they have not lived in a time when abortion could only be found by entering a criminal underworld, nor are women of many ages fully aware that poor, young, and geographically isolated women are still often deprived of this right. Younger women may have heard of the Equal Rights Amendment, but they probably know little of the intense and ultimately heartbreaking struggle for its passage, or the reasons why we still need full inclusion in the Constitution. Some customs those of us who were adults in the 1950s and 1960s grew up with—for instance, separate "Help Wanted" ads for women and men, like those for "Colored" and "White" that existed almost as long—may seem incomprehensible now. We also forget that terms like "battered women," "sexual harassment," or "the feminization of poverty" were so nameless and normal that they were just called "life."

Young women rarely have a way of finding out about events that were distorted or left uncovered by the media—moments of personal revelation, the crucial support of small groups of women, and the lives of struggle that were the unseen context of almost every news story—yet they are the wellspring of the women's movement. They are also the messages in this book. But telling women's stories is urgent, not only for the sake of younger women who will be nourished by them, but also for those of us who have been working for decades. There is no better source of renewal than returning to what got most of us started in the first place: the daily lives of individual women, and the support and insight that come from no other process but sharing them.

Among other things, I hope these complex and textured stories will inspire scholars and journalists to consider a simple rule: *People over paper.* Before going to the library for secondary sources, or doing a computer search that colors our thinking forever with the interpretations of others: *Talk to the women who were there.* Activists can also use these stories as sources of tactics, so fewer wheels need to be invented. And this populist history, the most rare and precious variety, may encourage each of us to tell and preserve our stories. As the great feminist historian Gerda Lerner has pointed out—and as Mollie Hoben explains in these pages as she founds a newspaper—the slender record that exists is still interrupted by silences. The most common characteristic of women's history is to be lost and discovered, lost again and rediscovered, lost once more and re-*re*discovered—a process of tragic waste and terrible silences that will continue until women's stories are a full and equal part of the human story.

In the Company of Women affirms the importance of every woman's story. It affirms the power of hearing our own and each other's words unfiltered by interpretation. It reminds us that the shared themes of our experience are the only source of trustworthy politics. And it tells us that we need this book and more like it. Stories create the country of our hearts.

INTRODUCTION

The modern American women's movement seemed to emerge spontaneously in the 1960s. It began at kitchen tables and in company cafeterias, at PTA meetings and in legislative hearing rooms. It happened in the lives of individual women who responded to the messages of the early days: the personal is political, sisterhood is powerful.

In the Company of Women is the story of this movement. The book is not a chronology of names, dates, and events. It is, instead, a history told by those who experienced it in their public and private lives—as artists, explorers, secretaries, and police officers, as housewives, antiwar activists, and women's studies students. The purpose of this book is to illuminate the movement from the perspective of its participants, speaking not in essay form or from the podium, but one-to-one in a quiet room.

Concerned that these stories might be forgotten or lost, we interviewed people who identify themselves as feminists and who have been active in some way. We asked these women how they came to the movement and how it affected their lives, how they felt about it and what they did about it.

Listening to their stories reminds us how the world has changed in 30 years. We heard from middle-aged women who had longed to play sports in high school. We heard that rape victims were once required to ride in the back seat of police cars with their attackers. We heard from a bank officer who was supposed to quit her job when she was pregnant.

We are also reminded of the excitement of the early days, the sense of discovery, the naming of the previously unnamed. A college teacher speaks of "that marvelous, marvelous early period of small support groups—our confessional groups, where we told each other about our lives." A poet says, "I remember vividly reading that first issue of *Ms.* magazine and just being thrilled, overjoyed, that someone was finally telling the truth for us." We are also struck by the significance of large gatherings and marches for many of the women. Recalling a national meeting of the National Organization for Women, one woman reflects, "We forget those conventions, the impact they have. The incredible pride at being a woman, the power and the beauty of gathering with other women."

Our most striking discovery, however, was the continuing strength of the movement. We found feminism alive and well in the 1990s—greatly altered from the late 1960s, but deeply embedded in everyday lives. One woman observes, "I don't know a single feminist from that time who isn't still an ardent feminist. And working. But now a lot of us are working quieter." The heady days of discovery are over for some women, but for others they have just begun. The women's movement has changed how women see themselves, their relationships with men, and what they want for their children.

Between 1991 and 1993 we taped interviews with 127 women. *In the Company of Women* includes excerpts from 76 of these interviews, providing a glimpse of how each person's life was affected by the women's movement. Some stories show what life was like before the movement. Some describe how women set up organizations or services. Others explain the strategies of the activists.

We interviewed women who call themselves feminists and whose words and lives reflect that perspective. For most of them, the meaning of feminism goes well beyond a standard dictionary definition such as "organized activity on behalf of women's rights and interests." A farm woman says of her friends, "Some of them would probably balk at being called feminists. But *I'd* call them feminists. They're strong women, all very much in tune with themselves." A secretary asserts, "If it hadn't been for feminism, some man would be in charge of me. I wouldn't feel as good about myself, as self-assured as I do." Others refer to feminist goals. A peace activist says, "A feminist wants equality, but equality does not mean your share of a rotten pie. You've got to want to make a new pie." Many women in the book believe the women's movement extends beyond what they do to who they are: "Feminism is not a philosophy you just adopt. You become a feminist, all the way through," says one.

We interviewed women who reflect the diversity of the movement. While we did not attempt to provide a statistically representative
sample, we wanted to provide a balance by age, race, class, urban or
rural residence, political and religious affiliation, and sexual orientation.
We also looked for women who were active in issues important to the
movement—abortion, racism and sexism, the Equal Rights Amendment, employment, violence against women, welfare, and child care.
While many interviewees joined the movement in the 1960s, some
came to feminism as recently as the 1990s.

The women we interviewed ranged in age from 21 to 93, although
most were in their forties and fifties. Introductions tell ages and circum-
stances at the time of the interviews. Some of our choices are obvious:
a founder of the nation's first battered women's shelter, the first woman
supreme court justice in Minnesota, and women who helped start the
National Organization for Women and the Women's Political Caucus.
We also chose some women who were less visible: child-care workers,
ministers, physicians, labor activists, journalists, and many others.

Not surprisingly, the majority of the women we interviewed are
white and middle class. Lobbying the legislature, applying for grant
money, filing a lawsuit—these are next to impossible for women engaged in a daily struggle to survive. But women of color, working-class
women, and poor women are active feminists, too. So this book includes, for example, a Chicana beauty-shop owner, a welfare mom who
dreamed of buying an $8 sweatshirt, and a Hmong woman forced to
marry at age 14.

Our interviews averaged about one and one-half hours. We asked
each person for a brief summary of her life: family background, education, employment, current family status. The questioning after that
was open-ended and varied from person to person. We wanted each of
the women to reflect on the meaning and influence of the women's
movement in her own way.

We have edited primarily for length, choosing the most relevant
and unique parts of each interview. We generally used about one-tenth
of each interview. Other than adding brief introductions to provide
context, we have resisted the impulse to analyze these voices. To us, the
stories themselves reveal the women's movement in all its humanity—
rich, humorous, full of detours, eloquently passionate, and incapable of
being fitted neatly into labeled boxes.

The book is organized into two parts. "Beginnings" describes the process women went through as they became feminists, and it includes women who express ties to earlier activists. "Sisterhoods" groups interviews by areas of activity: art, politics, education, law, religion, and health. A glossary at the end of the book lists some organizations and terms mentioned in the interviews.

The women in this book live in Minnesota now. Are their experiences representative of feminism across the United States? Yes and no.

In population, Minnesota is about average, with approximately 4.5 million people. In square miles, it is larger than average. Like most other states, it has a mix of urban and rural people and of agricultural and industrial economies. Its ethnic mix is primarily northern European—German and Scandinavian, English and Irish—although there is more ethnic diversity in metropolitan areas and on northern Minnesota's Iron Range. Unlike many states, more than half the population is concentrated in one place—the Twin Cities metropolitan area of Minneapolis and St. Paul, which includes the state's centers of business and government as well as the main campus of the University of Minnesota.

Along with the other states in the upper Midwest, Minnesota has a tradition of rebellious populism. It is the only state that did not vote for either Ronald Reagan or George Bush. As writer Meridel Le Sueur —herself from a long line of activists—observes, "It is not unusual here that four or five generations have stayed where they were, being dissidents, radicals, mavericks, abolitionists, Red Republicans, and anti-monopolists. These movements have deep and meandering roots like alfalfa."*

The political system in Minnesota is relatively open. Feminists here are more likely than elsewhere to turn to the political parties and the legislative process to accomplish their goals. The Democratic-Farmer-Labor Party (DFL), in particular, provided a base for many of the activists. Minnesota's Human Rights Act (1967) forbade discrimination in educational institutions on the basis of sex before Title IX of the national Higher Education Act required equal opportunity in athletics

* From "The Ancient People and the Newly Come," *Ripening: Selected Work, 1927–1980* (1990).

in 1972, and the state ratified the Equal Rights Amendment in 1973, less than a year after it won congressional approval. Many years later, a fifth woman was appointed to the state supreme court, making Minnesota the first state to have a female majority on its highest court. It is still the only state with a comprehensive pay equity law for both state and local public employees.

The state also has a strong commitment to higher education, and many early feminists focused their activities on college campuses. The first college women's center in the United States was located at the University of Minnesota (1960), and some early feminist organizations, such as the Council for University Women's Progress, were also centered there.

All this has influenced the movement. Political activists in Minnesota are likely to know one another personally and can therefore work together. A predominantly white population makes women of color feel both more and less visible here. A strong Catholic church means that Minnesotans faced the struggle for abortion rights sooner than others.

While the women we interviewed live in Minnesota now, they are a cosmopolitan group. Their stories unfold at the North and South Poles, in the slums of Chicago, in a Yale University physics lab, and in a Bronx jail—as well as in small-town coffee shops, suburban church basements, and downtown banks. The women who contributed to this book have lived in 25 states and 18 foreign countries.

Ultimately, Minnesota women's issues are the same as other American women's issues. Being denied a job or experiencing a rape feels much the same in Boston, Houston, or Minneapolis. The difficulty of being the "other" in a male world and the delight of working together are the same everywhere.

From the earliest days of American history, women had few legal rights. Yet long before the modern women's movement, they made significant and varied contributions to the nation's public life. Women tilled the land, healed the sick, wrote books, made soap and candles, fought slavery, worked in factories, and created institutions to help the poor. They crusaded in the temperance movement and campaigned for the right to vote. Popular images of women include the schoolmarm, the bloomer girl, the Gibson girl, the flapper, the keeper of the home fire, and Rosie the Riveter.

In the 1950s, however, there was more pressure than ever to conform to a single ideal: that of the happy housewife, mother of Dick and Jane. To a large extent, the women's movement came in reaction to that pressure.

Demographic patterns of the '50s and '60s often clashed with the ideal. Though most women continued to marry and have children, their educational levels and labor-force participation rates grew steadily. The development and marketing of the birth-control pill and intrauterine device (IUD) in the late 1950s and early 1960s gave them hope for greater control over childbearing. In addition, women's life expectancy was increasing—a factor likely to influence their thinking about life roles.

Women of the era were segregated, however, into a smaller number of occupations than at the turn of the century, and "women's work" had low status and painfully low pay. A woman who returned to college after her children were grown says, "I don't think women have ever been pushed into such a narrow funnel, in terms of their expectations, as they were at that time."

Historians' analyses of the early years of modern feminism identifies two separate strands: the women's liberation movement and the women's rights movement. Women's liberationists, rooted in the civil rights and antiwar movements of the 1960s, tended to be in their twenties and thirties and were often college students. Many began noticing that the inferior status accorded racial minorities also described their own status as women.

In response, they rebelled against the traditional role of women. Street theater and "zap actions" were common strategies. At the Miss America pageant in 1968, women tossed symbols of the beauty mystique—girdles, bras, false eyelashes, and fashion magazines—into a "freedom trash can." Feminists protested the glorification of women as bland, apolitical consumers and the lack of African-American contestants. The media dubbed this event "bra-burning," although nothing was burned.

Some women's liberation groups were separatist and revolutionary, challenging marriage, motherhood, and other once-sacred institutions. While many Americans considered their actions outrageous, the groups' energy and creativity captured the nation's attention. Their writings were collected in the popular anthology *Sisterhood Is Powerful,* compiled by Robin Morgan and published in 1970. The activism that arose from the women's liberation movement created several enduring Minnesota institutions. The Amazon Bookstore, founded in 1970, is now the oldest feminist bookstore in the U.S., and in 1974, Women's Advocates became the nation's first shelter for battered women.

The women's rights movement, on the other hand, grew out of the state commissions on women and long-established organizations such as business and professional women's clubs, the League of Women Voters, and university faculty groups. Participants tended to be older women—homemakers who had read Betty Friedan's *The Feminine Mystique* (1963) or women who worked outside the home but had otherwise led conventional lives.

Unlike their younger counterparts, women active in the women's rights movement had goals that were more constrained. The purpose of the National Organization for Women (NOW), for example, was and is "to bring women into full participation in society in equal partnership with men." The major national feminist organizations—NOW, founded in 1966, the Women's Equity Action League (WEAL), established in 1968, and the National Women's Political Caucus (NWPC), formed in 1971—were the means to achieve these goals. WEAL's strategies were typical: "education, legislation, litigation."

Defining these historical roots, however, oversimplifies the early days of the movement. Many women that we interviewed did not fit neatly into either category. There were homemakers in the civil rights marches and young protesters who went home to babies and husbands. Women of all sorts wore "Make Policy, Not Coffee" buttons and "Ladies' Sewing Circle and Terrorist Society" T-shirts. Women from both parts of the movement found the early consciousness-raising groups significant in their becoming feminists. Historian Sara Evans has called consciousness-raising "the primary structure of the women's revolt."*

By the mid-1970s the distinctions between women's liberation and women's rights blurred as more and more women came into the move-

* *Personal Politics: The Roots of Women's Liberation in the Civil Rights Movement and the New Left* (1979).

ment. The messages of feminism had spread throughout the nation into small-town living rooms and suburban backyards, into college dormitories and big-city offices. Most often the ideas were passed along informally among neighbors sharing child care, between friends over the telephone, by home-made handouts prepared at kitchen tables, by little traveling bands of women, and at seminars sponsored by YWCAs. The insights and the vocabulary of the women's movement had taken hold.

Throughout the nation and in Minnesota, increasing numbers of women were elected to public office. More and more women entered graduate programs in law, medicine, and business. Schools began to open up athletic opportunities for girls, and women's centers and women's studies programs sprang up on college campuses. Feminist presses, publications, theater and arts groups, and bookstores were established. A women's music industry was born. Women were ordained to lead Protestant and Jewish congregations, while Catholic women started speaking out about their role in the church.

Throughout these years the push for the Equal Rights Amendment (ERA) to the U.S. Constitution and for a woman's right to abortion dominated the feminist agenda. Congress passed the ERA in late 1972, and the decade-long, eventually unsuccessful struggle for ratification by the states began. In 1973 the U.S. Supreme Court ruled in *Roe v. Wade* that women had a constitutional right to abortion. State legislatures, however, continued to pass restrictive requirements, and feminists continued to fight for a woman's right to choose.

The late 1970s and early 1980s saw an explosion of political action and the creation of social services intended to meet the needs of women. In 1977 the government-sponsored National Women's Conference in Houston summarized those needs in a 26-point agenda. In Minnesota, state funding was obtained for family-planning services, battered women's shelters, sexual-assault counseling programs, and displaced homemakers centers. Legislators revised rape and divorce laws and expanded antidiscrimination laws in education and employment. In 1979, more than 30 women's groups came together to form the Minnesota Women's Consortium.

By the mid-1980s many of the means to meet the needs of women had been established in laws and in state agencies, in schools and colleges, and in local social services. With the exception of a few landmark events like the nomination of Geraldine Ferraro as a vice-presidential candidate in 1984, the mainstream women's movement had become institutionalized and no longer front-page news.

The gains, however, did not come without cost. From the earliest days, feminists faced ridicule and outright hostility. Women's liberation was trivialized as "women's lib," and words such as "strident" and "shrill" were applied to any woman who questioned the status quo. In recent years, the word "femi-nazi" carries the same meaning. This stereotype of angry women who oppose "family values" has caused some to avoid associating themselves with the movement. It was and is common to hear women say, "I'm not a feminist, but . . . " and then finish the sentence with support for feminist goals.

In these later years, women began to recognize that discrimination had not disappeared, but was only taking more subtle forms. Women with new law or business degrees found that doors were not really open wide. Those who had moved up quickly in their careers discovered a "glass ceiling." At the other end of the economic scale, the impoverishment of women and children grew. Increased crime rates, a culture of violence, and the widespread availability of pornography made many women recognize their continuing vulnerability. In 1991, the Senate confirmation hearings of Supreme Court Justice Clarence Thomas and the treatment of Anita Hill for her testimony on sexual harassment re-energized the movement. The growing conservative mood of the country and the heightened power of the political Right brought home the fragility of women's gains.

For many early feminists, none of this came as a surprise. They had settled in for the long haul once the high spirits and optimism of the '60s and '70s had worn off. For younger women, particularly those who had taken women's studies courses, the swing to the right brought a new interest in feminism. For women who had been put off by negative media images, there came new understanding. One woman ruefully told us, "I'm your example of a slow comer, a slow learner. Before, I let all those early people like Gloria Steinem do the soldiering for me."

A pervasive myth about the women's movement is that it is a monolith with a rigid party line. In contrast, however, we found that most women discovered feminism on their own and then took some initiative alone or with a small group of friends. A suburban housewife organized coffee parties in local churches to talk about "Women Awakening." A police dispatcher filed a discrimination suit and eventually became the first woman police officer in her community. A secretary learned about a national clerical organization, put a notice in a downtown flyer, and established a local chapter. A single parent housed battered women in her own home before there were any shelters.

When we embarked on this book, we assumed that the stories would start sounding alike. Instead, we found incredible variety. A former prostitute tells of being a "dirty little kid" on the streets of New York, a homemaker laughs about her campaign to stamp out pay toilets, a lesbian comic tells of her attempted suicide, and a nun explains why she chooses to stay in the church.

While the stories we heard varied considerably, we discovered common threads. Many women joked about their naïveté in the early days. Jane Hodgson and Edna Schwartz believed that if they could just explain injustice to the state legislature, something would be done about it quickly. Sara Evans thought a flyer in the *Ladies' Home Journal* would transform society, and Martha Boesing was afraid to go to sleep at night for fear of missing the revolution. But everyone realized sooner or later that change would take longer: "I felt like a bulldog with lockjaw for years," says Sharon Vaughan. "I'd take them on just one meeting at a time, one conference at a time," says Joy Bussert.

For many women, feminism began with their commitments to family: Jeri Rasmussen needed information about thalidomide when she was pregnant, and Choua Lee organized immigrant women to maintain their families' culture while adapting to a new one. Terri Hawthorne planned a Mother's Day mass at her church, and artist Sandra Taylor celebrates traditional homemakers in her work, *Housedress.* Mary Ann Grossmann defends the "proud traditions" of organizations like the Junior League, Hadassah, and the Guild of Catholic Women. Betty Jerome had four children in five years, while Anne Truax had five, Arvonne Fraser and Marion Fogarty each had six, and Carol Connolly had eight.

In our interviews, we observed the importance of the printed word to the spread of feminism. Women's studies students were influenced by classics like Mary Wollstonecraft's *A Vindication of the Rights of*

Woman, published in 1792. Others read *The Feminine Mystique, Sisterhood Is Powerful, The Female Eunuch, Against Our Will, The Second Sex, The Bell Jar,* and *Our Bodies, Ourselves.* Local feminist bookstores and newspapers—such as the Amazon Bookstore, and, later, *The Minnesota Women's Press*—brought feminist thought to an even wider audience.

The stories we heard do not gloss over the disappointments of the women's movement. There have been divisions not only between lesbian and straight women, but also between white women and women of color, and among those who disagreed on strategies. An abortion-rights activist recalls being told her presence would "taint" the ERA campaign, and a lesbian remembers being moved to the last row of a protest march. Some leaders were accused of seeking stardom, and power struggles developed in many organizations.

Yet over and over, women told us about the lasting bonds they formed with other women. Rose Minar draws strength from an "invisible army of women" behind her: "I can envision all these women saying, 'Go for it, Rose!' " Meridel Le Sueur, JoAnn Enos, Laura Waterman Wittstock, and many others treasure their memories of strong mothers, aunts, and grandmothers. Carol Robertshaw and Kate Wulf get goosebumps recalling the exhilaration of conventions and mass marches. Joan Anderson Growe, a suburban legislator with a "pouf-pouf" hairdo, remembers joining forces with Phyllis Kahn, the "radical from the university." Norma Nuessmeier is sustained by lifelong friendships with women who have shared everything from sandbox play to support in widowhood.

The women's movement is more than marches and protests, more than laws passed and services established. It is the story of each woman who participates, with each adding to the whole. What follows are a few of these stories, told by those who saw the world through new eyes and found their lives changed forever.

PART ONE

BEGINNINGS

Roots

Roots are the grounding, the source, the origins. The roots of the women's movement extend into the near and distant past, bringing a sense of connection with women in other times and places.

Roots may be our own mothers and grandmothers, as in the recollections of Meridel Le Sueur. They may be cultural, as in Laura Waterman Wittstock's ties to the matrilineal Seneca nation. Among migrant workers, JoAnn Cardenas Enos explains, survival has always depended upon family members, male and female, supporting each other. Esther Wattenberg's understanding of women and poverty is rooted in a time period, the Great Depression of the 1930s.

For other women, feminism finds fertile ground in the more recent past. Sara Evans, whose experiences typify the "women's liberation" strand of the early women's movement, awakened to feminism in the 1960s while working for civil rights in the South. Edna Schwartz describes her experiences in the "women's rights" strand, including the 1966 conference in Washington, D.C., where the National Organization for Women was formed.

Meridel Le Sueur

Meridel Le Sueur, born in 1900, is often called the voice of the prairie. She has written short stories, poetry, novels, essays, history, biography, and children's books. Throughout her life, she has been part of the radical socialist movement. Her writing was well known nationally in the 1930s and 1940s, disappeared when she was blacklisted during the McCarthy era, and re-emerged in the 1960s. Among her recent works are the novels The Girl *(1978) and* Winter Prairie Woman *(1990). Her daughter Rachel Tilsen, 64, moves around the kitchen where they live and occasionally joins the conversation.*

Meridel: My grandmother was a librarian, she got $10 a week doing that. She never talked. I think I began to write because she never said anything. She had five children, but didn't know anything about sex. She didn't have the slightest idea what it was. I said, "How did you have five children?" And she said, "Oh, I just closed my eyes." She didn't know the names for the sexual parts of men. She had three sons, but she said she just didn't look.

My mother also was conscious of the suffering of women. She had to leave her husband and kidnap her three children out of Texas into Oklahoma. Oklahoma had just become a state and for one year it was a Socialist state, very radical. Women had the vote there, and the socialist movement didn't believe in human beings as property. My father came from Texas to get his property back, his children back. But he couldn't do it in Oklahoma, so he didn't take us back into slavery.

When my mother left my father, she had never earned her living in her life. Eventually she became a lecturer. She had a lecture on "Love and Bread"—that women had to have bread before love. She gave it on the southern Chautauqua circuit, and I'd give anything to have a copy of that. My mother lectured on the vote for women, for a nine-hour workday for women. She spoke on abortion and birth control.

She was tried in Kansas City for giving out birth-control information. The penalty at that time was 99 years. The state had a witness to use against her, a woman who had 14 children. But the woman refused to identify my mother, so that woman served three years in jail. And she gave her 14 children to my mother to raise.

My mother belonged to the Socialist Party, but I don't think the Socialists were very supportive of women. Eugene Debs was the only person I ever heard talk about the freedom of women. The Socialists inherited the old attitudes. Women did the cooking at the picnics. I didn't see any women running things. That's the last thing to go, the male supremacist.

I lived with Emma Goldman in New York for a while. She was a wonderful woman, a friend of my mother's. Emma Goldman was a good lecturer, an impromptu speaker, like my mother. She also did all the cooking for the anarchists. *(Laughs.)* She believed in work.

Rachel: She earned the money, bought the food, came home and cooked it for the anarchist men in that commune. I've always been angry at Emma Goldman that she did that.

Meridel: Yes, the anarchist men just preyed upon the women like that. Anarchist womanizers. Well, you don't change your sex when you become an anarchist, I suppose.

They didn't respect women as leaders. I think the men tried to undermine my mother. The Farmer-Labor Party* had this big women's organization. They were very radical. But the women weren't given any . . . The men just wished they would go away. My mother was fighting that in the last few years of her life. When she ran for the state senate, the men didn't support her. She and another woman, they got an old, old truck and they rattled around campaigning. They spoke in village squares, just the two of them.

In the Farmer-Labor Party, it was the women who organized these little Farmer-Labor clubs in every town, the men didn't. Those clubs educated people on what you could do. They used to meet every

* A populist party in which both Le Sueur and her parents were active.

month, or every two weeks, and they taught each other. They kept
charge of the governor. They didn't just elect him and leave him up
there. They went to see him, they had plans for him. Governor Olson*
didn't like the clubs, he didn't want power over him like that. He was a
leader, an elitist.

But the women pandered to Olson too, his being a handsome man,
a macho man. Even with his mistresses, women were kind of proud of
his conquests, I don't think it was a secret. Women have to fight men.
Farmer-Labor women had to fight men. To keep it going, or to keep it
radical, to keep it educational.

I wanted to be a writer. My mother and my grandmother were
horrified. My grandmother asked me, "How are you going to make a
living trying to be a woman writer?" Well, that was the question to ask.
(Laughs ruefully.)

I didn't know many women writers in 1916. I didn't have writing-
women models, but working women were my models, I didn't have to
have bourgeois women. I didn't have much respect for bourgeois
women anyway. I wrote about women in the mills, women on the
breadlines, Mother Jones.

Being a woman writer was pretty scary, to say the least, if you
wanted to make a living. I wrote in the labor press and the Left press,
even in the McCarthy period. The old magazine *The Masses,* for example, was remarkable, the things they published all during that period.
But they didn't pay you a nickel. I had quite a big working-class audience, even now they still remember stories they read in 1930 in *The
Worker.* I didn't get paid for that either. *(Laughs.)*

I sent a story to *Scribner's* magazine once, "Annunciation," about a
birth. And they wrote back, "You write so beautifully, but we can't
publish anything about *birth.* Our audience can't handle that topic. You
should write more like Hemingway." So I wrote back. I said, "I can't
write like Hemingway, I haven't had the experiences of Hemingway.
Fishing, fighting and fucking are not my major interests."

Women don't have to write like a man, paint like a man. How long
do you think it took me, how many years to write *Winter Prairie*

* Floyd B. Olson, a Farmer-Labor Party governor of Minnesota in the early 1930s.

Woman? For example, the descriptions of the body, that was a struggle to me. Even the ending, the feeding, she feeds the wolves with her body. You probably could have been arrested and hanged at one time for writing like that.

The end of *The Girl*—I should have given her a name when she has a child. A young woman wrote me and suggested that after reading the book. But that in a way is what *The Girl* was about, being a woman. About being a waitress, about being just used or not used. Having a child, this is the first thing she's had of her own.

Your subject matter was part of your struggle. In women's magazines, you could sell stories, but you couldn't write about any of the struggles of women. That's true even now.

In the McCarthy period, my stepfather was blacklisted. I was blacklisted too, couldn't sell any of my writing for 10 years. My mother at one time went door to door selling *Parents* magazine. We had my two brothers in this little house, they didn't have jobs either. One of their wives had a job because she was a beautician. They had beautician women in the stores, selling beauty products. She was the only one in the family who had a job.

At another time, I lived with my husband and his brother and his brother's wife in St. Paul, and I was the only one who had a job. My job was at a bookstore way over in Minneapolis, it took me two hours to get to it on the streetcar, and another two hours to get back. And I got $10 a week at this bookstore. We didn't have any cash for food or anything. I don't know how my sister-in-law was doing it, with her two children. And then she took care of my two children when I was gone on this job.

There used to be a big mill in Minneapolis, they were one of the places that would hire women. It's closed now, it's gone south. But women that worked there were always in trouble too. There was a strike there in 1935. I have such an impression of the struggle of women in that period, to do anything or get anywhere.

I had children, I had to feed them, I had jobs. I always had the problems of a woman. The "women's movement," I call it sometimes, because it seems like they *move.* I like that better than "feminism."

I'm against using power. I don't want to be a feminist to have power over anybody, over men. Let them go ahead, I don't care anything about them.

It's more like yin and yang. One is male and one is female and they change into each other. One doesn't get power over the other. There's no fight between them.

I suffer intimidation all the time. One time I got on a TV program between two great male-supremacist poets. I've known those two men for decades. And here I was, over 50 years old, and I got smaller and smaller and smaller. I was a frightened little girl sitting between these two great mountainous giants. They were talking over me, as men have always done. And pretty soon they were answering the questions that people were asking me. Pretty soon I was nowhere. I was paralyzed. It was like it was in your body.

I was so mad when I left. I promised my body I'd never sit in between two men, I'd never do that to my body again. It seemed like it was in my body, this intimidation. I think we all still have that inferiority. We cover it up. I'm still scared around men, because I know they're going to make me feel inferior.

Rachel: In America they always write as if feminism was invented when Betty Friedan wrote *The Feminine Mystique.* But there were feminists long before that. The suffrage movement. The Women's Christian Temperance Union. The Women's International League for Peace and Freedom. They were feminists.

And that's just in the last century. And don't you think St. Joan of Arc was a feminist? She wanted to be in the army. She was doing things women were not supposed to do. I'm just saying, we don't know who these women were. Cleopatra probably was a feminist. We only know a few names of women in history, but I think they were always there.

They didn't have the communication. You didn't have radios and television and newspapers and telephones. Betty Friedan writes a book and it's immediately all over the world. That didn't used to be true. But people aren't that different now than they always have been. Do you agree, Mother, that there always have been feminists?

Meridel: There always have been women, there always have been women. They had to fight secretly, they had underground sabotage things, always had some struggle. They had to hide it from their husbands, or . . .

The temperance movement of women. I think that's one of the camouflages that women had for their revolt. I'm sure it was my grandmother's camouflage for her revolt.

Oh, there isn't anything to compare to what it was then. You didn't even have a vote! It isn't anything compared to being a woman now. I have grandchildren women, one of them is a lawyer. Women are not as bad off as they were.

Edna L. Schwartz

Edna Schwartz is small, dynamic, and 83. She has been employed all her life: first with the Electrical Workers Union in St. Paul and then with the Electrical Contractors Association. She has always been an active member of Business and Professional Women (BPW). She was appointed by Governor Karl Rolvaag to the state's first Commission on the Status of Women in 1964.

I was on the original Status of Women. Oh, I remember that. That was very exciting. President Kennedy had already established the national commission, and Business and Professional Women—national—sent out a mandate to every state federation that they'd better get a commission on the status of women. Well, we didn't worry about that, we knew we could do that here.

It was 1964 already, and in July the national federation* convention was going to be in Dallas. Every president was supposed to be ready to come up to the platform and say that they had a commission on the status of women. I went to Governor Rolvaag and I said, "We've got to have it by July." Well, you know how those things go. It was this, it was that. I think I cried. I hate women who cry, although I cry very easily. I've got weak eyes. *(Laughs.)* He said, "You can tell them, you can go up and tell them you're going to . . . " I said, "No. I can't do that. I have to have something written up." He said, "No problem, no problem."

So I went of course to Dallas. I had even bought a new dress. It had red and white and blue fringe. It was gorgeous, white with red and blue, to go up there, to announce about Minnesota. But I had nothing to announce. The Minnesota delegation felt pretty bad too. Some of them thought I should go up there anyway, but I knew I couldn't do that.

* National Federation of Business and Professional Women's Clubs.

Then at noontime, they said there's a telegram for me. So I ran into the office and said, "Is there a telegram for me?" Well, it was from Governor Rolvaag. It said that the commission had been established by an executive order. So, that afternoon session, I want you to know, in my fringe dress, I get to go up there all by myself! Minnesota gets to go up there all by themselves and read this telegram from Governor Rolvaag that says we now have a status of women commission. That was pretty exciting.

I was appointed. We had some Democrats, some Republicans, and we really worked. One of the funniest things that happened was when we were trying to get state discrimination laws in, to get "sex" to go along with "racial." Well, they just said, "That's not going to fly. If you put 'sex' in there, you'll lose the whole darn thing."

We took a vote. One person, maybe two, said, "To heck with them, let them lose it." Well, you know you have to compromise. But the funniest part was when the chair got up and said, "Well, we will agree not to have 'sex' this year, but we'll be back next year." Well, of course the paper thought that was . . . *(Laughs.)* She didn't mean it like that, but she was so worked up. So then the paper said, "Commission agrees to give up sex, but Senate doesn't." Well, we got "sex" in eventually.

We never had any money, we had no support, we had nothing. We just begged. We would go out to speak about the Equal Rights Amendment, or equal pay, and we'd get maybe $5. We each pledged that somehow we'd get $25. That wasn't so hard for some people, but for some of the rest of us, $25 was kind of hard. Even $5 was quite a bit then, for a little organization in Ely or Marshall or someplace like that. We used the money for printing, to do the reports.

We had committees. The employment committee, the education committee, the legal committee. I was always employment. We would lobby. Minimum wage law, I lobbied for that. We lobbied for equal pay for equal work.

I can remember at one of the hearings. I always liked lavender, and I had this lavender jersey dress that was pretty snazzy. The weather was terrible the day we were going to testify for equal pay and the Equal Rights Amendment. I drove a Volkswagen then. I've never been a good driver and I knew I couldn't get up there to the capitol—so I came in a taxi.

When I was testifying, they asked me if I felt I could be a truck driver. I said, "If you were stupid enough to hire me as a truck driver, you certainly ought to pay me the same wages. But I couldn't even get my Volkswagen up here today, so I don't think I'd be a good person for you to hire."

The paper said, "Petite woman in lavender dress . . ." I'll *never* forget that. "Petite woman in lavender dress says she doesn't qualify as over-the-road truck driver." You know, they messed it all up. They missed the whole point of it. People who know me have never let me live that down. Would they have said that about a man who testified in a blue suit? No, they wouldn't have said that.

At that same meeting, the chamber of commerce was disputing us. They testified, and they said they represented all the employers in St. Paul. All the employers would have to go out of business if they had equal pay. Well, this woman who owned a business got up and said, "I have to make a correction. You are not speaking for all the employers in St. Paul. You are not speaking for me. You will have my resignation from the chamber by the time you get back to your office." We always loved her for that.

We were so enthused. We were so sure that this was going to solve all the problems, if we could just get everybody to know about all this. We got a lot of coverage. I got clippings, and we got our picture in the paper, oh my goodness. Why, you'd have thought someone like myself was a celebrity. It wasn't until later on that the media got into this joke business. It wasn't until much later, it seems to me, that they began the "Oh, just a bunch of silly women" stuff. We were taken quite seriously.

One reason, I think, was that we were still quite ladylike. I wore white gloves when I testified. I wore a hat when I testified in front of the senate. I did not have jeans and stuff like that. I laugh about that now. When Minnesota ratified the Equal Rights Amendment, it was very exciting, of course. We were so optimistic. There wasn't any question, you know.

I was in Washington as a member of the state commission at the time NOW was formed. I think the Department of Labor or something had invited us. I forget what the issue was, but we wanted to send a telegram to the president. We couldn't send it as members of the commission, because we hadn't any instructions. And there were other commissions who said, "Oh, we couldn't do that. We'd have to go back and talk to our commission."

We said we'd think about it overnight, and we all came to the thought that we'd do a new organization. So we did. We plunked $25 down and we were now a new organization. Then we said, "What are we going to call it?" Well, then we had to sleep another night, because we had to think about that. We came to breakfast then with Betty Friedan, and she suggested calling it the National Organization for Women.

I came back, and I think I got 10, 15 members right off the bat. $25 from each of them because—you see, they did it for me. They didn't know anything about the organization, but they were taking my word for it. These were members of Business and Professional Women, you see.

When the women's movement came along, it felt right to me. I felt all along that somehow we were not equal. But you couldn't expect anyone who was brought up in my generation, with my background, to be—you see, I've never picketed. Naturally never the bra situation, not for a person like me. That kind of upset me. I thought they were pushing too fast.

We were brought up—and in Business and Professional Women—our whole culture said that you bring about change through education and legislation. You knew you had to wait. You knew it wouldn't come overnight. But that doesn't mean that I don't appreciate what was done. It was just that I didn't feel I could be that way. I wish I could have. I would love to be young today, and in the women's movement.

Do you know, one time on the Status of Women we were going to meet at the Minneapolis Athletic Club. Do you realize that women had to go through the kitchen? And Senator Coleman,* as a man, could walk in the front door? Then we all ended up in the same room? I wouldn't do that now. But we were so doggone ladylike.

That's another thing that was hard for women, you know. Men could get off work to do things. They could go to their Kiwanis Club, they could go to a senate hearing. We were always having it happen that the hearing would be set, and we'd get somebody down from out of town. And then they'd postpone it.

It wasn't so hard for me. I worked in St. Paul, and my employer would let me off. I could come back again if I had to. But if we were

* State Senator Nicholas Coleman, a member of the 1964 commission.

going to have a crowd . . . I can remember one time we were going to have a hearing, and it was for equal pay, and there were only four of us there. We saw some tour going through, homemakers going through the capitol, we said, "Lookit, would you come in and sit in this hearing?" So all these women came in and sat down. I don't think they knew what they were doing. *(Laughs.)*

And we had women working for the banks, and insurance people. You really couldn't ask somebody who had a good job, like secretary to the president of a bank or an insurance company, you couldn't ask her to be up there saying insurance companies are unfair to women. They just couldn't do that.

I had relatives who thought there was maybe something wrong with me, because I worked night and day. Saturday, Sunday, evenings. They just didn't understand what it meant to me. But that never bothered me too much. I conformed, you see, I wore the white gloves and the hat. We should have been more aggressive, but that had to come. We really didn't have the courage then.

I was on the St. Paul Ramsey hospital board in 1973, at the time of *Roe v. Wade*. Oh, that was rough during that time. People would call me at midnight. St. Paul Ramsey did abortions, and they wanted it eliminated. They're still trying to eliminate it. *(Laughs.)* Then they said they were going to sue all of us. There was one well-to-do person on the board, I don't remember his name—well, he resigned. But I thought, "Sue! Well, sue me!" I didn't own a house, I didn't have any money, I had only my job—what would be the point? I didn't pay any attention to that.

But those were rough times. People would call and say, "Are you the one who is down there killing babies?" When you live alone, at 11 o'clock at night, it's no fun. And just before a vote, when you have to drive on that slippery highway down there, and then they call you just before you're going to leave. And it's snowing, and everything. I was not used to that. That was one of my worst times. That went on for quite a while, and it wasn't easy.

Did you think of yourself as a feminist at that time?

Oh no, that was much earlier. When I was 14, although I didn't know what the word meant. It happened when I was 14. I'll give you the brief version: My mother always wanted me to have proper shoes, because as a youngster she didn't and had bunions and things. At that time, "ground-grippers" were a high shoe and laced up. I'm sure they were good for your feet, but oh man, they were awful. My mother said, "If you wear these shoes now, you'll have neat ankles. When you get to be a woman." Apparently neat ankles were going to be important. I never found it so, but anyway . . . I was the only one who wore those stupid ground-grippers. I hated them. And for overshoes—we couldn't afford the ground-gripper overshoes, too. So I had to wear overshoes that didn't fit right.

One day while I'm trying to get my overshoe off—oh, those cloakrooms were dark!—some boys get me and they're holding me like this. And Carl, who I liked pretty well—they're pushing him over, and they said he's going to kiss me. I was so scared. I wasn't too sure that you might not have a baby. Because that was what I had heard. And Carl, he didn't want to kiss me either. He was scared too.

So they're holding me, and they're pushing him, and the teacher comes in. She says, "What's going on here?" They all say, "Carl is going to kiss Edna." They never said a thing about my being *held* there. So she says, "Well, go to your seats. Edna, you go to the library." So I sat there and sat there. Then when school's out, she comes in, she talks to me, and tells me what an awful thing I'd done. I didn't know what I'd done. I hadn't done anything. She said, "We can't have things like that going on in school." And I'm crying.

When I get to confirmation class, everyone has told the pastor that Edna was kept after school because she was going to kiss Carl in the cloakroom. So after the lesson, he says, "Edna, you will stay." So he comes over and sits down next to me, and he tells me what a terrible thing I did.

He said, "Do you know the commandments?" I said, "Yes, I do." So he says, "What is the sixth one?" I said, "Thou shalt not commit adultery." He said, "Do you know what that means?" I said, "No, I don't. It's something you're not supposed to do, but I don't know what it is." He went on to tell me how serious this all was, that's how women and girls would get in trouble.

Well, I didn't know what he was talking about. Then he broke my heart by saying, "I'm not going to tell your mother about this because I know how badly she would feel." Well, *I* was going to tell my mother all about it. But I thought I'd better not, if it's going to make her feel so bad.

Right then, I became a feminist. I didn't know what it was, but I knew somehow the treatment was never going to be the same, if you were a girl.

Laura Waterman Wittstock

Laura Wittstock, 55, is president of Migizi Communications, a media production company. Migizi means "eagle" in the Ojibwe language. Her company offices are decorated with Indian paintings, Hmong needlework, photographs of Albert Einstein, and Japanese prints. Laura, wearing a T-shirt and slacks, relaxes behind her spartan desk.

I come from the Seneca nation, which is part of the Iroquois Confederacy, and which is matrilineal still today. You gain your identity not from your father, but from your mother. So I had an unfair advantage over lots of other women, of never having to shed the father domination.

My mother was my role model. At the age of 63, she founded the San Francisco American Indian Center. This was during the relocation period when Indians were being seduced into cities with promises of jobs and training. They were beginning to die in those cities, and families wanted the bodies sent home, but there was no money. So my mother formed a women's sewing group, and they did what they knew how to do. They made beautiful things out of cloth and yarn, then sold them and paid to send the bodies back.

I first identified as a feminist in 1975. I had done an article called "Little White Dove"* about the groupie women who follow male Indian leaders around. Some of them actually were Indians, sad to say, chasing after these men. And a few years earlier, I had been asked to review the draft of *Our Bodies, Ourselves.*** I felt really privileged to do that. I instantly recognized it as an important work. But I didn't really

* A reference to a country-western song in which ill-fated Indian lovers drown trying to reach one another.
** By the Boston Women's Health Book Collective (1973).

see the potential of women until I attended the International Women's Year conference in Mexico City in 1975.

One thing that hit me right between the eyes was, these women from other countries, women of color, thought that Indians had it soft. They didn't separate Indians from the "ugly Americans." We were considered pets of the "ugly Americans" because we lived in the fat country. And there we were in Mexico City, where there are Indian beggars on the street, Indian people starving.

Then I realized that many of these women were high officials in their countries. I was more or less a peasant, and these women were more or less the elite. For them to be talking about Indians in that way, I realized it was a political statement. The northern European women were very educated, they had written numerous books. They were extremely rude, extremely arrogant. Even in those early days, in 1975, the stratification of women was apparent.

But our major themes were very much in agreement: the more "civilization" that occurred, the more the deterioration of women. In earlier times, almost everywhere, the marketplace had been a place for women. But with industrialization, men were taught to drive the big trucks, men were taught agribusiness, and the women were subjugated. Women were made into the childbearers, the beasts of burden, and the prostitutes.

There were 10,000 women at that conference! And despite all the tensions, I recognized the tremendous potential. There actually was a great deal of accommodation that took place, a lot of eagerness to understand one another. In terms of an awakening, I realized then that you have to seek out ways to work with other women. It's not going to come naturally or easily. But the potential is there.

One practical thing that came out of that conference for me was, I never again had a secretary. All that stuff has nothing to do with efficient work. It's everything to do with prejudice and the willingness to enslave others. Unfortunately, as women took over men's roles they also took over men's prejudices, class distinctions like not typing and pretending not to know how to use a copier.

Thirteen years later, in April 1988, I went to the pro-choice rally in Washington, D.C. A million people walking is an intoxicating, rejuvenating experience. I saw all kinds of women there—Indian women, Black women, Asian women, Hispanics, European-Americans. It made me realize that the pro-choice issue isn't only about a woman's right to choose. It's about women being allowed to be human, fighting the power of the elite to call the shots. At times I felt like we were almost angels, transcending the veil of control. Then at other times, I felt we were lab rats—thinking that we have something to express, but that nothing will really change.

We have got to do something about the racial question. Right now, the discussions I've been in, some women are saying, "I didn't cause your pain. I wasn't there when Columbus stepped on the first Indian's neck." On the other hand, women of color need to say what they need to say and they have to be heard. I think there's right on both sides.

There are plenty of women of color who are conservative, who would not share my views at all. But simply by virtue of having color we are manipulated by people in power. They say, "Oh look, we've got women of color and they think thus!" So the rest of us stand outside the window looking in.

The leadership of the national women's organizations has got to change color. They can't play the game of getting a few who have the skin color required, but whose philosophy is so close to that of the leadership that it's indistinguishable. They have got to get people up there who don't agree with them. I don't mean on choice. I mean on strategy.

I've also seen diversity within the European-American culture that isn't getting heard: rural women, older women, farm women. Poor women, those that are on welfare, those that have to struggle with issues like single parenting. Think about welfare people who have to spend hours in their day just maintaining their poverty, standing in line for this, filling out that, answering to the various authorities about your children, and so on. Being poor is a time-consuming job, and getting women in poverty involved in decision-making is very tough.

Some of my views have been considered too radical for native people, which is understandable. Native culture is conservative, that's one of the ironies we have to deal with. You don't have a society that has been around for a hundred thousand years without it being con-

servative. And when something like feminism comes along, it has negative connotations to a people who are used to a thousand years not
being a very long time.

The whole idea of individuals over groups is the idea of the dominant culture. In native communities, it's group over individual. So
feminism is seen as a betrayal. But it's only a problem, it isn't an impossible barrier. It's a problem of, How do you work in the context of
groups to advance women?

There's also what I call the cowboy mentality or the playboy mentality. That is, native groups have readily accepted, without knowing it,
the male domination which comes from the external culture. Now we
have to understand and restore that balance of men and women, because it is out of whack.

For example, there's the treatment of lesbians in native culture. In
the old days, homosexuals of both genders were celebrated throughout
the native cultures. There's almost no record anywhere of them being
persecuted in any way. But now they are outcasts in the community. It's
bad enough to be a woman and be assertive, but to be a lesbian . . . So
that's part of the playboy mentality that has turned Indian culture on
its head. People that were once considered to have unusual abilities,
once cherished by the group, are now being ostracized.

Feminism is very unpopular. To look through the eyes of women
is considered abnormal. So in addition to being a minority as a female
of color, to be a feminist is another way to be a minority. That's a burden that many women of color don't want to take on. Understandably.
It's bad enough as things are, why make it worse?

Sara M. Evans

*At 48, Sara Evans is chair of the history department at the University of
Minnesota, Twin Cities, and the author of* Personal Politics: The Roots of
Women's Liberation in the Civil Rights Movement and the New Left
(1979). She describes herself as "southern, white, activist, feminist."

I grew up in South Carolina, in the segregated South. No one I knew—except my parents—thought segregation was wrong. I went to college at Duke University, where I became involved in civil rights through the Methodist student movement and the YWCA. I spent a summer in Africa in 1964, laying bricks in a work camp, and that was my first interracial experience.

Also in 1964, I read Betty Friedan's book* and I was an instant convert. I was not going to have the "problem that has no name." I was going to do it all. I was going to be Superwoman. And I recall a string of arguments I had that summer in Africa. There were men in my group who were arguing for traditional family relations. They looked forward to having families, wanted a strong intelligent wife who would stay home and have the kids and do a real family thing. There's a sense in which that was a turning point, but I didn't have a label for it.

At Duke, we had this little SDS** group. My role in it was probably enhanced by the fact that Harry, the man I eventually married, was a leader. He'd been arrested seven times in his freshman year. I was also a campus leader, but in more traditional roles. At that time, Duke had a separate women's campus and men's campus, and I was a leader on the women's campus.

In 1965, I went on the Selma-Montgomery march. That was when I called home and said, "I'm going to do this." I was afraid they would take my picture, it would be in the paper, my grandmother would see it and have a heart attack and die, and it would be all my fault. But I did it. I was the only woman with a group of nine men from Duke who drove down.

In 1967 my husband and I moved to Chicago where Harry was enrolled in school. Up until then, I had been somewhat sheltered from the sexism of the New Left. I was more in the religious branch of the civil rights movement. But when we got to Chicago, the campus was incredibly male-dominated. There's where I saw women speak up and the conversation go on as if they had burped or something.

So I was primed for the moment the women's movement came into my life. Somebody came by and said, "There's a group of women been meeting for a month or so, don't you want to come?" I was there, and I don't remember having a moment of doubt about it. It was a real

* *The Feminine Mystique* (1963).
** Students for a Democratic Society, a radical student group.

easy slide. And that's how I fell into one of the very first women's liberation groups in the country, in 1967.

We just called our group "Women's Liberation." Later the groups proliferated rapidly and we had to give names to things, so we called it the "West Side Group." Soon there were other groups and I was going to all of them. That year was incredibly transforming for me. The women's movement became fundamental to my identity.

In that Chicago beginning, I felt part of a national movement. People came through from all over, Chicago was a crossroads. There were people starting women's groups in Washington, Ann Arbor, Toronto, Boston . . . You got a feeling that something very powerful was happening.

The women's movement felt different from the other movements. It had a different kind of intensity, it had a different kind of ownership, it was without question much more personal. I could locate myself within it. The civil rights movement also had a personal link to me as a white southerner, but the women's movement was just part of my identity from the moment I got into it.

We were scrambling around to find what to read. We read Simone de Beauvoir,* and sex-role theory from sociology. But we also were busy writing things ourselves. There were all these pamphlets that got mailed around the country. I remember reading lots and lots of mimeographed pamphlets, some of which were very angry. Some said, "Smash the family." I tended to not like those, but I was aware of why people were feeling so angry, there was a feeling of release. And there were arguments going on among us, what this all meant.

In Chicago the model was a little different than in New York, where I think consciousness-raising was the primary focus. In Chicago, the group I was in was made up of people who already thought of themselves as organizers. Several had been in Mississippi for the Freedom Summers of 1964 and 1965. With that kind of background, our group was less interested in theory than in how to organize. How to get groups started.

We did think of little guerrilla actions, because we did believe if you just gave people the word . . . We'd think, what if we just did a flyer about how ads distort things, and stuck it in the *Ladies Home Journal* on

---

* Author of *The Second Sex* (English ed., 1953).

the newsstand? People would open their *Journal,* see the flyer, and go, Bingo! *(Laughs.)*

We imagined doing little plays in laundromats, where we would be literally doing the laundry and then engage in an argument over who should do the laundry, why do women always do the laundry, shouldn't somebody else do the laundry—bring out the division of labor right there.

That had a big impact on me, that I was with a group of people whose self-image was organizers, not intellectuals. Because I came back to North Carolina thinking of myself as an organizer, thinking of the groups I organized as needing some kind of action or outreach or something. Starting something like the Lollipop Power press, or campaigning for day care and then starting a center.

Becoming a feminist did not mean stopping antiwar and civil rights work. That was an active argument within the movement—what should the relationship be to the Left? Parts of the Left were getting very crazy by that time and exploding themselves. So it was nice to have this other thing that seemed to work and have meaning and made you feel effective, while the male-dominated Left was going a little nuts. Parts of the Left got more and more macho as they got crazy, as people developed a lot of pseudo-military fantasies about what they were doing.

I was never willing to simply walk away from the Left. The war seemed too compelling, we had to oppose it. But it was hard to know how to do it. That's why some of us got involved in founding the New American Movement in the early 1970s. It was an attempt to resolve that dilemma, to allow us to be part of the New Left and also part of the women's movement. The New American Movement had a much stronger feminist presence, a decision to have half the leadership be women. We held a national socialist feminist conference in 1972, which we thought was the first one ever.

We talked a lot about the problem of second-stage organizing. That is, you get together, do consciousness raising, you figure out something for yourselves, but then what do you do? We were very concerned that this not turn into therapy.

But support was important. Throughout my life, I've always felt I needed a support group of other women. I don't know how to live without that. But we didn't want to just exchange ideas. We were about changing the world.

JoAnn Cardenas Enos

I think it was 1964 when I decided that things needed to change. It was through Cesar Chavez,* through the boycott of grapes. My brother got me involved because I can sew. *(Laughs.)* He wanted to know if I would make some Black Eagle flags. Of course you do everything for your brother, right?

That's how I got involved in politics, because the workers were not getting adequate anything. They were being violated in every sense. So I got active in leafletting grocery stores that were selling grapes. My kids were little, and I remember being out there with them in the hot sun, and the police coming—because we were standing on the sidewalk, on property owned by the grocery store.

JoAnn Enos was one of the founders of Casa de Esperanza, the battered women's shelter for Latinas established in St. Paul in 1982. At 49, she now attends school, works for the Urban Coalition, and serves as state Democratic-Farmer-Labor Party secretary.

As a child I played hockey with my brothers, played baseball, climbed trees, I did everything. Of course I'm an Aries, so I definitely don't take any crap from anybody. I do whatever I want to do and have always done it. My mother always told me, "Just because you're a girl doesn't mean you have to push a mop around for the rest of your life."

My mother always told me I was like my grandmother. I don't remember her, but she was very independent, had three daughters like myself and had been married a couple of times like myself. I always recall my mother saying, "I don't know why your grandmother had to marry all those men, she did everything on her own anyway." So I think my grandmother probably was a feminist.

* Head of the United Farm Workers.

My family's roots are in the fields, they were migrant workers. My grandparents were born in Mexico, all four. They came here for sugar beets, except my grandfather on my mother's side who came to work on the railroad. My father was born in Texas and my mother was born in Kansas, but they all came here to the sugar-beet fields. I recall my mother talking about how hard it was to work from sunup to sundown in the fields. It wasn't just a man's thing, it was a side-by-side thing. It was a woman thing *and* a man thing. They had to work to survive.

I never worked in the fields because my parents thought it was important that we assimilate. I don't know if that's right or wrong, but because of the abuse that happened to them, they wanted us to assimilate fast. Spanish was spoken at home, our parents' first language. But we kids never spoke Spanish. My father said, "You're an American, you're born here"—though he was, too—"and I don't want you to grow up and get beat in school for speaking Spanish."

My background has been that women have always worked side by side with men. Men are responsible for the same kinds of things that women are, child-rearing, cooking. My father cooked all the time, he took care of me. I can remember going to school with braids, and one would be coming out the side of my head and the other one would be up here *(laughs)*, because my father didn't really know how to braid my hair to go down. So it was a partnership in my family, and that had a lot to do with why I became a feminist. I was raised to be equal. My brothers and I were always treated the same.

The only division I remember was in cooking tamales. During Christmastime we make tamales. Tamales is an everlasting long thing to do. *(Groans.)* It's not like you can make tamales in an hour. You have 50 pounds of *masa,* the filling. The men usually knead the *masa.* Today it's different, because today the *masa* is kneaded already. But in the old days, the men kneaded the *masa* because you had to have those big old hands to knead that. The women clean the *ojas,* the corn husks, where you put the *masa* after you get it all ready.

If you were small you got a little spoon and you were allowed to smear a little bit of *masa* on the *ojas.* And as you grew up, you would get more and more and more. Usually everybody in the family started out, whether you were male or female, by smearing *ojas.* I noticed last Christmas my grandsons were smearing *masa.* And I can remember my kids—"Ma, how did I do with this one?" "Well, maybe you should put a little more . . . How is your grandpa going to fold that?" *(Laughs.)*

I got married very young, I was 16, and I had my first daughter when I was 18—oh God, young. I was 20 and had three kids age three and under when I divorced their dad. I was a single mom for a long time, but I had a lot of help and support from my family.

In 1964, I had my own beauty shop. As a matter of fact, my name was still on the window there until recently. It was called "JoAnn's High Fashions," can you believe it?

It was really hard for me to get any money. I thought, here I am a single mom, how am I going to . . . I got a $500 loan from a small bank, that one over on East Seventh. I thought $500 was the absolute most money in the whole entire world. So there it was, my business. I had three people working for me and I was doing really good. I was never in the red. I was never making any money, of course, but I had my own business. And I worked at night besides, as a waitress, trying to supplement my income.

As I said before, I started getting real active in people's issues because of Cesar Chavez, and because women would come into the beauty shop and tell me about things that were happening in their lives. Like being abused. That was a real concern of mine, because I was a battered woman. By the time I was working in the beauty shop I was out of the relationship, but that brought me full-circle to what was happening to a lot of women. They'd come in to get their hair done and they'd be bruised and have black eyes. I'd always ask them what happened. I recall a woman who used to come into the beauty shop who ended up getting killed by her husband—who was a police officer. She had been in my beauty shop maybe two weeks before that.

There were all kinds of those dynamics going on and I didn't like it at all. But I felt helpless—I felt like, what can I do to help? How I felt being a young woman, uneducated, I felt worthless. Plus being a woman of color. But I was a caretaker, I took care of everybody always. Women who were all bloody would come live with me, even before shelters. I can remember my mother taking women in, too. And families, too. Eventually I did go and work in a shelter, because I've never forgotten about things that have happened to women in my lifetime.

Because we come from working-class people, we have learned to organize a lot sooner. That's the way Chicanos have always done things, because we were never wanted in our own country, the United States. That's part of my history.

The women's movement—we had already done that in our community. Women in our community had worked with Rosie the Riveter, and worked in the fields back in the 1800s, you know? Fought in the Mexican revolution in 1910—women were already carrying pistols, way back then. So the women's movement here was not like the women's movement I was raised in. We were doing that already.

Esther Wattenberg

Esther Wattenberg, who is in her seventies, was a member of Minnesota's first Commission on the Status of Women in 1964. She was later instrumental in establishing the more permanent Council on the Economic Status of Women in 1976. She teaches social work at the university and calls herself "a loving critic" of the women's movement.

I was born and reared in a western Ontario town in one of the few Jewish families in a very Anglican community. But I was always made to feel that we could bear the brunt of intense anti-Semitism. It was the current of the times—very intense, often quite vicious. But we were given a sense, from our families, that we were the chosen people. I can't tell you, but that brings an enormous amount of inner strength.

I've always had a vivid interest in what happens to poor women. I don't know whether it was because I was a Depression child. I suspect so, although on the surface I grew up in a family that was very middle class. There was terrible suffering in the Depression, it was a searing time. Our next-door neighbor gathered up grass clippings, and made a cream sauce for it, because in those days there was no safety net. She was a widow. I have haunting memories of how terrible it was to be poor. And how terrible it was not to be able to give children what they needed.

It was women who had to head households. In those days they

were widows, of course, because of World War II. And . . . men abandoned families. In very large numbers. We never wanted to recognize
the number of men who just left, and were never heard from again. I
remember a number of my friends who lived in single-parent families,
where there were simply no fathers. It was just common gossip that he
was a drunk, or he hit the rails, that something had happened. It was
not uncommon, although we weren't aware of the single-parent phenomenon in the way we are now.

I think this country is more driven by social-class distinctions than
it's quite willing to recognize. What is of such consuming interest to
poor women doesn't surface terribly much in the women's movement
generally. I think particularly of a terrible law, a really really bad law,
which criminalizes women. We've never had the guts to take it on—
AFDC, Aid to Families with Dependent Children. The relationship of
work and welfare.

You think women aren't going to work to put bread and butter on
their table and a roof over their heads when their grants have lost buying power over the last five years? You think they're not going to work
when they have to buy boots for their kids? You think they're going to
report it? We've got a law that's got 73 pages of regulations, that no one
can understand, and you think they're going to obey it? When nobody
can even tell them what part to obey?

A bad law. We invite corruption. We invite criminalization. So
where is the women's movement on that? That's the life of poor
women—trying to thread their way through really bad laws, and hoping to God they don't get caught. We haven't taken that on. We took
care of the elderly, we took care of the disabled, we took care of widows, but we could never take care of young families.

I think it's associated with race, I think it's deeply racist. We think
it's just young black women who are having babies and are on public
assistance. We don't think there are suburban white women who are
doing it. I just came from a meeting early this morning . . . One could
hardly sit there to hear about what was happening, the overwhelming
needs of young families. They don't have transportation, they don't
have phones.

Can you imagine having two small children and living in a place
where there's no car and there's no phone, and your child is sick? And
you have no health care, and you have to get into the emergency clinic,

and there's no way to do it? And it's three o'clock in the morning? I mean, there were stories . . . I mean, there's a certain kind of terror in which poor people live.

We've never been able to make it vivid, or understandable. There's all this ideological talk amongst women, but can women ever introduce two concepts without being laughed at as being silly and sentimental? What I mean are "love" and "compassion." Can we ever say those words without feeling embarrassed? I don't know.

I regret our incapacity to bridge the social class distinctions. I regret that our solidarity with minority women was always so fragile. That's the limitation, I think, of living in a culture where we're still very individually absorbed. We don't live next door to each other. We all lead quite segregated lives. I live near a low-income housing development, but it would be absolutely fatuous for me to say we have close intimate relationships.

I often think back to the most remarkable thing that occurred. I believe it was in the late '70s, possibly earlier. Saul Alinsky,* toward the end of his career, decided that the promise of a low-income workers' movement to radically transform social institutions was not working. That it was the wrong expectation. That poor people did not have the power we had assumed they had. Indeed, they were so absorbed in their struggles to survive, one couldn't expect them to bear the cost and the emotional investment of social change.

His target then, most interestingly, became middle-class suburban women married, quote, to men of power, unquote. A very interesting event took place at a cocktail fundraising party. There, in this most unlikely setting, we had the appeal being made to well-to-do, middle-class, educated women who had always savored as part of their persona a social-justice theme. But when I think of it, the appeal was made to women who slept with men of power! It just shows you how the culture has changed. I mean, he quite nakedly addressed women as appendages to men. If only they could use their well-known manipulative strategies, they might indeed get some things done!

I think the great gift and legacy of the women's movement was that it changed that culture. Our relationships with men changed forever. We would never go back to the relationship of being, of permit-

* A nationally known community organizer.

ting ourselves, to be victimized and exploited and subservient and so on. The equality of marriage as a healthy partnership has become simply the expectation of how life is to be lived. The women's movement did that. It changed the expectation of how women live their lives, it changed the expectation of the options that are open.

I told you the story, really, because I think you cannot talk about us, and our contributions, and our movements, without relating it to what is called the *zeitgeist,* the spirit of the times. There were a few brave souls who broke loose of that and went to the outer edges, but most of us stayed within the spirit of the times. Pushing at the edge, but still retaining our own sense of propriety. Women of my generation stayed pretty much within the boundaries of, quote, acceptable, unquote, social change.

We assumed, I think, that there was a shared consciousness among very large groups of women about what the goal was, what the strategies should be, and what we ought to do in our political life. That began out of perhaps the naïveté, or the wanting-to-believe phenomenon that occurred in that marvelous, marvelous early period of small support groups—our confessional groups, where we told each other about our lives.

The one I was in was very small, just a few women. Mostly we just laughed a lot. We laughed at what we had tolerated and put up with. And then, in a confessional way, we no longer had the need to tell each other what perfect lives we had. What perfect children we had. How absolutely wonderfully lucky we were. We ripped that away to tell each other that a lot of life was really very anguishing, and full of disappointments.

I can think of one woman who shared with us the fact that her husband was an abusive drunk. And how impermissible it was to let anybody know that. Totally impermissible, and the energy it took never to disclose that. And how much it worried her about whether or not her children would be scarred by those internal domestic horrors that she had to deal with. I mean, before then, women never told each other about that.

We told each other about our children, about terrible things that had happened. And the endless grief, as I have had, of a child who committed suicide. Endless grief, and I could talk to these women about the quality of that incurable wound. At one point, three of us who lost children this way got together, and you know what we did? We put hands together, and we told each other that none of us had experienced a heart breaking before . . . and now we had.

That's the great gift of the women's movement. It changed the culture. It changed institutions—imperfectly, struggling, a lot of work to be done—but it opened the possibilities up. Maybe that's enough.

Awakening

Does the process of becoming a feminist occur suddenly, or is it a gradual dawning? Some of the women we interviewed identified sudden flashes of insight that left them changed. Rose Chaltry-Minar experienced it with a frying pan full of fish in each hand. Angie Flynn was driving home from her therapist's office when she realized that "the answer" was not movie star Robert Redford. Diana Diego's world suddenly made sense when she read a book assigned for a college course on the family.

But for most women understanding came more gradually. Mary Ziegenhagen's activism grew from modest Mother's Mornings Out into the recognition, "This is that women's liberation stuff." For Cecelia Jones, feminist consciousness was not an intellectual process but came from protecting herself and her children from a violent husband. Jane Greathouse tested the men around her, exploring new meanings for friendship, and Margaret Boyer learned about feminism as a VISTA volunteer. Legislator Phyllis Kahn felt a new consciousness in 1973, when six women—an all-time high—entered the state legislature.

Mary Ziegenhagen

Mary Ziegenhagen was out of the United States during most of the 1960s as a Peace Corps volunteer and as the wife of the Peace Corps director in Samoa. She returned to the country in 1970 to find the women's movement in full swing. She was an early co-chair of the Minnesota Women's Political Caucus, started a successful string of suburban newspapers from the basement of her home, and later was the first woman editorial writer for the Minneapolis Star. *She is 55.*

I remember the moment when I changed my mind on abortion. In my medical-records training, and in my work in hospitals, and in my own Catholic background, I had considered abortion a grievous sin. Truly murder. When I was 19, I had quit a job at a hospital because they did therapeutic abortions. I mean, it required three or five doctors' approval and all kinds of medical screening—but they did do them. I quit that job because I couldn't be part of that. It made me physically ill.

Then later, when we were back from Samoa and I was pregnant with our second child, I read in the *Washington Post* a really good, fascinating, long story of four women who had found a way to get illegal abortions and who wound up in the hospital with real injuries and infections. I remember those women's stories, which I read when I was pregnant, as being profoundly moving. It convinced me that we had to get them into hospitals . . . *(Her voice remembers.)* I remember what I was wearing the day that happened, I remember what the light in the room was like . . .

It could be that my feminist consciousness started then. At that time I was extremely interested in what women were doing in the United States, but I'd been out of the country for most of the '60s. I came back, and I was really confused by it. I was interested in what these women were doing, but also frightened by it.

At that time, probably one of the most profound experiences I had was . . . We were new in our house, a new family, just back from overseas. I was very much in the culture of the early '60s. I had on a polyester dress, and I sprayed my hair and teased it. And my sister, who is 10 years younger and was in college, came over with four or five friends to see me.

They wanted to see our house, they wanted to talk about Samoa—they were interested especially in the sexual habits of Samoa. *(Laughs.)* I remember I didn't like them at all. They had long scraggly hair and they wore army boots and they sat on the floor. They didn't use the furniture, which really bothered me. I thought they ought to sit up on chairs.

And then they said "fuck." They said it a lot. I thought, "Who are these terrible people?"—although I thought they were doing really interesting work. They were setting up a health directory of some kind. The next morning, my sister said, "Wasn't that fun last night?" And I said, "I thought it was just awful. Who are these awful people?" My sister and I had a frank talk, with my saying, "Well, it's important to be civilized, it's important to be a lady," and she just took me on.

I realized that if I were in another country, in the Peace Corps, I would be saying, "How curious that the younger women dress differently from their mothers, and talk differently, and their behavior is so changed. What is that about?" I would be much more analytical about it.

Arvonne Fraser* helped me understand what it was all about. There was a story in the Minneapolis paper about her getting together with a group of congressional wives to talk about "this woman thing." I wrote her a letter and said I thought that was so interesting, and I certainly hoped she was including *my* congressman's wife in her group. Arvonne wrote back and said that what she found useful was women, right in their own neighborhoods, just getting together with some others. Saying, "Why not come over and we'll talk about this women's thing?" She said, "If you do it, I'll come and be part of it."

So I did. I got a group of women together—in June or July of

* A founder of the Women's Equity Action League and wife of Congressman Donald M. Fraser. Her story begins on page 75.

1971, I think. I was in a brand new neighborhood in the suburbs, everybody was in brand new houses and most of us were first-time occupants. Most of us had young kids, we had created a baby-sitting cooperative. Just so we could somehow get some time for ourselves. And it was a way to get to know people.

Out of all that, I found a couple of others who were interested. We said, "Gee, we've got to tell more people." We set up a meeting over at the little Lutheran church out here, they seemed to have interesting things going on there. So I asked, "Could we use your hall for something we'll call 'Mother's Morning Out?'" They said yes. So then we went to the Presbyterian church and asked, "Could we have a little seminar for mothers and women? We'll call it 'Women Awakening.'" Yes, sure.

We'd take a coffeepot, and we'd put something in the church newsletter, and we probably had some political lists or something. There was some way we got people to know about it, although there wasn't any community newspaper then. But there was a woman reporter on the county paper, and the first story to appear there about the women's movement was my being interviewed. The headline read, "Mary Ziegenhagen Spearheads Women's Movement in Dakota County." *(Laughs.)*

We had consciousness-raising groups. Various ones got started. I'm not sure I stuck with one very long, there were all kinds of odd little dynamics. I remember one in St. Paul where three of the women would always knit. They would never make eye contact, and that was uncomfortable.

In my own neighborhood, out in the suburbs, there were a couple of ongoing ones. But usually they only lasted five or six times. Then women would more or less decide what they were going to do. Some of them got divorces, some of them went to college, some of them had another baby, some of them ran for school board. They didn't need much. People were ready to move, and all they needed was any teeny little group that would say, "Good for you, go do it."

We read books. We read *Sisterhood Is Powerful*. And I ran off all kinds of copies of "The Politics of Housework,"* and Gloria Steinem essays. That was the format I used most often—to have lots of stuff to hand out that were quick reads that would get people thinking. There

* An essay by Pat Mainardi in *Sisterhood Is Powerful* (1970), Robin Morgan, compiler.

wasn't anything like year-long book groups or anything. I'm not sure we really knew enough about supporting each other. It was a time when women were very much alone.

It was about this same time that Koryne Horbal* had these little panels of women, called the DFL Women's Caucus or something. I went along on those. I remember loving the work because I had generated a talk about the history of women in America. Koryne, when she introduced us, would say, "Now, this isn't any of that women's liberation stuff. We're just talking about women in the DFL. We're just talking about needing our share."

I'd think, "Why does she say this isn't that women's liberation stuff? This *is* that women's liberation stuff." As I think about it, at that stage, there were enough women being safe that I sort of pushed the boundaries a little. I remember once being on television, talking about the Women's Political Caucus, and this charming afternoon interview guy said, "Why, you don't look like one of those women's libbers." And I smiled proudly and said, "Oh, but I *am*." I had little Mark along, this little freckle-faced kid along, so I was purposely trying to say that traditional women in traditional roles have a place in this movement too.

Rose Chaltry-Minar

Rose Chaltry-Minar is 50, a legal secretary. She is curled up on her sofa, wearing a hot pink T-shirt and white painter's pants, nursing a beer. She's a founder of West Side Women, a neighborhood pro-choice group, as well as being active in Women Against Military Madness and president of her neighborhood crime-watch group.

I became a feminist when I was living in the bush in Canada, 200 miles north of Thunder Bay. The only way to get there is by water or by air, there aren't any roads.

I had been corresponding with a man who built a log cabin there.

---

* State Democratic-Farmer-Labor (DFL) Party chairwoman and a founder of the DFL Feminist Caucus. Her story begins on page 222.

It was the end of the '60s in San Francisco and I was turning 30, it was time for me to be making a change in my life. I asked myself, "Can I live like that, in the wilderness, in seclusion?" I got to the bush in the middle of the winter, and didn't see anyone else until ice breakup, four months later.

At the end of my first summer there, some journalists came to interview Wendell as a back-to-the-land person. We were going to have this big fish fry, someone brought all the fish.

I was feeling that I was not the interesting one, and that was okay. However, I found myself doing all the work. And when you're living in the bush, it's not like you're turning switches or anything. It was in the summer when it was hot, and I cooked in the big fireplace.

I remember getting all the water, carrying buckets on my shoulders, making the kindling, bringing in the wood, making the fire, standing over the fire dripping with sweat with two huge frying pans full of fish. While these guys—they were all men, of course—were sitting around the table discussing all these important subjects.

So I was starting to get mad, martyrish. I served the food, and the men were sitting there enjoying the fruits of my labors. There were only enough places around the table for them. So I went and sat down separately, and one of the journalists said, "Come over here and sit." Somehow I said to myself, "I'm never going to do this again—do all the work and then go huddle in the corner, wait for someone to invite me to come and participate in the conversation at my table."

I started feeling the strength of myself as a person. You had to cut down trees and make wood to keep warm, that was how we survived the winter. I had to learn those things. I assumed he would cut the wood and I would cook, but that got old real quick. So then I'd follow him into the woods, I'd take a little hatchet at first. Then later I took the axe, and eventually I could go out and log myself. I got so slim and tough, strong.

A woman canoeist had come through in 1971, she later sent me that book, *The Female Eunuch*.* As soon as I heard about feminism I said, "Oh, yes, that's who I am."

If it hadn't been for feminism, some man would be in charge of me. I wouldn't feel as good about myself, as self-assured, as I do. If

* By Germaine Greer (1970).

something happened to my husband, the last thing that would be necessary for me would be to go out and find a man.

I'm so proud of women when I see them doing activist things. I'm not afraid to take on things any more. You know you've got this invisible army of women behind you. Whenever I had to stand up to a man I felt tall and strong because I felt I wasn't alone. I could envision all these women saying, "Go for it, Rose!"

Angie Flynn

Angie Flynn is a standup comic who often appears at the Dudley Riggs comedy club in Minneapolis where she is part of the show, "What's So Funny About Being Female?" One of her characters is Mother Attila, the dictatorial head of a girls' school—a perfect role for her scrubbed Irish looks. A volunteer at the Minnesota Women's Consortium, she often performs at benefits for women's organizations. She is 43.

We were terribly, terribly Roman Catholic. My oldest sister is Mary Gretchen, the next is Mary Theresa, and I am Mary Angela. *(Laughs.)* In the late '70s I was a housewife and mother, active in my church, a member of the Altar and Rosary Society, a good Republican, and pro-life. I was one of those people who derided "women libbers." I was a person who was doing all the "right" things.

In 1980 it all started to fall apart. I realized I was not what I was pretending to be. This happy Catholic home which I was trying to build was just crumbling around me and we had . . . we had no idea. Bob was a nice guy and I'm a nice woman, we had a beautiful baby, we had a lovely home, he had a good job, we had all the pieces. But we weren't happy. We were miserably unhappy.

Of course, being raised Catholic, I knew it was all my fault. My mom reaffirmed that one time. When I told her we were going to counseling, that Bob and I were trying to straighten out our marriage, she said I could save a passel of money on therapists if I'd just lose some weight and put on some makeup.

It was through individual therapy that came the dawn of what was wrong. I got in touch with the fact that part of the reason our marriage wasn't happy was because I wasn't attracted to men. I was attracted to women. At the age of 30, to come to the realization, and actually state it out loud, I was terrified. I knew I would lose my husband, I was quite sure I was going to lose my baby. She was only two years old at that point. I didn't think they'd let a lesbian keep her children.

My therapist asked me, "In your fantasies, who are you being sexual with?" I just glared at her. I said, "Robert Redford," and stormed out of the session. On the way home, I burst into tears, because I knew it wasn't Robert Redford. Bette Midler, maybe, or Lily Tomlin . . . *(Laughs.)* I could list a number of women. But I was just terrified because my family had made it quite clear that there was just one narrow path you could walk, and that path was definitely heterosexual. I knew what would happen if I came out as a lesbian—I would lose my family of origin, and I was afraid that I would lose my daughter Rachel.

The day after I realized the answer was not Robert Redford, I felt my world was falling apart. If I couldn't keep my daughter, I just didn't see any reason to live. I did indeed attempt suicide and ended up in the hospital in a locked mental health unit.

I was terrified to come out of there, so it became something of a womb. My husband came to see me one time and said, "What the hell is going on here?" And I said, "Well, sit down, Bob, because I have something to tell you." And based on nothing more than my feelings, because I'd never so much as touched a woman, I told him that I thought I was a lesbian. He didn't say much of anything, he just left. But he came back the next day and said, "If the truth be known, I'm a gay man." I said, "Oh, that changes everything, doesn't it?" *(Laughs.)*

Then there was a whole period of anger when I realized he'd known this all along. I had to work through a lot of rage with him. I worked through everything from, "I don't want to lay eyes on you again," to being at a point where we're very good friends. We have a wonderful divorce. We have a much better divorce than a lot of people have marriages. He's a good dad to Rachel, and he's a good friend to me.

He knew he was gay?

He knew all that time. He was going to a therapist at the time. We'd started by joint therapy, but then the therapist suggested that we split up and Bob would go to one therapist and I'd go to another. And the whole time, his therapist was saying, "Tell her. Tell her the truth." Then when I was suicidal, my therapist kept telling his therapist, "Hey, look, you jerk—she's in there ready to off herself because your client will not tell her the truth." It all worked out, but it was a terrible time.

It was during therapy, and then afterwards, I started to get all these lightbulbs going off. I was exploring sexuality, I was exploring feminism, and I was starting to put names to some of these things.

That was a good period of my life, exploring my own values. I didn't toss out everything Mom and Dad taught me. Lots of things they taught me—fidelity, monogamy, honesty, an honest day's work for an honest day's pay, sense of humor, all those things—I kept them. There were lots of things of theirs that I kept, but there were enormous boatloads of junk that I threw out because they had no place in my life.

It also played out the way I thought it would. My relationship with my mom was always strained, because she is very strict, a very traditional Catholic. She is very unbending, everything is black and white. My family of origin has now not spoken to me in about 10 years. And my mom lives just down the street from here.

Did you try to talk to her?

Oh, yeah. And my therapist talked to her and said, "If I gave you the name of some priests who would give you a different perspective on the lesbian lifestyle . . . ?" No, my mother wouldn't hear of it. "If I gave you some books you could read . . . ?" No. My mother wasn't interested. She wouldn't budge.

My sisters were also devastated by this. But what's so scary is, what they disapproved of most strongly was the divorce. They wanted us to stay together. "This is it." "You took a vow before God." I was the first in our family to get a divorce, I was the first to break a lot of rules—not the least of which was going to a therapist and divulging the family secrets.

You just didn't do that. They felt that was a betrayal, and they felt that the divorce meant losing my eternal soul. They couldn't support me and be true to their faith.

It was like a death. Ten years ago, six years ago—it took me a long time to realize that this is just the way it is. That is what I lost. What I gained was an entirely new world. What I gained was worth that. I wish it could be different, but since it can't be different, I'm happy with the choice I made.

One day I got the courage to call Sheila. We'd worked together at the phone company. I said I'd like to have dinner some night and tell her what's been going on. So we got together and it was through her that I got to meet other women—the phone company's a great place to meet women *(laughs)*—and these were women who dressed like you and me, and had the hair like you and me. They spoke with intelligence, with a sense of humor, they were aware and alive. It was really like spring, everything was beginning to blossom.

There was also: how do I forgive myself for 30 years of lying? That was how I saw it. I saw myself as having been really dishonest. I had to forgive myself for that.

I believe human beings can change. Just growth, and reading, devouring every book I could get my hands on, and lightbulbs going off, and my eyes opening. Most of the books I read at that time were coming-out stories. In fact, there was one called *The Coming Out Stories,** in which I saw myself many, many times. There were lots of little Catholic girls in them who went to Catholic schools, in fact they had the hots for several Catholic nuns.

And the books couldn't talk about lesbianism without talking about feminism. One of the authors suggested that you couldn't be a lesbian without being politically active, because the very process of coming out is a political statement. Lesbianism is much more to me than just the attraction to other women.

I think the feminism came as my own self-worth developed. With lesbianism and feminism I discovered how wonderful women can be. How marvelously creative women can be. I hadn't seen that before. I'd seen women as making dinner, and then the men went into the living room, and the women cleaned up. And then the women do the laundry. How insidious, and how subtle it all was.

When I came out as a lesbian, my friends mostly said, "Ummm— so what's your point?" It just didn't make any difference to them. They were more concerned about what was happening with our marriage, or what was going to happen with Rachel. They were very, very supportive. Most of them were straight friends, married couples and so forth, they had the feelings that all friends have with a divorce. You know, "If we have a party, do we invite them both, or do we . . ." It

* Edited by Susan J. Wolfe and Julia P. Stanley (1980).

changes their world, too. And if she goes into the lesbian world, do we ever see her again?

In fact, they have seen me again. But I'm different. There's no question, I'm a different person than I was.

When you talk about the lesbian world, just what do you mean?

Well, the lesbian community is just south of Eagan, it's in a new development, take a left turn . . . Oh, I'd love it, it would be a lot of fun. It's like the straight community, who are they and where are they located? They're really diverse. When I talk about the lesbian community, I'm talking about my network of friends. In our circle of friends, we have a member of the Minnesota Orchestra, a concert pianist, we have realtors, we have doctors and teachers. And they're moms, a lot of them have kids.

When I look over the last 10 years or so, I think the most important thing is learning to like myself. For 30 years I did not like the person I was. She was a phony. Absolutely the best thing that has come out of it is that I have a lot of confidence. There just isn't an obstacle that I can't handle. I have hundreds and thousands of resources that I just didn't know were there before. I have friends I didn't know I had before. I have strengths I didn't know I had before. My friends are my greatest treasure. You know I lost my family of origin, but the family I have developed since then is just a really loving network of people. They accept me for who I am.

If there's one thing I could change, it would be phrases like, "Well, I'm not a feminist, but . . ." and "I'm not a women's libber, but . . ." That really irritates me. What's so terrible about being a feminist? I think the single most evil thing that Reagan and Bush have done is to turn the word "liberal" into something evil, and to turn the word "feminist" into something evil. If there was one thing I'd ask my sister feminists to do, it would be to take the gunpowder out of "lesbian," too. Don't make that such a terrible thing to be called.

My experience has been really positive with feminists. I haven't had one encounter with one women's organization where I haven't felt free to say, "I am Angie, and this is my partner Sheila." My own experience is that they're very accepting. They seem to understand that the essence of feminism is that we accept women where they are.

But I would also like to say one thing about *men*. Men in comedy. And what I think about men dressing up as women. I want this on the record. I want folks to know that I'm deeply offended by—and want us to get beyond—men dressing up as women. Having that be such an instant predictable hilarity. It's been going on for hundreds of years. I wish people, particularly the men who do it, could see how demeaning it is to women.

It's right up there with Amos and Andy. When two white guys get on as two black guys, we just wouldn't accept it. It's demeaning to black people. It makes fun of their lips, and curly hair, and we just wouldn't accept it. So why is it that we still accept men dressing up as women, and it's so funny, it's so goddamn funny, to see these guys demean themselves. It's such a sure laugh-getter. I see it over and over and over again. You see their hairy bow legs sticking out of a skirt, and usually the breasts are enormous, and the lips are fiery red, the wigs are simply dreadful. I wish we could come to a point where there wasn't the constant put-down of women in comedy.

Any regrets?

If I had it to do over again, would I change anything? No, I wouldn't. All the good and all the bad that's happened in my life has happened for a reason. I wouldn't be the same person I am today if all of the things that happened didn't happen, in just the way they happened. There's not a single thing that I'd change. No, at this very moment in time and space I have no regrets. I am who I am.

Diana Diego

Diana Diego, 27, came to Minnesota from California to attend Bethel College, a conservative Baptist school. She is the second in her family of four girls and a boy. Abused as a child, she is still working through problems of depression and a dissociative disorder. She lives alone on Social Security disability.

My family was traditional, very religious, Baptist. My mother's job was to take care of my father, and that was taken very seriously. He doesn't have to get up to get food. He's brought his food. It's pretty sad, but that's been her life. My father's a very angry man, all the time. He'd come home from work, he'd eat, he'd watch TV, he'd go to bed. I don't have much idea of what he's really like . . . It's just, "Stay away from me." Real traditional, real traditional. They would be against everything I do now.

My father wanted a boy. He would not name his daughters. My mother named all of us. Finally he got James. I was in the role of being my father's little boy until James came along. It's amazing, because the moment he was born . . . I mean, it wasn't like he could *do* anything. This little baby, like, "Let's go out and play catch." But I remember from the moment he was born, it was a whole different world. I was 8. I was mowing the lawn with my father up 'til then. I continued to mow the lawn, but alone. From 8 until 13 I was just kind of lost out there. I wasn't anything, I was just wandering around.

When I hit 13, my mother and my older sister decided I needed to be a little lady, and proceeded to educate me on what that meant. It really freaked me out too, because I couldn't do that. High heels, and all that. I was too loud for a girl. Much too active for a girl. I was given a list of things I needed to stop doing. It wasn't too successful, but they tried.

I shut down from the time James was born until I finished high school. Then something clicked and I thought, "I've got to get away from here, I can't survive living like this." I applied to Bethel, a good Christian school, a good *Baptist* school. I pushed my way here. I have no idea to this day how I actually got here. I got here on my knuckles.

I had a professor who taught early childhood, she dealt with family stuff. She went beyond the early childhood training and dealt with what happens in families. We read *Growing Up Free,** and that dealt with how it went from the time you were born . . . as in boy/girl, pink/blue. Everything. That really opened my eyes. Growing up with my father, and his thing about getting a boy, made me ripe for anything like that. It was like, "Feminism? Yes, yes, yes!" I was really ready for that.

I think a feminist is someone who believes in people. Growing up, I felt like I wasn't a person. It was like I couldn't be a person in the church. I couldn't be a person at home. I was not a *male*. To me, that was totally insane. Even though I'd grown up with this abuse that told me all along that I was evil and bad and everything . . . *(Trails off.)* My church and my father saying women aren't as good as men was just to-

* By Letty Cottin Pogrebin (1980).

tally insane to me. I couldn't grasp it. And I couldn't understand how that lined up with the idea of God being a loving God.

As a matter of fact, I'm a flaming feminist. I mean, I'm the "hate-males" kind of feminist. Most aren't. For me, part of it is fear of men. I would much rather be with women. I like being around women, I like the intellectual stimulation. Women are always talking about all kinds of different things. It seems like men are always talking about things like sports, or business.

I think feminism is one of the most empowering things I've ever had in my life. Usually I don't like labels that much, but to me feminism is like empowerment.

I go to the salons of the *Women's Press,* and they keep me alive. There are all kinds of women there. There are college students. There are women who are, like, 80. There's a woman whose main thing is to get rid of high heels. *(Laughs.)* There are women who are lesbians. There are women in long-term marriages. There are women who are in long-term marriages and are considering ending them. So many different people, so many different lives.

When people talk the way they do at salon, about their lives and things, you can learn to have compassion. I've learned more about my mother from going to salons, because there are women there who grew up when she did. Women who've lived the way she lived, and are now living a different way. I think, "God, it's so sad that she's still so trapped in that." But she can't see anything different.

There's a part of feminism that saddens me. In thinking about my mother and my sisters. How they have been so enclosed in a male world and can't see anything else. They can't be anything. They can't believe in themselves. They can't feel worthy of fighting for themselves. I get so sad about that sometimes.

I just want to go to my mother and say, "Come with me. Leave him there. This man is ... *(hesitates)* ... always angry. He's emotionally dangerous. He beats on you every day, telling you you're worthless in one way or another. You don't need that." It's like, "Come and discover this world." It just kills me there's no way for me to do that.

Phyllis Kahn

Phyllis Kahn has been a DFL state legislator representing a section of Minneapolis for more than 20 years. She came into office with the group of women who passed landmark legislation for women's rights in the early and mid-1970s. Small and energetic, she runs marathons, rides her bicycle to work, skis cross-country, and crusades against smoking. She has a Ph.D. in biophysics from Yale and did post-doctoral research at Yale and Princeton. She is 55.

When I came to Minnesota in 1965, I started looking for a job. That was a shock. That was the first time—I mean, I really had very good credentials, very good qualifications. I had recommendations from people tops in their field, and I was just shocked at how uninterested they were. It was kind of overt—it was, "Are you looking for a part-time technician job?" I said, "No." I finally did find someone who agreed to let me apply for a grant, but I wasn't allowed to do it in my own name.

At this time, the women's movement was just starting. I'd always been an activist, someone who marched in antiwar marches, in civil rights. But I was never real active, I'd been too busy taking care of kids and being a scientist. So when the women's movement started, I thought, "Oh, maybe this is the reason I've been having problems."

One of the first things I did concerned a new building being built, a new science building. A couple of us discovered that it had no women's rooms. So another woman and I wrote a paper about it—it was like a scientific paper, a spoof—with tables and data and all that. We showed how women needed more bathrooms than men, not less. We did it as a draft copy, and copies went everywhere. To the president of the university, to the EEOC,* to the congressmen, to the newspaper. The dean wasn't happy, but they did change the building.

* Equal Employment Opportunity Commission.

At about the same time, I was recruited to be a member of a group called Women Against Male Supremacy—WAMS. One of the first campaigns was trying to get rid of the sex-segregated want ads. I plunged into the campaign. I was too late for the group that planned to chain themselves in front of the *Star Tribune*—which would have been fun—but I remember making a linoleum woodcut of the woman's symbol with a fist, and printing it all over the place—on newspapers, on posters.

Remember how the women's movement was very touchy-feely? And nobody had any leadership, and we all did things by consensus? WAMS was like that. There was a meeting about what we should do about the *Star Tribune,* and I said, "Let's just call the publisher at home." I said, "Let's call him and tell him the *New York Times* has changed their want ads." People started discussing this, so I just went to the phone and called him.

As I remember, there was a certain amount of talk that I was misbehaving, that it was not an appropriate way to act. One of the women told her husband, who taught physics, that people thought I was behaving like a man—that I thought like a man, that I wasn't a good participant. Her husband laughed, and said, "I know exactly what Phyllis is doing. It's not that she's thinking like a man. She's thinking like a physicist."

Anyway, the women's movement seemed like a movement just made for me. And as I got more involved in the women's movement, and making more complaints, I filed a complaint not only with the university, but a formal complaint with the EEOC. My situation went from bad to worse. People don't take kindly to you when you do those kinds of things.

One day a friend of mine came into my lab, and said we had to go down and lobby at the legislature. We anointed ourselves as the NOW lobbyists, we went down as the NOW lobbyists and nobody objected. I don't even remember if we asked anybody. In '71, we came down and hung around the legislature. I'd never seen a legislature before, or even thought about one before, but it was fascinating. And you saw how hard it was to change things, to do anything from the outside—from finding a place to park to getting an appointment to see somebody.

In 1972, I had all this energy—so I ran for the legislature myself. Of course that was a redistricting year, and I ended up in a new district, a very good district for a woman. This was an area that had elected women before. Myrtle Cain was elected at the time of suffrage, Alpha Smaby had served two terms, and I was the third. You also had the consciousness of women at the time, which you didn't have before. It was the right year for that campaign, there's no question about it.

There ended up being no endorsement at the DFL convention, but I won the primary. I remember talking to somebody, a reporter I think, who asked, "Why should you be elected?" I said, "I'll make a real difference in the legislature, I'm very different from the others"—and I could see his eyes glazing over. He said, "What do you mean by that?" And I said, "I'm a scientist, and there are no scientists in the legislature." *(Laughs.)*

After getting elected, one of the things that was so wonderful about that session was that everything was so new. First, there were six women, the most ever. And the speaker was wonderful. He really could see—I don't know if at heart he was a feminist, or whether he could see that this was a movement that was coming, and he was going to be in front of it and not chasing it. We don't need to look at motives. He appointed the women to good committees, he gave us lots of good appointments.

People were real helpful. One of the things I remember about that first year was . . . an older Republican man sat here, I sat behind him, Linda Berglin sat next to him, and Joan Growe* sat in front of him. He helped us. He did everything every time we were in trouble in the house. He would write amendments for us, he told us what to say, he told us what to do. He was this wonderful, gentlemanly person—and his obvious assignment was to take care of us. I can remember at one point he was holding his head in his hands, he said he couldn't believe how many rotten things he'd voted for. But he said we were always so serious and working so hard, he couldn't bear to let us down.

In my first session, the bill I worked on hardest was for no-fault divorce. I also worked on some bicycle stuff, and some nuclear stuff. I had a moratorium on nuclear power. Just like now, a lot of bills which all failed. A lot of bills which got a lot of publicity but which all failed. *(Laughs.)*

I started trying to do repeal of laws against prostitution in '74. I

---

* Her story begins on page 227.

think one of my legislative accomplishments in '74 was getting equal penalties for men. When I couldn't get repeal of prostitution, someone suggested, "Why don't you just go for equal penalties? Then if they ever enforce the law and start arresting men, there'll be a real clamor to get rid of it."

One other thing. They used to get up and address the house as "gentlemen." So we had this rotation where one of us would get up and call them to order for "defamatory words in debate." It was nice to have a group of women there because the same person didn't always have to do it. We just alternated. I got up, or Joan did, I think we even had the Republican woman do it. It was nice because we were all so different, you couldn't put us in a box. We had different interests, different backgrounds. You couldn't say this is a stereotype of a woman legislator.

Just the other day I was listening to the radio in the car. It was a program on public radio, on Sunday, and I was driving somewhere. It was on women and science . . . and I actually found myself crying because I wasn't a scientist anymore.

I thought, this is ridiculous, I haven't wanted to do that for 20 years. But it's still there, it still hurts. Most of the time, when I see the people I went to graduate school with, I usually think my life is more interesting, what I'm doing is more fun. But obviously there is still something back there.

I remember when I was in college going to this advanced physics laboratory where you did independent study, where you did some of the wonderful classic experiments in physics. It used a high-energy voltage machine, and I was going into biophysics, so this was something I needed to do to look at the structure of molecules.

I remember going into this guy's office. I remember his saying as he took me into the lab, and giving me this look, "The most important thing for you to remember about this experiment is not to put one finger here and one finger there. If you did, you might be electrocuted." I remember thinking, "Gee, that's weird. What a weird thing to tell a senior physics major, that you don't want 50 kilovolts running through your body." Only 20 years later did I figure it out, that he didn't say that to *everybody* who walked into his office. *(Laughs.)*

Cecelia Jones[*]

My introduction to feminism came from staying at a battered women's shelter 10 years ago. We used to hold meetings every night, group support sessions. One of the advocates . . . *(Trails off.)* I'm not a feeling kind of person, but she was the only one who could make me cry, and this was just by reading poetry about self-esteem.

Cecelia Jones grew up in a working-class family in Chicago. She was elected vice president of her sixth-grade class because she was the smartest girl—and the president position was reserved for a boy. At 46, she's now an office manager.

I dated off and on throughout high school. Never went steady with any guy because marriage was the furthest thing from my mind. I was in love with the Beatles and had every intention of going to England to meet them with my friend, Arlene, right after school. We were both going to find jobs, save our money, and go. Well, Arlene proceeded to get pregnant. She ended up with a shotgun wedding and our dreams went down the tubes. So I embarked on my career as a secretary.

Before I got married, I was still living at home. My father and I used to have lively philosophical discussions over dinner, and on many occasions we agreed to disagree. But that all ended when I got married. One time my father and I got into one of those discussions and my husband walked out, probably because I wasn't paying attention to him.

I was married for 12 and a half years, and left my husband due to domestic violence. I'm really ashamed to say exactly how I got married, because this is embarrassing to me. I met this guy on Monday and I married him on Saturday. I would call it obsession. It was stupid, it was dumb.

* Not her real name.

But at the time it was really romantic. Every waking moment other than being on the job we were together. It was nothing I had ever experienced before in my life. I should have just let it play for a while *(laughs)* instead of rushing into this. It wasn't that I was starved for male affection, I had these other guys out here. I don't know what happened—hormones, I guess—that's it.

He had strong opinions about women's role. I can remember cleaning the house once and honest to God, I swear he would find dust that wasn't there. He'd say, "I hate this, it's dirty"—yeah, right. He got me where he wanted me, I was right there.

We were married 12 years, had three kids. I was a tough cookie, and I thought, "Aaah, I'm pretty stubborn too." Maybe the Polish in me— I see it in my kids now. But I decided I'm going to ride this out no matter what, I'm going to be the best wife there has ever been. It was my personal goal.

I'd say a month and a half after we were married, actually while we were still living with my parents, a fight started where he figured he wasn't getting enough sleep or some BS like that. It was too noisy, he said, and he . . . *(hits her cheek)*. So he leaves, and I got mad. Right after that I got into this discussion with my mother about marriage, and I took my ring off and just threw it. My mother said, "Hey, you can't do that, you just got married." Okay, we all made up.

Then we moved out of my parents' house and into an old apartment building. We got into an argument about—I was working. I felt I was entitled to my check, or some of it anyway, and he felt otherwise. He thinks he gets the whole kit and caboodle. Well it ended up . . . *(whooshing noise)* . . . that's how it ended up. So we got into this physical battle, and I used to fight with my sisters, so no big deal, right? But he got me down to the floor—I was okay up until then—and he got my head and pounded it on the floor four or five times, and then I thought, "I cannot fight this person. There is no way I am going to win."

And of course in a typical battering situation, after the fight they promise you the stars, take you to dinner, buy you things, promise they'll never do it again. And I always lived with this hope that, hey, maybe . . . I still had that personal goal of being the best wife ever so the man would have no reason to complain, but after 12 years . . . it wasn't constant, but . . .

The first time I actually left him, that night he came in—he was drunk, and he was accusing me of having sex with his best friend. Come on, give me a break, I'm really a femme fatale seducing guys all the time—I mean, I've got three children! And he's accusing me of all this from three years ago or something, bizarre. So he socks me. I have a scar to this day right here where my eyebrow split wide open.

The man who lived downstairs from us was up here while all this was going on. Everybody was terrified of my husband, he was big. That guy wasn't going to say anything or do anything. Here I am, just dripping blood, and I had to sit there and listen to all this BS about how I cheated on him. So finally I said, "Listen, I have to go to the hospital, this won't stop bleeding," so this guy from downstairs took me to the hospital.

He left me in the emergency room, and I of course lied to the doctor. They stitched me up, and I got on a bus and I rode most all night long around town, thinking, "What am I going to do?" So I called my friend Amy. She's the one who told me about this shelter, so I called them and went in. And the next day I decided, I want my children. So I called the police and they sent an escort to my house. He had the next-door neighbor watching my children. So we put some clothes in a garbage bag, and we went back to the shelter.

One of the rules in the shelter, which I think is a good one, is do not have any contact with him. Because if you do, everybody has regrets, everybody is sorry, everybody has promises, "Never again, never again." But after three days I called him. "Can you at least meet me?" he says, "for a hamburger or something, with the kids?" He was crying, I was crying, everyone was crying. So I met him, and I just never went back to the shelter. Life was fine, life was good for a while.

One night in 1983 I decided I couldn't take it anymore. The straw that broke the camel's back was when he took my daughter by her ponytail and threw her. She was 11, my oldest. The day before, she had made her first communion, and I went to church with a black eye, and my father was in church. My father said, "What happened here?" "Ah, I fell into the coffee table." Yeah, right. So I'm supposed to take care of the coffee afterward, I've got this party going, right? It was terrible, my youngest child was scared to death of me when she saw that black eye, even to this day she'll talk about how it was "fuzzy." She was scared to death of me, my own child.

I can recall him using a belt on my son one other time, when he was four and had been playing in the street. But up until that point when he did that to my daughter, other than that he didn't physically hurt them or sexually abuse them. But that day . . .

I could always tell when something was going to come down, I don't know if it was intuition or what. I would be extremely physically nervous, and get into diarrhea, before any of this would happen. My body would tell me this is going to happen. And all day long on that last day I had this feeling. I was terrified. I called my parents and I said, "I want to take the train, I'm coming to see you." But then the day before I was going to go to them, this happened.

He threw Judy. Then he says to her, "Oh, go out and play in the freeway." So she walks out the door. This is like 10 o'clock, 11 o'clock at night. I went after her. Her and I, we ran down the block together and cut through somebody's yard, down the alley to Amy's house. I said, "Amy, please keep Judy here. I have to get out of here." So from Amy's house I called the police. When I called the police, they said, "We'll meet you at your house." I said, "Are you crazy? This man is extremely angry."

Finally, when they did show up, it was an hour later, at Amy's house. Then we all went to the building, and my husband was lying on the couch like nothing happened. Carol was out there eating watermelon, I'll never forget this. (Laughs.) On the coffee table this seven-year-old kid has got this humongous slice of watermelon. Mark was in his room with the door closed. My husband said to me, "What's this?" I said, "I'm going to take my kids and I'm leaving." He said, "Oh fine, what are you going to do about the truck, what are you going to do about the car?" Big important things, right? I said, "I'll sign them over, I don't care."

So I'm glad he did that, because I grabbed all the papers together with birth certificates and all that. I took the title to the car that I had, and I gave him the damn titles that he wanted. As we're going out the door he's screaming and yelling, making all kinds of threats to me, to my parents. The police are saying, "Don't say this, she has witnesses. If anything happens to her parents, we'll know who did it."

I got in the car with my kids and I thought, okay, now what? Where do I go, what do I do? I was not going to go to my family's, because I knew he'd go there first. So I just hit Highway 94 west. I thought, okay, there's some big cities this way, maybe I can find a job. The first city I came to of any size was Madison. It was July but it was kind of cool out. I had brought eight sweaters for my kids. They were 11, 10, and 7 years old then. So I hit a phone booth and asked for directions to the women's shelter.

Later on, finding an apartment was a little difficult because I had no references. But I lucked out and found a place. I met the landlady, and she was sympathetic to my plight. I found out later it's probably because she was in the same situation.

Even after we got to Madison, I was terrified he would find me. It was terrible. I had to cut it off even with my parents for a while, because he might find me. And even after I left, my parents would have to call the FBI because there were threats, and I didn't want to endanger them.

Now every once in a while I still get paranoid, but for the most part I'm not. I don't have any regrets about leaving him—oh heavens no. Never did have.

I keep hoping for the day when a letter comes that says he's dead.

Margaret Boyer

Margaret Boyer's one-person office in Minneapolis is a hole-in-the-wall stocked with coffee mugs left over from fundraisers and with pamphlets from child-care studies. Margaret has an unassuming manner, but legislators that she has lobbied know that she never, ever gives up. She is 44 and has been working on child-care issues for 21 years.

I grew up in western Pennsylvania on a small farm. My claim to fame was that I was the first girl born in 50 years in the Boyer family. My father was a farmer, and he worked in a steel mill, so he had two full-time jobs. Except he was laid off a lot. We were a poor family.

I had a hard childhood. Part of it was my personality. I was definitely one of those overly sensitive kids. When my dad would kill a cow, I would run up to my bedroom and put my head under a pillow and start singing and holding my ears. But I would still hear that sledgehammer hitting the cow over the head and that shot. Whenever they killed chickens I would enslave myself to my mother, promise to do all the dishes and clean the house for a week, if I didn't have to help kill the chickens.

My father and I had a tumultuous relationship. I suppose he would be considered abusive today. But it was the time where people felt comfortable disciplining their kids by hitting them a lot. They felt like they had to break your spirit. And my mother tells me that she does not know anyone more stubborn than I was. Instead of breaking my spirit, my dad just made me more stubborn.

In some ways it was good, too. I loved living on a farm. My dad did too. He would take us on walks, he knew every single tree on our farm, he would go show us these special trees. We lived on top of this small worn-down mountain. We'd wake up in the morning and there would be fog all around us, and it would look like we lived on an island. Our land had two veins of coal under it, so my dad could have stripped it and been rich. But he loved that land so much that he never did strip it. Instead he worked really hard, struggled to make a living.

My mother was from a farm family. She had nine brothers and sisters. My grandfather owned the farm over the hill and my uncle lived two farms away. The whole county was our relatives. I liked that—we had like 50 cousins. So we had lots of family reunions, or people coming over to share farm work. My mother was a great cook and a great canner, a great sewer, one of those farm women. My grandmother, her mother, had been in the women's temperance union. She was one of those bar-smashers.

I was always a little mad at my mother for not protecting me from my father. I definitely grew up in a very patriarchal family. My mother was not the secret power behind the man. She accepted my father as the boss, which was really frustrating to me. I learned from both my parents, you should always speak up for what you thought was right. I would in my family, knowing that I might get hit for doing it. But I still would do it because it was valued.

I was the first Boyer to ever go to college. The way I picked my college was, I looked in the catalog for the cheapest school there was. Slippery Rock State College, I remember it cost a thousand dollars a year for room and board and tuition and books.

I loved college. It was so much fun to be away from home. I found people like me who were kind of naïve, we hung around together and had fun. We short-sheeted each other's beds. Some people I know now were smoking dope then, but I didn't even know dope existed.

I remember a speech class, we had to pick a controversial subject to learn debating techniques, so the teacher assigned abortion. I had never heard of abortion before. I assumed I would be against it, and I signed up for that side. But after reading about women mutilating themselves and being mutilated, after debating it, I decided I supported the right to have an abortion.

I often get really nervous before I talk, but once I start I feel so strongly, I lose my self. My voice has always been an issue for me. Especially men, they have said my voice is like a little-girl voice, and discount it. I've had other people tell me that because my voice contrasts so much with the content that it's more powerful. I've thought about taking voice lessons. *(Laughs, embarrassed.)* I have a soft voice and I'm not afraid to say hard things. If that makes the message more powerful, that's good.

After college I joined VISTA,* and I was sent to Chicago for VISTA training. All these people were saying "fuck." I had never known anyone in my life who said that, except somebody had carved it in one of the outhouses, and I didn't know what it meant. And I was really shocked to know that women weren't virgins, that they had lovers without being married.

I had always been this real patriotic person. I was the one who every morning put the flag up in our family's house, and I would reverently take it down every evening. I knew that politicians were corrupt and that presidents kind of came and went. But I always thought that with the balance of power—that was sacred. I was always so glad we have this check-and-balance system, and I always thought judges were wonderful.

Well, one of the things we had to do in VISTA training was go to a courtroom and observe. When I went, this judge was setting bail. First of all, I was surprised that all the people coming up were black. Then there was one man with a policeman on each side holding his wrists. He just moved his arms, broke their grip, and said, "I want to stand alone."

* Volunteers in Service to America, a government-sponsored organization.

I thought that was a proud thing for him to do. But about 20 policemen that were sitting around in the court, they all got up and started beating him with clubs, right in front of that judge. They dragged him to another room. You could hear him yelling. They were beating him, and that judge didn't say anything. I got up, and I started yelling at the judge because I was taught you should stand up for what is right. The other VISTAs dragged me out of there because they were afraid I was going to land up in jail. I was saying, "You can't do this. It isn't fair."

It was like my whole world just shattered that day. I felt like, what can I believe in now in the United States? It was so obvious that black people weren't being treated fairly, and that the justice system which was supposed to be the final check wasn't working.

In 1971, after training, we stayed with welfare mothers for six weeks, to learn about poverty. But my welfare mother was richer than *our* family ever was. All the other VISTAs were from upper-middle-income families. Here I was living with and organizing people who had more or the same amount of money that I grew up with. But in some ways I had never felt poor, because everyone around us was the same. Anyway, to me it looked really rich.

They called me the "virgin VISTA" because I was really naïve. As far as being poor, I wasn't naïve, I knew more about that than a lot of the others. But as far as swearing and the Vietnam War, I knew a lot less than other people.

People from our VISTA group started the health clinics, the tenant union, child-care programs, and some of the people kept an old neighborhood from being torn down, turned it into a thriving neighborhood. We felt like we could change the world. It's really fun to get together now and look around and see the impact our VISTA had.

That's when I learned about feminism and the Vietnam War. My roommates went to the March on Washington, and I went with them. My family's response was, "If we see you on television, we don't want to ever see you again." It was hard because my cousin was over there as a Marine, and he was killed. They felt what I was doing made his death meaningless.

Later on, in Minneapolis, there was this Southside Ministries—a man who ministered on the street. He had a group of parents that met once a week, and they needed someone to do child care. That's what I started doing. Later, the parents decided they would like a nursery school, so then I organized a nursery school and got it licensed. Then the parents decided they would like a full day-care program. So I did that. And that's how I got into child-care issues.

One reason I love pay equity as a feminist issue is that I've always felt like feminists only wanted to open up typically male jobs for women. They wanted to be lawyers and CEOs and plumbers and electricians. I think that's great, but for that to be the main thrust of feminism, it puts women far behind. I felt like they didn't value typical women's work. I wrote a letter years ago, about feminism needing to value typically women's work, like child care.

I've been in this women's group, I think it's been 16 years or something. We just talk about, what is feminism and what is our job as a woman. It started out as consciousness-raising—we'd read books and have discussions. We helped one woman out of an abusive relationship, and now she's a CEO. We helped another woman through a nervous breakdown, and now she's a really good lawyer. So there's a lawyer and a CEO and a psychologist, and I've been the child-care person. All these years, they were making huge salaries, and I was still struggling as a child-care person. Pay equity is important.

I wrote this grant proposal with an Indian woman to train 10 women of color to become head teachers in child-care centers. But as soon as they were trained, they could have any job they wanted in public schools. Child care pays shit wages, so they left the field. In some ways it was good because here's 10 more women of color who have good training who are working with kids, but it's not in child care. And that's where little kids are all day.

Behind every working parent is an underpaid child-care worker. We used to have that on a button. *(Laughs.)*

Jane Greathouse

Jane Greathouse is in her early twenties. A recent graduate of St. Olaf College, she is now working as a waitress, doing volunteer work for the Older Women's League, and trying to decide what she wants out of life. She came to feminism through her college women's studies classes.

Identifying myself as a feminist changed everything, from my physical looks to the people I choose to hang out with. I don't shave my legs and that totally weeds out a lot of people *(grins)* . . . because they just can't deal with it. I wasn't sure at first if I wanted to weed people out, but I don't mind it anymore. I like the people who are my friends.

I can't be friends with the men who are blatantly sexist and will not listen to a thing you say. They're not worth my time. I don't apologize for it, and I'm never going to feel bad because they don't fit into my scheme. That's too bad for them.

The women friends and men friends that feel the same way I do, that's wonderful. And people that don't feel the same way I do, I don't try to cram anything down their throat. But if they care about who I am and listen to me, maybe their ideas will change.

My parents were "good Democrats," you know. But they wanted us to be our own people. When I was in high school, I kind of became a radical, shaved my head and bleached my hair and all that. It was really hard for my parents. My mom wanted me to go to the prom and be normal and have a boyfriend. Now my mom is proud of who I've become.

When I first became a feminist, I cut down homemaking and taking care of children. It hurt my mom a lot. Now that I've got my head on straight, I realize what a wonderful thing she did for me, what a wonderful occupation that is. I respect her now more than I ever have. I think a lot of young feminists are learning that.

When I was in college, at first, I wasn't as articulate because I was just learning about things. So I'd find myself getting into a lot of arguments with men and not understanding how to argue. Because women don't know how to argue—we're not taught how to argue within the male system of argument or the male understanding of it. So I'd just get myself really angry and these men would just be like, "You don't know what you're talking about." And these were my considerate, sensitive, New Age guy friends, and they really made me mad.

As I finished college, a lot of my male friends had started to understand where I was coming from. As they learned that I was not going to compromise, they learned that they better change their minds or they're going to lose me as a friend.

So it became better with men, but I got really worried when I graduated from college. I was thinking, "Well, God, these are the most liberal men I know, what's going to happen when I get out into the real world? I don't know if I can even *talk* to men." And I started working at this restaurant, and as time has gone on I've made just a massive amount of male friends, more than I've ever had in my life.

I'm much more articulate about what I think and I compromise even less than before. And these men who are fraternity boys or whatever, they listen. They want to change their views, or they're working at it, and so my relationships with men have changed for the better. But it's because I'm really sure about what I want.

Do you think men have changed very much?

I'm not sure. My sensitive male friends who try to be so understanding of women's issues end up saying or doing something that proves it's hot air. They learn what they are supposed to learn and say what they are supposed to say, but they eventually get caught in their own lie. You catch them, and they're either like, "You caught me," or "Oh, I guess I don't understand."

And yet there are men who have no idea about anything and they're like, "Wow, I never knew that." They want to change, and I think men have changed. With mothers and fathers both working and more divorce, a lot of my male friends were raised by their mothers. They don't question the power of women, I guess.

I don't want to get married. But I do want to have children. I have a joke with my men friends. I always say, "Well, you know, the only purpose of men is to make women." And they are like, "You're so awful." *(Laughs.)* But I want to have children, I believe in that whole generativity and needing to leave something behind, I guess. Bringing a child into the world—I can't think of anything more wonderful or more beautiful than that.

Pioneers

Some frontiers pioneered by women in the last 30 years have been physical, like Ann Bancroft's polar icecaps and Choua Lee's Chicago skyscraper. Other frontiers are less tangible. Sharon Rice Vaughan mapped uncharted territory by starting the nation's first shelter for battered women, and Carolen Bailey showed that a woman could be a police supervisor in a high-crime area. Arvonne Fraser stepped across the invisible boundaries of her role as "congressman's wife" to become an activist. Jane Hodgson crossed her frontier in a hospital one spring night, knowing she could be arrested and lose her livelihood as a physician.

These women paid a price for being female "firsts." The pressure to represent all women, Dianne Arnold notes, can be a burden. None, however, regrets her choices. Entrepreneur Kathryn Keeley finds life on the edge exhilarating, and Bailey credits the women's movement for giving her the confidence to pursue her career in law enforcement.

Ann Bancroft

Ann Bancroft, age 37, is an elementary-school teacher and an explorer. In 1986 she became the first woman to reach the North Pole on foot. In 1992–93 she led the first all-woman trip to the South Pole. As a result, Ann is the first woman in history to have traveled overland to both poles. Despite all the publicity surrounding these "firsts," she is an intensely private person, and she speaks quietly.

I was drawn to the outdoors right away when I was growing up. I wanted to disappear a lot of the time, being fairly shy and introverted. I have a learning disability, and so school was something I was not excelling at. Sports was a place for me to feel good about myself, to excel. I learned skills, and as I grew in my skills, the trips got longer. Pretty soon I was canoeing way up into Canada, bike trips, kayaking. I climbed Mount McKinley.

I wasn't a dogsledder in the beginning, I only had an aspiration to go to the high Arctic. The men that were leading the 1986 trip realized it would be a good thing if they took a woman. When they'd been on a training run in the Arctic, they'd bumped into this woman with her own dog team in the middle of nowhere, and they thought, ah-hah. It might enhance fundraising. It might be a nice mix, publicity, that sort of thing.

I had more questions than they did. I was scared to death, I didn't know if I was getting in over my head. I certainly didn't want to be on stage for all women and then fail. But Will Steger said, "I can teach you how to dogsled. Do you like dogs?" Well, I love dogs—they're a lot like

eighth-grade boys. *(Laughs.)* He said, "You can learn dogsledding relatively quickly. The winter camping you have. But I'm looking for a
personality who can be out there for days on end doing the same kind
of work." So that's how I got on the trip.

We trained at Frobisher Bay. Between the training and the trip, I
lived primarily with men for 10 months. My mother, my sisters, my female friends—they were a long way away. There was no rest really, no
chance to come back and recharge my batteries. And to do it with all
this other added stress, the publicity, needing to be successful in order
to pay the bills. Then people would write and tell you, "You've got to
do this for women." My intellect is saying, "I've got to do this for me.
Because if I start trying to prove myself as a woman, I'm going to start
making stupid mistakes." In the wilderness, if you make a mistake, it
often costs you your life.

The time I spent with these men allowed me to learn some valuable
lessons, to experience a kind of loneliness and deprivation that I
wouldn't have otherwise. I felt like I knew what sexism was, but I hadn't
experienced it to the degree I was experiencing it then. When
I first approached the men about sexism, I was ranting and raving.
We were in training at Frobisher Bay and I was exhausted. So were they.
We were all very lonely, very homesick. But one day—we had two al-
ternates in the event one of us would get injured. One was a woman
and one was a man. Our group understanding was that they were just al-
ternates, the woman wasn't an alternate for me and the man wasn't an
alternate for the men. The woman was involved longer and had probably more skills than the man. Well, it came out during a meeting that
this woman was really an alternate for me—and I flipped out.

It represented to me the fact that I was a token, a marketing ploy,
that I had no worth whatsoever. So I became the irate female *(laughs)*
and blew up. We had everybody at our camp sitting at this long table,
right after a meal. The men could not understand what the problem
was. One thing that hurt the most was there were no team members
saying, "Yeah, it's outrageous that this woman is an alternate just for
Ann. She has earned the right to be an alternate for any one of us."
There was silence.

The kinds of sexism I experienced on the trip—physically I was
the smallest and the weakest. I'm 5'4" barely, the biggest guy was 6 feet,
230 pounds. We had five dogsleds and the sleds were about 1,400

pounds apiece. Ten dogs per sled. We'd get separated from each other, but you could usually hear and catch up. Occasionally you'd have a sled all by yourself, which I absolutely loved. I did love the dogs, they were an awful lot like kids—and I loved being off by myself. You're in these vast places, but actually you seldom have privacy.

I had a team all by myself one day, and I was having the best day, a day that sticks out in my mind. I came into camp and two tents were already up. Three sleds were in and there were two of us still out, another sled behind me. One of the guys came up to help unharness the dogs. He greeted me and said, "My, you're running dogs well." I noted in my journal that this was 43-some days on the trail, after months of training together. I just blew up at him! I realized after I cooled down why that was so irritating—that every day there'd be this inflection of surprise in their voices. I knew he intended it as a compliment and a greeting, he was being warm and tender.

I traveled with seven good guys, really liked them. We shared everything, we worked fine together. But this trip afforded me a lot of time to learn some subtler things. It was hearing that inflection over and over again. It wasn't until the 43rd day that I realized—"You're damn right I'm running dogs well, I've been running dogs for a long time." There were four of us that didn't know how to run dogs before the trip. Four of us that were much more skiers. I later apologized and tried to describe why I was reacting that way, and again I was met with this blank look.

What really capped it off for me was when the fifth sled came in. There's Geoff all by himself, the biggest guy on the trip, never run dogs before this trip either. He comes in last every day because he's got the most unruly bunch of dogs—and no one says a word to him. He arrives the last person, and the tents are always up, and no one says boo to him. I said, "He doesn't get a greeting? Why should I get a greeting? Not only do I get the surprise but I get an undeserved greeting, special treatment." That's the kind of experience that allowed me to see the subtle sexism.

Edged out of the conversation physically, just by the turn of a shoulder, those kinds of things. You feel them but you can't name them until you feel them every day. Then you realize you don't have a voice. You're speaking out, but they're not acknowledging you. They're showing you that in the language they use, the subtle ways they deal with their bodies.

What I also experienced was, they always expected me to dole out the emotional piece. At one point I finally said, "I'm not the emotional babysitter here. You got the wrong kid because this is the one area where I don't have a lot of strengths, I'm not a big sharer of my feelings." On the trip, they would come to me and say, "Would you check this out?" if they had a wound, or . . . I'd say, "Why don't you check it out with your own tentmate? You have three others over there, with just as much first aid." But I was the nurse, expected to listen to their homesickness, their woes.

Consequently they robbed themselves, we all robbed ourselves of opening up to everyone. I certainly bought into the system and I played by the male rules. They got nothing out of me, and I didn't get my needs met either. But I couldn't fight that with the conditions we were under, and I'm not talking about Arctic conditions. I'm talking about it wasn't okay to have shortcomings, to feel weak and scared. If they did express anything, it was expressed to me. It felt like a burden. On a trip like that, if you give emotionally, it is the same as giving physically.

On the South Pole trip with women, we were carrying 200 pounds apiece. And if somebody was having a bad day you might take 40 pounds to lighten her load, if she's sick or something. If you're giving to an individual who's homesick or ailing emotionally, it zaps your energy—it's like taking the 40 pounds. People don't know that. The emotional piece doesn't get acknowledged.

I had always thought about leading a major all-women's trip. It seemed appropriate that after the '86 trip I would go to the other end of the globe. The way I planned the Antarctic trip was very different. I wanted everybody's emotional batteries to be charged, and the way to do that is they needed to be around their friends and family. We would train, go home, and then start the trip.

They dropped us off in Antarctica in a 60-mile-an-hour wind—they weren't so sure they wanted to do that. We heard some patronizing comments before we left, too. For instance, they wanted us to radio in every day. I said, "I know what it takes to radio every day, a lot of time and effort. We don't need to." I said we'd call every three days. They said, "No, no." If we were a male group it would have been "Yes, sir."

We had four and a half years of preparation. Had calculated exactly what kind of mileage we were going to make when, based on the weights of our sleds and the terrain we were studying and our condition on past trips we had been on together. That's what training is all about, to mathematically map out this trip. It was not a reckless risk, a half-baked dream. But I remember being on the radio during the trip, and hearing that same element of surprise at our mileage.

These women, like other outdoor people, are all introverted. Which is an element that you really need, particularly for this Antarctic trip where you're single file. You're all by yourself all day, in a sense. It's not like running dogs. Dogs—it's very social, you're talking to them all the time, you have to motivate them. This was different. You have to like being alone.

When the women went off on a training trip for 35 days to the Northwest Territories, one of our first long trips, we failed miserably in our dynamics. It was so much like the North Pole trip, it was spooky. We put up our tents every day, we skied, we worked as a group very well, but we did not talk, and we did not like each other.

So we came back, and this is where the difference is: women have a higher commitment to wanting to communicate better because we are socialized that way. The men get a bum rap because they're told not to talk and that they're wimps if they do—so they don't.

So with the women, right after that training trip, we talked for two days. We said, "This is what I don't like about you, this is what I do like about you. This is what I feel we didn't do as a group, how can we change this?" I hate that kind of group-process stuff. Just hate it with a passion, I'm the first one out the door. But I knew we had to do something or we were going to just live out the blueprint of the North Pole trip.

So we talked, and it changed. We made little rules for ourselves. If you pass me in my tracks to take over the lead, you no longer can pass in silence. You just have to grunt, if you can't muster a word. The wind's in your face, you're wearing a face mask, skiing single file for 10 to 14 hours a day, you're exhausted at the end of the day, so you're not talking much. At lunch your backs are against the wind, so everybody's facing the same direction, and the elements are totally against you.

What can we do as a group to counteract these things we know are going to be there?

When the wind wasn't blowing, I would make a conscious effort to turn and face people. Sometimes as leader I would pull everybody in the tent at once. I also used humor a lot. But mostly it was just talking to each other as you're passing, and changing jobs. We changed tents every eight days so you had to deal with a new face. When communication breaks down, and it's gonna break down, you need to re-evaluate and then try again. Re-commit, have everybody be an owner of what you're shooting for.

To have the four of us stand at the pole was a really important moment for me. I knew we could do it physically. I know a lot of people don't think women can pull 200 pounds, especially when they only weigh 105. But we knew we could, we had done it before. Frostbite, tendinitis, the aches and pains were pretty normal. What we didn't know is some of the other things. Can you overcome the adversities that are out of your control, that Mother Nature will dish out for you, or the physical limitations of each other?

You are in that bind as you are achieving firsts. I'd be lying if I said I wasn't out to prove a few points. But I like to stay away from the word "proving," because I'm truly going on these trips for different reasons than just to prove. One of the things I feel the most triumphant about on that trip is, we wanted to go across the continent and come out as friends. That happened. People have accused us of having way too much fun. *(Laughs.)*

Sharon Rice Vaughan

Sharon Rice Vaughan is known for her work with battered women. She sheltered women in her home in the early 1970s and was one of the founders of the first battered women's shelter in the United States in 1974. Her house is a big, rambling Victorian duplex, not restored or manicured like many in the neighborhood, but slightly rundown and homey. We talked over coffee and cookies on her sunny upstairs porch.

I got married when I was very young. I'd had just one year of college. I married a man I'd met on the St. Croix River, and one of the things that held us together was that our grandmothers were best friends. I grew up with a grandmother, two grandmothers, that I dearly loved. One was all Irish, from the potato famine, my Grandma Maggie. My other grandmother had two houses, cottages really, on the river.

We had a great romance. Here this boat would come across the river because *his* grandmother lived right across from the sandbar where we went out to swim. I would take my little brother and sister out in a little 10-horsepower boat, and I found if I got there at noon every day, a boatload would come across with these young studs— Peter and his cousins—with a big cooler full of daiquiris. I had just graduated from high school.

It was one of those incredible romances, on the river, in the summer. He wanted to get married but it was never a good relationship. It was really built on what might be called the paradoxes of the '50s.

The Vietnam War was going on when I was married. Peter was a reporter, and our friends were his friends, and we'd sit around during this terrible war. We all hated it. We'd sit around drinking wine on a Saturday night. There was a heavy level of cynicism about the war, but as reporters they couldn't protest it. The minute Peter and I separated, I got involved in the antiwar movement. After a long period of being depressed by events, I got involved and joined the Honeywell Project.*

But feminism was harder. I can remember reading about feminists and feeling turned off. I come from a classically liberal family that believes in moderation, and that often meant not taking a stand. In the neighborhood where I grew up, everybody said they'd never object if their daughter married a black man. But there were no people of color in that neighborhood of Minneapolis. There were no black men to meet as peers. So we ended up taking these liberal stands, but they never got tested.

Feminism to me was a sort of stance that I couldn't connect with personally. I didn't call myself a feminist until long after I started working with battered women.

Shortly after Peter left, I got evicted from the apartment where we'd been living. I came home one day and there was a notice on the

* A group protesting that company's military contracts.

stairs. I was so shocked. We'd lived there for three years and had a child there. That was my first real experience of discrimination. I was a single parent and not married, and that was the only reason I was evicted. The people downstairs were Jehovah's Witnesses, they owned the house, and the disapproval was thick in the air.

That was in 1970. I decided to buy a house, even though I was living on $300-a-month child support and going to school. But my mother, she was wonderful, she said she'd lend me a down payment. I ended up buying this house. It was very inexpensive, on the market for a year and a half, and was in terrible shape. So I bought the house and moved in downstairs. Put all the kids in one bedroom and had one room for myself, and a 30-foot living room.

I'd always wanted to be a hippie, but I never quite made it. A good friend I'd met in the Honeywell Project was someone who was sort of free-floating in terms of getting involved in things. She wore old Indian bedspreads for skirts and things like that. I just loved her strength in being herself.

This was in the middle of the hippie movement, and really a great time in many ways. It was dreadful for women sexually, but this is all afterthought. You were supposed to be part of the new sexual freedom, and part of that was to be free for anybody—and considered frigid if you weren't.

It was my friend Susan who pulled me into a group she'd gotten involved with called Women's Advocates. It was a phone service at the legal assistance office in the county. They had started as a support group—no, as a consciousness-raising group. I had never been in one. I had had women friends when I was married, but I was hungry for something more—some kind of real contact.

I remember going to these Tuesday-night meetings. The group had reached a point where they wanted to do a project, and they decided they were going to have a house. It was to be called Woman House. It was to be a retreat house where women in the group could go, but then other people could also come who needed housing. We were going to teach classes.

We needed money, and that's where I came in. I remember going to the mental health center one night, and we used all the phones, and we phoned people to get pledges. I became completely absorbed in this. You have to be really compulsive and obsessive in terms of getting into something like this, and then just not let go. I know I felt like a bulldog with lockjaw for years. *(Laughs.)*

From the calls that were coming in, by working on the phone service, we found there were a lot of women who needed to get restraining orders. At that time you couldn't get a restraining order unless you had initiated divorce proceedings. And in this Catholic town, divorce was not simple. It was before no-fault, so a lot of women felt they could only get a legal separation, not a divorce. It was pretty complex.

The restraining order was a civil order, I think it was called a peace bond. I mean, it was perfectly worthless. We didn't have any understanding at all about battering. That's important when you think about the history. All we knew was we were getting requests from women who needed to get their partner out of the house. And they didn't have any other place to stay.

We also had a lot of other calls that weren't really legal problems. No woman's problems are neatly separated the way systems fragment them. So we learned a lot about social services in the community, and there simply wasn't any place where a woman could go. It was so shocking. She could go to the Grand Hotel or the Andrews Hotel. Overnight, from the time the welfare department closed at four o'clock until it opened the next morning at eight o'clock. Or on a weekend. And she had to qualify. She had to be eligible for welfare. They were horrible places. They were literally dangerous places for women and children to be in, and that was it.

There was no sense of battered women as such. It was completely uncharted territory. The language didn't exist, there was no language for what was going on. *We* didn't even know what was going on. But I had my house, this house, and my kids were too young to say no . . . so I just took people in.

This is a pretty yuppie neighborhood. There are no single parents here, and there were all these people coming in and out all the time, and they weren't all white. One summer the power went out and I ended up sitting on the front porch steps with my neighbor. She said to me, "Just what is going on in your house?" She told me that people had been coming to her to sign a petition to get me out.

I can remember reading the early *Ms.* magazine at this time and being really angry with it. I felt like such a failure compared to all these slick women. If they were married, they had husbands who loved them. If they weren't, they just sort of sailed on this path of liberation. I felt as though I struggled so hard, and I couldn't keep my house clean. I never had enough money. I always drove on an empty gas tank because I could only put a dollar in it.

I can remember coming home and my kids would be in the kitchen, and they would all start crying. There were no microwaves—I still don't have a microwave—and I'd never remember to take anything out of the freezer. I'd be chopping away at this block of frozen hamburger, and they'd all be crying. I felt so inadequate. I would think, "If I had any sense, I would take all these kids down to the High Bridge, push them off one by one, and follow them." I would go through this litany: "If I had any sense I would take my children to the High Bridge . . . but I don't have any sense. So what the hell are we going to eat?"

I thought to myself, I feel I can't cope, yet look at these women who come to my house with a garbage bag full of whatever they could grab. With their kids. They seemed to have such spirit and such survival. In many ways they kept me going.

Were you ever afraid?

It got really, really scary sometimes. I remember once when a social worker called and said, "There's a woman here and she's been badly beaten. We think she may have kidney damage." They sent her over in a cab and I remember she slept for about the first 8 or 10 hours. I was really worried about her.

Another social worker told the guy who had beaten her—who turned out later to be her pimp—where she was. He said he had this important message from her family and he had to get it to her. He started coming over here. We had a meeting, we had one man who worked with us who wanted us to leave, to get out of the house, but the rest of us decided we weren't going to leave. We would have a watch, someone would be awake all of the time.

I can remember sitting up in this house downstairs, with these great big old windows which are so low to the ground. It was summer, and it was really hot, and I felt so vulnerable. Almost like facing death on my watch. But we were doing this together, and that felt good.

Another time I served papers on a guy. The guy was a professor, and I thought, no problem. Well, he beat me up.

Literally?

Yes. I can remember, we ran and ran and ran and we got away. I was with his wife and we hid on the floor of a bus. We got to Taco Bell, or whatever it was then, and I called the lawyer on the pay phone. He said, "Well, you've got to press charges." I said, "No way." If my husband ever found out that I was hurt, he would take his kids away.

And then I really understood why women don't do it. The lawyer said, "You're not going to press charges? You're going to let him get away with this?" I said, "Absolutely." Now, of course, I wish I had done it. But at the time, that was really real, and it was probably the right decision not to. I thought Peter would have just freaked out, not for me, but for the children. It was hard, but there was a certain amount of risk for the children. I never pressed charges, and that guy got away with it.

By 1972 or '73, we started writing proposals. I'd been housing women here, but we knew we needed to buy a house. We got somebody who had written a proposal to show us how to do it. We'd come out of the Vietnam War and we did not want to get what we called dirty money. We wanted to get the money for the house out of our pledges, but we were getting only about $400 a month from pledges. So we went to the foundations, and we got the money.

We opened up the shelter for Women's Advocates in October 1974. By that time we started really understanding that we were dealing with battered women. We had the house by then, and we were conscious of the need for women to have a place to stay in a hurry. It's what I'd call in retrospect the brick wall of revelation. You walk into it, and you then realize that the women who are coming in are battered and that it's an epidemic.

I think, in our ardor, we associated the women's movement, the white middle-class women's movement, with the other systems that oppressed women. What we saw was that battered women hadn't been helped in this whole system. These women were falling through the cracks like crazy. They were completely invisible.

The systems themselves were really the impetus for our collectivism at Women's Advocates. It didn't come out of any abstract belief in sisterhood. It was that we had to completely recreate a new system that was radical and revolutionary. We saw the traditional women's movement as . . . well, if they really were feminists, why hadn't they seen this? They didn't seem to listen to us.

Then in *Ms.* magazine, every time they did a story about something, it came out of the East Coast. It didn't ever really deal with the women . . . *(Trails off.)* I mean, I had this terrible love-hate relationship with *Ms.* I always wanted to cancel my subscription because I felt it put me down so much. But it was also the only place where you could get information about what was happening to women. They had wonderful stuff, but I thought they had a terrible attitude. The women who were the feminists were privileged women.

What I learned from the women I worked with was how divisive the class system really is. How complete it is. In England, it's obvious. You open your mouth and the minute you say anything, they can tell what class you're from. People work and work to come up with a BBC pronunciation. That's how they overcome it. But here, we think of ourselves as a classless democracy. It was partly through confronting all these myths of a classless society that I came to believe that the women who came here, the women who were poor and struggling, were my role models.

Our collective experiment at Women's Advocates didn't succeed. What I wanted us to do was to be able to value all work: the person who answered the phone, the person who cleaned the toilets, and the person who went out and raised money. We were becoming more and more sought out as leaders in this field. It was exploding all over the country as shelters were started up everywhere. We were being asked to go and speak, but my leadership wasn't accepted by the collective.

I wanted my leadership to be accepted as being as important as what everybody else was doing. But it wasn't. I also wanted us to do it right. I didn't want somebody to go out and speak simply through drawing straws.

A woman who had come out of prison and had been recently hired as an advocate was the one who won when we drew straws to go to New York to speak on a national TV program. I was furious. They had asked me to come, and the group wouldn't let me go. When the people in New York said they didn't want the other woman, they wanted me or nobody, my peers and co-workers turned against me. It caused a terrible split in the organization which I don't think ever healed. I was just devastated by that.

And I think I was pretty burned out. I mean, there was a time when it was so painful. I'd been with Women's Advocates for six years,

it had started in my home, it was just terrible. I left and went to work at
another shelter—Harriet Tubman, which was just opening.

By 1985, I was really burned out. I felt the movement was getting
out of touch with the needs of the women and was acting more and
more like a patriarchal institution. I wanted to recreate what had been
the heart of the revolution. The battered women had radicalized me. I
had become a feminist through women's stories, and I had been lucky
enough to have women staying in my house and to hear their stories.

I decided to do this other dream I had, to get women's stories on
the radio. I've always been passionately in love with radio. I've never
watched TV, but I believed in radio. I thought at the time that these
stories would radicalize the movement, bring it back.

I insisted on being producer, even though I didn't know anything
about radio. I knew what I wanted to do, even though I didn't know
what it was. Of course I didn't have any money, but KUOM* gave me
a studio to work in, and time from the engineer, and the help of an accomplished producer. I did that for two years.

And I met every month with a small group of women I'd worked
with in shelters. They helped transcribe tapes and critiqued whatever I
had ready for them to listen to. One did the bookkeeping. I raised
about $19,000 in two years for supplies and to live on.

It was terribly hard, but I think on the whole it was successful. We
did 10 programs in almost two years. I really worked hard. I cried a lot.
I had to learn all this stuff, I was completely machine-phobic. I was so
broke. I had lived with a poet for years and I began to understand what
his lack of security was like.

When the engineer, whom I loved working with and who was a
wonderful man, was saying that he thought he'd ask for overtime for
being stuck in the elevator for half an hour, I just lost it. I wanted to
physically attack him. Just the thought of overtime—I mean I had no
vacations, I couldn't pay my bills, I had a terrible credit rating. And I
just worked all the time. I'm sure it could have been done better, but I
did the best job I could. And when we sent these tapes out, they won
the most incredible awards.

During all this time, my women friends have really, really sustained
me. When you wake up in the middle of the night and feel that terri-

* A public radio station.

ble bleakness, it is those friendships that make the morning bearable. Feminism has allowed me to make sense of the world. In some fundamental way, it's about listening to people, respecting people.

We need to look past the atrocities. We need to name the atrocities, because they've never been named before in a man's world. Battering is certainly one of the processes of that naming. I've been very lucky in being able to do the things I've done. I wouldn't change anything. *(Very long pause.)*

I do have one really big regret. The one thing in my life I would change is that when I was 13, I was attacked and raped. I was on a glorious adventure out into the country to my grandmother's. It did so much damage to me. It should never have happened. My daughter's illness, my marriage, all the things which have been very painful in my life have given me so much, I would never change a bit of that. But that incident, of being pulled off my bike, made me realize . . . *(Trails off.)* I can remember seeing this guy in his car, waiting for me to come by. Before that, I didn't think anything could happen to me. But when that happened, when I realized that I'm not exempt from anything—and maybe it's a valuable lesson to know that—it killed something in me. It created a wound which never healed.

Arvonne S. Fraser

Arvonne Fraser, 68, moved to Washington, D.C., in 1962 when her husband, Don Fraser, was elected to Congress. In Washington, she was a founder of the Women's Equity Action League, and in Minnesota she supported the beginnings of many feminist organizations. She was an official delegate to the first United Nations Conference on Women in 1975, she worked for the Carter administration recruiting women, and she later became international coordinator for Women in Development. She returned to Minnesota in 1981 and now teaches at the Hubert H. Humphrey Institute of Public Affairs.

I'm a farmer's daughter. I went to the Lamberton, Minnesota, public schools and then to the university. Started in the Humphrey campaign of '48, worked in the DFL office as a secretary, married Fraser, had six kids, was a DFL Party activist. Went to Washington, was a feminist activist. Came back, and here I am!

My father was an alcoholic and my mother was a frustrated housewife. She had always wanted to be a doctor, but she ended up being a country schoolteacher. My father was a radical, left-wing—not really a political activist, but he talked about it all the time. I was always told, I was always shown, how women were treated. That they shouldn't be treated badly—although they were—and that I should never tolerate that. As I think about it, my mother gave me mixed messages—get a good husband, but always be able to support yourself.

After I moved to Washington, I was really depressed. And everyone thought I should be so *delighted*. I'd been a DFL Party officer, as well as a mother and community activist, and had had sort of an independent career. I was on the Minneapolis Board of Public Welfare, and then I was obviously very active—I semi-managed Don's campaign. But when we moved to Washington, all of a sudden I'm just a suburban housewife. And Washington was a culture where you are just a wife. A lot of the dinner parties were where the men talked, and the women listened. It just undid me. I'd had to give up my career, give up my independence.

With a brand-new baby, in the winter, in the suburbs—everything. And no sense there was any hope to establish anything but be the congressman's wife. And so I hired a maid and went down to Don's office, which I always said was cheaper than a psychiatrist. But I'd read Betty Friedan's book,* and knew perfectly well that I could never be content just being a mother and a wife. That book described the way I was in Washington.

I had a friend who was in as bad shape as I was, a woman who had organized the Minnesota Nurses Association, and we'd been reading about the new consciousness-raising groups and the young feminist activity. We decided we were too old, probably, to join these young people's groups, so we organized one for ourselves. It was in '69, or maybe '68. We'd sit around, and of course no one could make a fancy lunch. You had to bring a bag lunch, and the hostess could only provide coffee. It was a mixture of young and old. When it got bigger and

---

* *The Feminine Mystique* (1963).

we tried to divide up by age, both the old and the young refused. They liked it that way.

At first we were just a women's group, although ultimately it was called the Nameless Sisterhood. You were to introduce yourself, and you couldn't introduce yourself as being related to any man. One woman said, "This is the first time in 20 years in Washington that anyone has asked who *I* am." The women's movement was real dinnertable conversation at that time, and the way the group got named the Nameless Sisterhood was that a reporter heard about it and came to see me, and asked who the women's *husbands* were!

It was professional women, and housewives, and mothers. And it was smart women. We took on the abortion issue, and then sterilization. That was just surfacing in Washington, and we discussed that. We didn't have books to read, and we didn't always have a discussion topic. We just came together like any other consciousness-raising group. Nobody called themselves feminists, at least at first. It was just a zinging group.

Out of that I was asked to form a WEAL chapter—Women's Equity Action League—in Washington. And because I was on Capitol Hill, working in Don's office ... you see, Bella Abzug was there, Shirley Chisholm, Patsy Mink—there were a number of activists on the Hill.

I'll never forget sitting in George Washington University. We decided we'd write a women's educational-equity act. Well, I knew how to write a bill. We thought this would be for consciousness raising. We'd just hold hearings, Patsy Mink would hold hearings. And when we got to the clause about money, the appropriations paragraph, we casually put in $30 million or something like that. Mink held hearings, and Mondale held hearings, and it went smack through just like that. Within a couple of years, we actually had about $10 million. *(Laughs.)*

It was easy. When you know systems, and how to work systems, and when you have a cadre of staffers and congresswomen like the ones we had ... but it was a very different political atmosphere, a liberal political atmosphere. All the stuff was just in the air. The ERA was starting up there. Even though this was in the days of Nixon, it was a Democratic Congress, and we got all kinds of legislation passed. We formed all kinds of organizations. It was great fun.

I lived in two worlds. I came back to Minnesota every summer. I remember somehow as soon as I got known, people sent me things. I'd been getting more and more feminist stuff all the time. Then when I came back here, I was always talking to groups. It was interesting how people in Minnesota responded to my interest in women's issues. Women would come up to me and whisper in my ear, "I can't say anything publicly, but boy I'm proud of what you're doing." I was as fascinated with the women's movement here as they were with me. If there was a down side, either they didn't tell me, or I didn't listen. *(Laughs.)*

Because I had organized the WEAL group, and because I was on Capitol Hill—and I suppose because I was a congressman's wife, too— I got invited to places all over the country. My political background helped with speaking to groups. I was used to speaking to big groups, although I'll never forget the first time I spoke up at our DFL ward club. *(Laughs.)* I guess I'm half ham, because I now like to speak. And watch audience reaction.

I read once that the first thing in a good speech is that you get the audience to identify with you. Men do it by telling a joke. That's a way of leveling, of flattening out the hierarchy. Women don't have that problem, because we aren't in the hierarchy. *(Laughs.)* Being political, I figured ideas were important. I believe half of being active politically is educating people. And that's what speaking is.

I could always predict the questions. But I also learned that you had to have a sense of humor. If you can deal kindly—but with a sense of humor—with the stupid questions, the audience likes you better. And the fact that I got grey fairly early, that I was never gorgeous, that I'm short, and usually fat, and so on—that helped. I didn't look like people's stereotype of a feminist. And I was older than many others, that helped a lot. A friend said, "She looks like everybody's grand-mother, and then all this *stuff* comes out of her mouth."

The younger feminists made me look respectable. I was able to get much more done because there was an extreme. I was middle-of-the-road, even though an awful lot of people thought I was pretty extreme. *(Laughs.)* I've always been very respectful of the more radical feminists and their function. We knew at the time it was a useful strategy. I have a clear vision of some meetings where we were together and some of us would tell them, "Go ahead and do it, because that's helpful to us." I'm not sure they always understood that, nor did a lot of our people, but it's very important.

WEAL died because it didn't take care of its constituents. That's why I have a real admiration for NOW. NOW went out and got members all over the country, and took care of those members, and listened to them. WEAL concentrated on getting laws and policies changed first. It started out as mostly lawyers and college professors, kind of an "elite" group, and that was about it. Then, after I left, they went the way of getting foundation grants, and then ultimately government contracts. So they had no base, and what base they had was lost.

Dianne E. Arnold

Dianne Arnold was executive vice president of a large Twin Cities bank before leaving to form her own management consulting service. In 1982 she was featured in Fortune *magazine as one of the nation's top women bankers. She is 49.*

I remember being aware of differences at a pretty early age, challenging the unwritten rules of who did what and how things happened. My parents belonged to a Baptist church—a conservative Baptist farm group in North Dakota. By the time I was 9 or 10, I was openly questioning some of the dogma.

It was mostly between my parents and me. We would come home from church to the typical Sunday dinner—which was always fried chicken—and argue. I mean, I would initiate the arguments about what had gone on in Sunday school or the church service, or something the minister had said. And I would pick a fight. You could just count on it. I don't think my mother thought it was so wonderful. It really frustrated her because she's a very good woman. A teacher and a very good wife.

I got a degree in economics and statistics in 1966, and went to work for First Bank System. I'd gone to a job fair, and First Bank was one of the companies I'd talked to there. They were one of those who quizzed me about my birth control practices—I was married at the time—which in retrospect just blows my mind. These starchy men sitting there asking these outrageous questions!

I was hired as an operations research analyst. That was a job they could put me in because I had a math background, and not have to put me in the management-training program. They really didn't want women in there. But the operations guy, he didn't care if you were male or female. I got into doing some programming of my own, building some models, analyzing work flows in the production area, and some cash-flow forecasting. I built a model we could sell, so I got to travel a little bit into the hinterlands calling on small banks—and that was fun.

By 1970 or '71, I was very aware of things that were happening as an outcome of the women's movement. Particularly the movement by teachers to get maternity leave—because I was pregnant in '71. The bank at the time had a policy that said that when you were six months pregnant you terminated your job. It wasn't terminated and then came back. It was just terminated, period.

In fact the policy required women to have a signed statement by their doctor attesting to their last menstrual period. Well, I found that just to be outrageous, and never did submit one. I refused to submit it, and nobody had the courage to demand it. Finally, at about the sixth month, six or seven months along, I did ask my doctor to give me a statement. I don't know where this came from, but I had decided I wasn't going to leave.

The things that were happening with the teachers were very helpful to me. There was a lot of stuff in the newspapers and it gave me the courage to move ahead in the private sector. I remember being very conscious of that, and used it in my discussions with the bank, to try to help them understand that the world was changing. That the way the policy was written and the intent was kind of ridiculous. It had nothing to do with your ability to do the job. They sort of assumed your brain died or something.

At any rate, my doctor, bless him, an old time OB/GYN guy here, wrote this note saying the due date is approximately such-and-such and that, "As far as I am concerned, she can work until she goes into labor." Signed his name and said, "This ought to do it."

The nurse who got it here in the bank went, "A-a-a-agh," but the fellow who hired me originally supported my effort to change the policy. To the point where he went to the mat. It had to go all the way up to the holding company, and it was a huge flap. The banks here operated very independently, and you didn't go up to the holding company for anything. This was a major brouhaha.

I was granted a leave of absence—which was a major break-through—and by the time I came back the policy had been redrafted to allow for these leaves. As I think back, I was more involved in the cause than in thinking about the long term, about whether there'd be damage to my career or not. I was more outraged by the arbitrariness of it all. I mean, there were days when I was so angry so many times, days when I'd get in my car and collapse in tears. I'd cry all the way home, and cry all the way to work—and then go at it another day. There was lots of agonizing over whether this was all worth it.

I don't know what the other women thought. I felt absolutely alone in doing this, I was just out there doing it alone. I'm sure there were other women who supported it, but they weren't supportive in the way we use the term today. They wouldn't have done it themselves, probably. It was a very strange thing to do.

I still have a visual of one of the men about my age coming up to me in the hall—I suppose I was seven or eight months pregnant at that point—and him saying in all genuine friendliness *(her voice shows amaze-ment)*, "Are you still here?" Kind of, "Are you still working?" It wasn't malicious. Underlying it was, why would anyone want to do this? Why wouldn't you just want to go home and put your feet up? So I had to explain that that wasn't what I had in mind, that I liked what I was doing, and that my brain wasn't impaired.

In 1974 I decided I wanted to get out of operations, because that's not where the game is played, and into commercial banking. By 1974 things were starting to open up a little bit, the bank was realizing that it had to look for women. So when I came wandering in and said I'd like to come back full-time, and maybe I'm speculating here a little bit, somebody said, "Hey, here's one! We found one. And we know her. We think we could manage her." That was the first mistake they made. *(Laughs.)*

I don't know if I can point to specific instances where being a woman was an advantage going in. There were certainly times when I was able to carve out good client relationships both with existing cus-tomers and some new ones. I think it was due to what I would call the

more "feminine" style. My style was different. I spent more time getting to know people, probably on a different level. I spent less time trying to impress them with my title, or with the fact that I represented
the "big bank." More time just understanding, asking questions. And, I
think, being a woman was probably less threatening to them. You
know, the expectations were lower. *(Laughs.)*

There were also customers who said to the bank, "We do not want
a woman on our account," or, "Thank you very much, don't bring her
out again." And the bank was pretty good about not just caving in.
There were a couple of accounts where I either pulled out or I
switched with somebody else, because life is too short, after all. And of
course, there wasn't anybody who said, "Please send us a woman." But
I was a little bit of a novelty, and that sometimes helped get me in the
door, or get a conversation started, or get somebody to agree to see
me. And I had no inhibitions about using that, whenever I thought I
could.

In many situations I've been "the first woman who . . ." or "the
only woman who . . ." Many times I was the only one because whoever had been first had moved on or been drummed out. As you learn
to survive in these situations, it's sometimes useful and fun to be the
only one. You get a lot of attention, and everybody likes attention. So
it's not the most awful thing.

On the other hand, the pressure you put on yourself, and that gets
put on you, to represent *all* women can be a little overwhelming at
times. I contributed to that also, because I tended to feel that the mistakes that I made were not only going to have consequences for me but
may make the road harder for others. I've gotten over a lot of that, but
I know that put pressure on me during those early years. I became a little too invested in the "I've got to do something to help other women,
and boy I'd better do this right." It's a burden an individual really
shouldn't take on themselves, but it's hard not to.

One of the hardest parts of being the only one, or the first one,
was that many times you had no clue about the unwritten rules of a
particular group. It required an awful lot of hard figuring out about
what's going on, figuring out who you could trust. You had to make
quick judgments, and you had to be pretty right on it. It wasn't always
obvious. People would put on behaviors and appear to be one thing

when, underneath, they were really something else. This was so new for them, to have a woman there.

I tend to be outspoken, or plain-spoken, many times. I learned the hard way more than once about the feelings of my male colleagues. A lot about the male ego that I never really knew. I tended to attract attention because I was a "first" or "only" many times, attention in terms of newspaper or magazine quotes, or just some attention inside. It took me a while to realize that while it may have been good for women, it was very threatening to men. I remember one article where I talked about some of the difficulties of being the "only." Well, I mean to tell you, it's very hard for people to see stuff in print that they think reflects on any possible shortcomings they may have.

You get so . . . *(she searches for the right word)* so *calloused* after a while. I get so tired of men apologizing when they curse in a meeting. And they still do it. Even 25 years later, it's still going on. One of the things I've found hard is the accumulated effect of that stuff, to keep sloughing it off. Keep not taking it personally. And to keep saying, "It's out there, it's not directed at me, it's directed at a large group of people, it springs more from their insecurities, their inabilities, whatever." But I find it can be debilitating.

Equal opportunity laws have made a big difference. And the reason I mention the laws is because I think that whatever limitations they have—and there are many—I think their enactment played a key role in the ability of women to get many kinds of positions. It's a stick. It's a club. And I don't think the bank or many other companies would have bothered with the effort if it hadn't been that they knew they *had* to show some activity. They didn't know what they were vulnerable to, but it was easier to do something than not. It opened doors that I don't think would have opened for a long time. I still don't know exactly where I come down on the quota issue on any given day, but I'm here to tell you that if you don't have some goals, you don't reach them.

I believe the women's movement made a difference, and mostly positive. It takes lots and lots of people in lots of places to make change happen. Personally, just to keep body and soul together, if you know there are others out there with at least the same goals in mind . . . for me, it's much easier to keep going. I benefited particularly from those women who were willing to risk ridicule. Public ridicule, like getting in the press for things that women needed to be recognized for. You have to have somebody willing to do that. To keep the attention focused.

Then those of us who work more quietly can keep chipping away, and can say, "Look, this is not going to go away, guys." It takes a lot of courage, I think, to put yourself up for that kind of ridicule. Some of them did things that I did not think were necessary, or that I didn't approve of necessarily, but it's nice to have somebody out there on that leading edge.

I played the political game, and that's maybe more male than not male, but I saw it as a survival technique. I got to the place where I knew what I wanted. You don't get there just by sitting at your desk and doing a good job and waiting to be anointed. I tried to be careful, to know where to draw the line at the substantive stuff. For the life of me I can't figure out what is so terribly offensive about men cursing in a meeting, or telling reasonably clean jokes. I mean, if it really gets crude and degrading, I'll walk out, or I'll say something. On the other hand, I've rarely been subjected to that—the harassment, the innuendo stuff. What I've been subjected to is more subtle. Maybe bankers are too uptight to be quite that crude. *(Laughs.)*

Carolen Bailey

When I made lieutenant in 1985, they asked me if I would be willing to go into patrol. I was absolutely delighted to do that. I went into patrol to be a commander in the northwest patrol team, which is our highest crime area. They'd never had a woman supervisor of any sort before, and I'd never worked patrol.

In addition to that, I got braces on my teeth the first day I started. Came to work and discovered that the sergeant who did roll call was sick. I had to give my very first roll call with brand new braces on my teeth . . . in front of a hundred men. *(Laughs.)* I want to tell you, and I've told other women, if I can do *that,* you can do anything!

Carolen Bailey was on the St. Paul police force for 30 years, retiring in 1991. She worked in the juvenile division, the sex/robbery unit, the sex/homicide unit, and as commander of the vice unit. In 1969 she was instrumental in establishing the first multiagency child-abuse team in the United States. Tall and rangy, she has an infectious smile—and straight teeth. She is 56.

When I started in 1961, the job was policewoman. There were gender-based titles. The policewoman had to have different qualifications from the policeman. They required that the woman have a college degree and experience in social work. The man only had to have high school. However, they did hire at a higher level, so I was actually hired at a detective's salary.

I had been a social worker, working child protection. I had a huge caseload, it was the highest in the county. One hundred six families, or something. And I loved it—I've always loved every assignment I've ever had. I quit as a caseworker to have a second baby. I was home for almost a year, and then heard about this exam being offered. I thought police work would be a challenge for lots of reasons, but one was because you're dealing with people in crisis. You have a much greater impact at a time of crisis than dealing with a family over a period of years. You can have a greater impact in helping people, I felt. And I still feel that way after all these years.

Secondly, it was a male field, and I thought there ought to be more women involved. Third, being a male field it paid far better than social work. *(Laughs.)* Fourth, I thought it sounded like a whole new challenge, and it gave me an opportunity as well to work varied hours so I could sometimes be home with the children during the day.

I was no threat then, because I worked in juvenile division. Mostly with girls. I was also given opportunities to work special details, like undercover morals division and that sort of thing. I've always loved to act, so I was very successful in that. *(Laughs.)* Opportunities to prove myself really opened the door for a lot more, and they took me out of juvenile division and into the sex/robbery unit—the detective division. They said they'd taken a poll, and they'd like me to work there.

After that, I worked homicide investigations for a number of years. Dealt with all kinds of violent crimes. I eventually took a promotional exam for lieutenant and came out clearly number one. It was at an assessment center, which I think is a tremendous advantage for women, because they actually measure your ability to do the work. However, that's the last time they did it. I think there's a device now that's used more commonly called a "promotability index," in which they ask the good old boys of higher rank to rate the candidates.

I'll tell you one of my favorite little stories. I had always felt that enforcing street prostitution was very biased. That to arrest the women prostitutes and leave the male customers alone—when the crime applied to both—was very discriminatory. At one point, in the middle '70s, a judge ruled that indeed it was discriminatory to use male decoys to arrest female prostitutes without using female decoys to arrest male customers.

With that ruling, our assistant chief decided he would use me as an undercover. But our primary problem was that it was 11- and 12-year-old girls working the streets, and he said, "Well, we'll try it, but I think you're way too old." *(Laughs.)* The first hour and five minutes I arrested 11. That night I arrested 60. And I've never let him hear the end of it. *(Laughs again.)*

I found it a new challenge. It was sort of fun, it was a diversion from . . . I was working homicide then. It was interesting, I mixed a little with the street prostitutes. In fact, some of them would ask who my pimp was. I remember on one occasion I was asked in a very threatening manner. I said, "If you don't quit bothering me, you'll find out who my pimp is!"

When I was a rookie, we had a series of purse-snatchers. They were quite dangerous, they would drop-kick older women in the back, and break their backs in some instances. So I was asked to help dress and do the makeup, to help decorate a male officer as a decoy. My first reaction was that I stormed down to the chief's office and said, "Why can't I do it?" He looked at me with a chuckle and said, "I'd wondered how long it would take you to get down here. But it's too dangerous, and that's it."

He wouldn't let me do it, so I did the makeup. But there were other areas in those days where they absolutely did need women, so I guess that's how we got a foot in the door in the first place.

The male officer, I think even today, is a little uncomfortable in dealing with interrelationships, family relationships. Our culture has allowed women to become much more versatile that way. I found it was helpful just in working homicide cases. Because so often, especially in whodunits that might involve acquaintances, relationships are real important. You need to analyze them and to deal with them. Because of that, I think men stayed out of the domestic violence area, whether it was child abuse or battered women. They felt uncomfortable, they weren't well trained in it. It was easier to say, "Well, this isn't a police problem. *We* deal with bad guys with guns."

The homicide unit was getting all the violence-against-children reports, among other kinds of "crimes against persons." I had worked that when I was at the county welfare department, so I knew both sides of the scene. I was very frustrated because we would build an investigation, go to court, and then we'd find the children back in the home. And really, we were desperately seeking coordination in the area.

We had a two-year-old little boy who was brought in by the babysitter. She brought the child right to me, at the police station. The child was rushed to the hospital, and he had not an inch on his body that wasn't bruised. And his buttocks had obviously been dipped in hot water, there was no skin left. You could see the water line, and so forth. Somewhere there's a photograph of this particular child. You could get a good . . . *(She trails off.)* They could print the picture from the back showing all the injuries without exposing the child's face. In that case, we could charge. We charged with aggravated assault. Aggravated assault is a crime of great bodily harm or with a dangerous weapon, such as a gun or a knife. We charged aggravated assault, considering the boiling water as a dangerous weapon. The judge convicted the mother, but reduced it to simple assault because he didn't think there was great bodily harm or a dangerous weapon. We had some real problems in the early days of applying adult criminal codes to the treatment of children.

In 1969 we formed the Ramsey County child abuse team, which was the first community-based team in the country. Starting that team was a huge improvement in dealing with family violence. The participants in the team included the police department, the mental health center, the county hospital, the county attorney's office, the visiting-nurse service—and later, the schools had a liaison.

We started the team out of frustration. I had just a lot of frustration, in fact I continued to after the team started because initially the team would only take physical abuse. And I was seeing incest, sexual abuse as well. They are to me the most difficult cases, even to this day I say that. The only reason I never got burned out is that any time I really felt frustrated or overwhelmed with sexual abuse cases, I would take on a nice clean murder. *(Laughs.)*

I can say it was my ranting and raving and frustration that got the child abuse team eventually to consider the incest cases as well as the physical abuse. In fact, there's a tremendous overlap. Most sexual abuse cases involve physical abuse, or fear or threats. And we also found the reverse. When you saw physical abuse, many of them turned into sexual abuse. But they weren't asking the right questions at the time.

I believe, firmly, that women can do all aspects of law enforcement. I have believed that for a long, long, long time. I suspect it's cultural— I'm not sure—but I think women care about people more, and care about relationships. I think women ask more questions about, why has it always been this way? Why does it have to stay this way?

And I think women are less likely to use physical violence to solve problems, and more likely to deal with people with respect. I've had a lot of people ask me how I could be civil and question an incestuous father. But you look at people, there's some good and some bad. I've always found good in everyone. I really believe in treating people with respect, even if their behavior doesn't deserve it.

I think the women's movement has had an effect on law enforcement. I think the women's movement has had an effect on everything—fortunately. *(Laughs.)* Just as an individual, for example, when I was challenging the right to take the sergeant's exam. The women's movement gave me confidence. It's the whole philosophy of support, that you're not crazy, you're right, that you can do the job even though everybody tells you you can't. I didn't have women ahead of me to be mentors. But I think I got my early support and confidence from the whole philosophy of the women's movement.

When I first started at the police department, I never questioned why I was being put in juvenile division when the men weren't. I mean, it was the culture, there were a lot of things we didn't question then. I did all the traditional things in the early days. When women were two or three percent of the force, a lot of women we saw coming in were trying to fit into the male mode. In fact, the uniforms do that.

You put a male uniform on a woman, and it looks like little boys trying to be big men. You'd see the occasional woman coming in who would try to be the man, and she'd adopt their language, and it was very unsuitable. Not because you should be feminine, but because you should use your qualities to their greatest advantage. Abandoning any qualities you have is superficial and ineffective. And you're never going to be part of the good-old-boys' club. As long as there's just one woman, they can control her. Put two women in, and they have a little bit of support.

How could any one of us have tolerated the situation without the women's movement? I am a strong advocate of the power of women. I don't think there's anything more powerful than organized women. It shaped my career, there's no question about it. If women didn't care about sexual assault, I might have been focusing on something entirely different. It provided a support for me, and besides that, it's fun. I loved going to the women's groups and speaking. I enjoyed the men's business groups, and I had more requests from them, but I always felt at home with women. I strongly believe in sisterhood.

People have asked if I've been scared. When I was a rookie, I was in some very difficult situations. Once there was a shooting of a police officer, and I was responsible for getting the voiceprint that matched the phone call that lured the officer to his death. As a result, there was an organization that had a contract out on me. But, you know, I never thought twice about it.

I guess I never really was scared because I always knew I had backup close. You know you have a radio there, and that within minutes you're going to have help. I always felt that I was not alone. In fact, when I was a social worker I had a lot of clients in a high-crime area, and I used to go there in the evening, and never think twice. When I became a police officer, I thought, "How did I ever do that? Without a gun? And without a radio?" *(Laughs.)*

Jane Hodgson

Jane Hodgson, 78, is a physician specializing in obstetrics and gynecology. In 1970 she challenged the anti-abortion laws by performing an illegal abortion, for which she was tried and convicted. The trial made front-page headlines.

My father was a country physician, the son of a Methodist preacher, and he was very conservative. He was a very deeply religious man, but most of the time he couldn't get to church because he was working. He was the county physician, and he took care of all the jail prisoners. I remember going to the jail with him and the prostitutes were there. I remember particularly how he treated these women. I know my father would have never, ever performed any abortions, but he probably took care of plenty that had been self-induced.

I made rounds with him a lot. We were very close, but he'd never particularly encouraged me to enter medical school, it just wasn't done. I don't think it occurred to either one of us. But after college, I worked in Chicago for a year, and I decided I wanted to study medicine. So I applied at Northwestern, and was told there was a quota. Four Jews, four women, and four blacks, they had filled their quota and were very sorry, and very nice. The strange thing is I accepted that, I never even questioned it.

So then I applied at Minnesota, where I got in without any trouble. When it came time for my internship, I wanted to get out of this part of the country, so I went out to the Jersey City medical center. I got married there, and my husband was also an intern. We lived in Florida for a while while my husband was in service, and then came back to Minnesota to practice after the war.

When I started out in practice I got going fast because women loved the idea of a woman doctor. The public didn't think they would, and the men didn't either—they felt kind of sorry for me. This little struggling woman, you know. So they'd just send me stuff, and I had more than I could do. I had no problem getting started.

After about 25 years, I got a little upset about our state abortion laws. It was probably an accumulation of frustration over the problems, it seemed like such horrible medicine to me. I was seeing a lot of it, almost on a daily basis, the complications after criminal abortions. I got more than my share. I saw the young women particularly—the mothers would bring their daughters in, their young daughters, who were pregnant.

I had been taught in medical school that interfering with a pregnancy was about the most dangerous thing you could do. And we didn't have any reason to believe that didn't always have to be the case. You had the idea that the invasion of the uterus was just this horrible thing, and that every woman would get infected, and maybe die or hemorrhage to death.

I tried to impress this upon patients, then knew they were going to ignore it. I'd tell them, "No, I can't do an abortion," and I'd see how desperate some of them were, and I'd know they were going to go ahead anyway. And sure enough, back they'd be, and I'd be taking care of them and worrying about them and sitting up with them all night. They would insert anything from knitting needles to catheters.

There were women right here in town who would go to another woman, who for a few dollars would insert a sterile catheter that would get her bleeding and get her started. Lots of times, I think, doctors were fooled, including myself. Patients would come in and they were bleeding. They'd say, "I'm pregnant and I'm bleeding," and you'd think it was spontaneous, but it really wasn't. It was amazing—after abortion became legal, you just didn't see that kind of case any more.

Then I spent some time in other countries, I went to a lot of medical meetings in Europe, in the Netherlands, in Italy. They were doing abortions way back in the '50s in the Netherlands, even though it was against the law. The doctors just disregarded it. They were using suction back then, and the Russians were using suction, and the Chinese started in the '50s.

I knew all this was going on in the rest of the world. Britain passed a law allowing abortions in '67. I was going to international meetings and realized the United States, and particularly Minnesota, were archaic in its attitudes. And it was bad public health for the women. Just gradually, I became weary of it. I thought, "This is wrong," and that all we'd have to do is point this out to the legislature and they'd change the law. *(Laughs.)* That's all it would be.

We tried to do that. I was on a committee with the state medical society in the late '6os, but nobody could ever agree. We met for about three years, and the best we could come up with would be that abortion would be available to women in the first three months, provided it was approved by a five-doctor committee. You can imagine getting five doctors together *(laughs)*, and the problems involved. But nothing happened after all, it was all tabled by the medical society. The guys at the top decided they didn't even want to reveal what the recommendations were.

During that process, it seemed like the only possible way we could change the law would be to challenge it. So this young woman, a housewife, 23 years old, she had three children, and she had been a patient of mine. She walked in and she had rubella the third week of her pregnancy. It was a pretty clear-cut case. She was about 10 weeks pregnant and she'd had German measles during the third week. We'd gotten all the blood tests, it was documented right, absolutely no question of the diagnosis, it was all perfect. She was a smart woman, a nice person, and she came to me very openly and said, "I want an abortion."

I could have sent her away, because at that point we were sending about 150 women a week out of the state for abortions. There was a clergy counseling service, the ministers here. There was a regular underground network. It was remarkable, really, the way the ministers would stick their necks out. Of course, we could all have been sent to jail for that, really. There was a doctor in California who was charged and tried and convicted simply for referring a woman down to Mexico. It was interpreted as "aiding and abetting."

Anyway, I said, "Well, we could send you out to . . ." I mean, I approved of her, I thought she should have the abortion, and offered to send her outside. But she said, "I don't want to leave my children, I want you to do it. You're my doctor, you ought to be able to do it right here. I should have the right." Well, I got to thinking, "She *should* have the right." So two days later we filed for an injunction to prevent the law from being applied.

I had to go to federal court because it was a constitutional law case. I was saying the law is wrong and I'd like permission to do this case. I'd like a declaratory judgment on the law, have it declared unconstitutional. And I said I'd have to do it by the first of May. But they were very slow, and I didn't hear from them, so I went ahead and did it anyway—on the 29th of April—because I didn't want her to go over 12 weeks.

I did it very openly, in the old Miller Hospital. It got in the headlines—I don't know who leaked it—but anyway, it was in the papers. Well, shortly after I'd done it, I got a response from the federal court saying there was no reason for them to interfere, to do anything. They would do nothing. Well, then the next day I was indicted by the grand jury. Arrested. The district court took over and arrested me, and I had to go down to the jail and get fingerprinted. They came to my office and took me out while I was seeing a patient.

I could have had a jury, but I waived the jury. I wanted to make this an educational thing, I thought a judge would be much better. I didn't want the emotions of the jury and the rest of it. We had the judge, and we got experts from all over the country who came in and testified. I had about five doctors from the Mayo Clinic who came up and testified on my behalf. We argued that the reason for the law no longer existed. It was all right back in 1851 when the law was established because it was a very dangerous procedure. It was to protect women at that time. But now it was working the other way. Women weren't being helped, but were suffering. We argued it on the First, and the Ninth, and the Fourteenth Amendments—privacy rights, and equal access.

We asked the United States Supreme Court to intervene. But the only one who voted for intervening was Justice Douglas,* bless his heart. His was the only vote to prevent my having to go to trial. Only after I was convicted could I appeal to the state supreme court, which I did. But they sat on it for over two years. I appealed to them and they didn't hand down a decision until after *Roe v. Wade* was announced. They just sat, and I waited, and that was the hardest part of the whole thing.

My sentence was suspended pending appeal, but if it had been upheld by the Minnesota Supreme Court, I would have lost my license. So I never knew, every week when they'd hand down decisions, but that they'd say my conviction should be upheld. I was just in a kind of state

* William O. Douglas.

of . . . of nothing. From the time of my trial in the fall of '70 until in 1973 when the Minnesota Supreme Court reversed my conviction.

While I was waiting, all this time, I of course lost lots of my patients. But at the same time I got new ones. I always had more patients than I could do. I never suffered any at all, as far as my patient load was concerned. But it bothered me no end because patients would come in pregnant and say, "You'll be here to deliver me, won't you?" I'd say, "I don't know." It just didn't seem fair not knowing from one week to the next that I might have to stop practicing. It kind of got to me after a while.

But I didn't feel I had any choice, really. I remember some of the newspaper people, this nice older man, he was so kindly, and he'd say, "Would you do this again?" You know, they would wonder if I regretted having got myself into it. Well, it just seemed that I had no alternative, I had gotten to such a point of frustration. If a woman came, a well-to-do woman, I knew they could have an abortion. One way or another, they could go to England, or Japan. They could get by with it, or even some of the doctors would put them in under the guise of another diagnosis. And they would get their abortion. But it was the poorer people, and the young, that really got such a raw deal. Such horrible care. There were two classes of medicine, really . . . it was so definite, it was so hypocritical. There were doctors who were rabidly opposed, but who'd call me and ask me to do their daughter. You just got fed up with it.

I was in a field—infertility—where you're trying to help women get pregnant, and you're dealing with live sperm and counting them, and you see the sperm wiggling under the microscope, and what a wonderful thing life really is, and how a sperm and an egg get together, and the whole process. When you see that, you look upon it as a process, rather than any one starting point. The idea of saving one sperm or saving one fertilized egg is kind of ridiculous when in nature there are so many surplus. So I looked on life as a sort of continuum, rather than in isolated segments that you have to protect at all costs. I didn't have any moral qualms, or believe that I'd burn in Hellfire. *(Laughs.)*

No, I never had any doubts. Of course, when the whole world is against you, and you're vilified so much, you get to thinking, "Well gosh, maybe I could be wrong." But all I'd have to do is see a patient. I would find that just seeing one who needed an abortion, a woman with an unwanted or unplanned pregnancy, that was all I needed. Obviously this is the right thing for her. And it's safer than anything else she could do. You can hardly ever condemn a woman for having an unplanned pregnancy, because we're all human. There was always some reason. She didn't have the money for the "pill." The kid didn't know. Ignorance. Poverty. That explains most of it. And then just human carelessness, in which we're all guilty.

I think I'm much more of a feminist now than I was 20 years ago, at the time I did this. That was really not why. I think it was more the lack of health care and seeing how women had to suffer. I can think of one in particular. A poor working farm girl who came to town and wanted an abortion. I think it was the only man she'd ever known, and she trusted him, and he left her pregnant. She came to me when she was too far along to send her away or do anything about it.

And she got all these complications with her pregnancy—phlebitis, and separated placenta prematurely—and nearly bled to death. It was horrible. Had high blood pressure. She was real sick, and no money. She worked as a domestic, and she developed a permanent phlebitis so she had swollen legs, you know. Suffered really the rest of her life. Absolutely no family, nothing, just here alone in the city. She'd just work, work, work, and she'd come to see me regularly over the years, and she never really got over that. Having to go through that pregnancy just ruined her life. She never complained, but it's that type of situation that makes you realize how important it is that women have some control.

Nobody likes doing abortions, it would be a wonderful world if we didn't have to do any. The patients—they still stop me, people I don't recognize, they'll thank me. And the friends you make, the new friends. I lost a lot of my old friends, and I lost my status in organized medicine. I'd been president of the state OB society, back in '67 I think it was, but I certainly lost it all. I've offered to serve on committees since that time, repeatedly, on the ethics committee. But I'm never asked to do anything here locally. They've never asked me to be on programs or to speak. It's always somewhere else.

Kathryn Szymoniak Keeley

I'm a DES* daughter. I have two health things I don't talk about
very much. I've had lots of problems because of DES. I've had problems with cervical cancer, and three miscarriages. And then the polio
piece is the other one. I had polio when I was two. I was in the hospital, I was in isolation for a number of months, I was in physical therapy
for about 15 years, I had surgery a lot as a kid. I didn't walk right, I
walked funny—on my tiptoes. I couldn't run, I didn't ride a bike until
eighth grade, many things going back to the playground as a kid.

So I got teased a lot as a kid, and that's where I really developed my
skills in ignoring what people think of me. I learned early on in my life
to make do.

*Kathy Keeley was the director of Chrysalis, a counseling center for women,
for four years. She later established WEDCO, the Women's Economic Development Corporation. She is 43.*

I've started a lot of projects. I started a non-profit when I was 19. I
was the director of an agency, I mean I was the boss, at 19. It was a
crisis center, suicide prevention. I had a roommate in college who had
attempted suicide. This was the spring of '69, when mental health centers closed at five o'clock. I figured what she needed was a telephone
hotline, so I went and started one the next year. And was director and
never understood why all these adult people let me do this. *(Laughs.)*

I ran it for the last three years of college and grew it to an institution in this college town of Iowa City. Actually, it's still there—it's been
23 or 24 years now. I found myself doing three things at the center.
One was suicide prevention, and I was on call throughout the middle

* Diethylstilbestrol, a drug given to pregnant women and later found to cause cancer
in their daughters.

of the night. The other was drug overdose—that was the time of LSD, mescaline, and lots of drugs on campus. And the third was abortion.

I found myself, about two or three in the morning, going to this park in Iowa City and picking up kids my age who'd had illegal abortions. There was a man who picked you up at a pay phone in the park, took you out to a farmhouse, and did abortions. This was '69, before *Roe v. Wade*. He did them on a dining-room table, these young women reported. He did abortions and about a couple of times a month he perforated the uterus. They'd be bleeding in the park, and I'd pick them up and take them to the emergency room and stay with them.

Having gotten blood all over my car a few times, and seen these women and talked to a number who'd been through this, I was outraged. So I organized a referral line at the crisis center and called abortion clinics in New York, where it was legal. I got the Concerned Clergy, or whatever the group was back then who was doing that kind of stuff, to send me to New York. I was about 20, it was my first plane trip, and I went to New York City by myself and interviewed abortion clinics. I cut a deal that if we would refer paying clients, they would do so many free ones per month. I found a clinic that would do that, a very reputable one on Park Avenue, and arranged all this. We got about seven a month, free, and sent college women to New York, paid the plane fare. I made the arrangements beforehand and then saw them when they came back to make sure they were okay. That's probably how I became a feminist *(laughs)* . . . in a very practical, very real sense.

It was at the same time that I was very active in the antiwar movement. We shut the university down, and did all kinds of things. But the antiwar movement was very much run by men. We were supposed to bake cookies, run the mimeograph machine, hold their hands, and *(rolls her eyes)* probably have sex with them on the side. That was our role, and that wasn't enough for me. So I quit that, basically, and decided I was going to work on these other things. I decided I was going to spend my life building things up, rather than tearing things down. And I was going to do that in the company of women.

I went to graduate school and started a rape-counseling program as my master's thesis. Instead of writing a paper, I convinced them to let me start this program. This was in '74 and '75, and there was nothing for rape victims in the whole rural part of southern Illinois. I remember . . . again, I had a friend who was raped. They made her ride to the hearing in the police car with the assailant, in the back seat. That was standard operating procedure. I was outraged, and so I convinced the faculty that instead of doing a thesis and all the research, I needed to do something more practical. Rape victims called us, we went with them to the police, and then took them through the court system. We went to court 52 times, and we never won a case.

When my husband and I decided to move, we came to Minneapolis. We did a national search of the best places to live and decided it was between Seattle and Minneapolis. We had all these lengthy criteria, including feminism and good democratic politics. And money to do social causes, which was the top of my list. As well as Chinese restaurants, a Jewish community, a football team. It was quite a list *(laughs)* between the two of us.

The state planning agency recruited me. The first month on the job, I ended up at a retreat. There was a new administration, a lot of chaos, and this new commissioner took us on a retreat so we'd all get along better. The first night, we went out to a bar, and the next thing I know my boss is drunk. He's putting his hand all over me, telling me he's fallen in love with me, that's why he recruited me for this job. He wanted to know if I'd have sex with him.

I got out of there. I got a ride back, went to my room, and in the middle of the night he tried to break into my room. It was in a dormitory, with all these state agency people, and no one did a thing. No one came to my aid, no one did anything because he was one of the most powerful guys there. When I got back to work, he continued to touch me and say all kinds of things.

I went to Personnel and was told it was all my fault. I was young, I was attractive, obviously I was doing something. So I went higher, to the next step at Employee Relations, to see if somebody couldn't help me. Again I was told . . . well, this time I was told, "It's *not* your fault, but he is very powerful at the legislature." They said, "We knew something was going on because you're the fifth young woman in that position in the last couple of years. But there's nothing we can do. You should take care of yourself." This was prior to sexual harassment being a term. I didn't know what to call it, but I knew it was wrong and I wanted to get out of there.

I immediately started applying for jobs, and the third month there

I got the job at Chrysalis. I was desperate to get out, I was applying all over town. My husband didn't have a job yet, he was studying for the bar exam, and I had to work. I didn't talk about it when I left there, I really felt there was something wrong with me. I've never put that three months on my resume. I just bleeped out that whole time because there wasn't anything I could do about it.

Chrysalis was formed in about '75 or '76, and I was the second director. It had been a collective. It had started at the YW as a kind of volunteer program, and then it evolved into this mouthy group who couldn't get along with the Y—so they parted ways.

In the early days it was really exciting and heady to be part of transforming the organization. We did a lot of the stuff that's been written about now, without knowing we were doing it. We spent a lot of time talking about language, and male/female communication. And about our own female communication. We spent a lot of time talking between straight women and lesbian women, trying to break down those barriers. We had a lot of meetings and retreats to work on feminist management. What were the elements? How were we going to make decisions?

Then later there was a decision, which I opposed, that the organization could choose to become an institution. To me the institutionalizing represented professionalism, standards, United Way money, forms, rules, all the traditional stuff. Or it could stay on the cutting edge.

That's what I think a women's organization should be. I've always believed women's organizations should be out front, designing new things, getting other groups to institutionalize them, and then moving on. I don't think women's organizations should operate shelters, for instance. I think they should get the men with all the money to do those long-term things. (Laughs.)

Unfortunately the board decided they wanted to do both, which was the worst possible decision. It set up inherent conflicts, I think. At the end, it was very frustrating. It was a schizoid kind of time—they wanted to be out front, but when I took on the United Way on a particular issue, the agency was very nervous because of the money. There were changes happening in the chemical-dependency world— Hazelden, Johnson—all those places were now serving women. I was arguing, "We should let go of our chemical-dependency program. We won, let's declare a victory. The guys have got it. It's not as good as ours, it's not perfect, but we'll never be able to compete because they've got millions of dollars."

I had gotten divorced about a year into Chrysalis. There were a lot of people who were delighted, hoping that now I'd become a lesbian . . . which wasn't my bent. *(Laughs.)* I got a lot of flak for dating men, who would sometimes come by and pick me up for lunch. There would be women in my office who immediately said, "Who was that man? How dare he come in here?" Men did not come into Chrysalis, which is one of the things I tried to change.

Anyway, my last year there I decided to get married. That was bad enough, but on top of it I decided to change my name. I was oblivious to the turmoil that would cause. I got people in my office picketing, I got calls and letters saying I had no right to be a feminist. It was very hard, because I was the person who in my first marriage in 1969 . . .

I had kept my name, and I had gone to court to keep my name. I was the first person in the state of Iowa to do that. It made big headlines, a blitz. And I had a court decree, a legal-size document of three pages, explaining how this Kathy Szymoniak became Kathy Beller became Kathy Szymoniak. It was a dumb law, and I had to carry that legal document with me wherever I went.

I thought I'd paid my dues, but at Chrysalis women were angry. Actually, it was a very personal thing. I got married because I wanted kids, definitely wanted kids, and I was joining a family with two children. It was important to those kids, to accepting me as stepmother. I wouldn't have done it for anyone else but those two kids.

I had lived 10 years with these damn court papers, and I thought, "I'm joining a family, I want to create a family. It's hard enough being this blended group, and to throw this in . . ." But everybody was so disappointed, and I was unprepared. I thought—and this is the classic— I thought I had paid my dues. I thought I was accepted, I thought people knew my feminism was unquestioned, that now I could do what I wanted. I found out, wrong.

I started planning WEDCO as my way out of Chrysalis. I went to the foundations and said, "I want to run something that addresses women's economic issues, but I don't know what." I just knew that I couldn't watch 1,200 women a month come through this place, prop them up, give them all this self-esteem, make them feel great, and send them out when they can't make money. I couldn't watch any more, this sort of revolving door.

I had a vision in starting WEDCO that I'd make it a kind of premier women's economic agency. I'd start with the business stuff and then move into economic development, and economic literacy, and job training. I wanted it to become a full service agency over a period of time. We knew that economic development had huge sources of money. Women's stuff was always guilt money, social-service money, and we needed to change that.

WEDCO sort of grew and grew and grew. I originally thought that the business piece, the entrepreneur piece, would only last a year or two. To me it was just an opening. But with the shifts in the economy, and what's happened, obviously it's going strong. Congress last year did a $53-million appropriation based on WEDCO, to fund groups like WEDCO to do loans to low-income women.

For me personally, I'm happiest when I'm kind of on the edge, doing something different and new. Feminism has given me the chance to be a different kind of entrepreneur.

Choua Eve Lee &
Pam Deu Yang Thao

Choua Lee, 23, was elected to the board of the St. Paul public schools in 1990. She is the first Hmong person elected to public office in the United States.* During the interview at her family-run insurance agency, her two-year-old son, Useng, sleeps on her lap, while her husband, parents, and nieces pass in and out. Her sister Pam Thao, 29, joins us for the beginning of the conversation. Pam is a homemaker and student.

Choua: We came from Laos. Pam is six years my senior, so there's an age gap between us, but we were always very close. She is always my

---

* Southeast Asian hill people who supported the United States in the Vietnam War and became refugees when American troops withdrew in the 1970s.

protector *(laughs)*—that's her role. My role in the family was to be the baby, do things and get away with it.

Pam: She's doing pretty good so far. *(Laughs.)*

Choua: Shortly after we left Laos, we spent a year and two months in a refugee camp in Thailand. Then we came to Chicago when I was 7 and Pam was 13. Pam got married shortly after we arrived.

Pam: He was a relative, a distant uncle. He was an interpreter for us. When I married, it was kind of jumping from the frying pan to the fire. Seems like that to me.

The early age is not the original custom in the Hmong community. My mom's generation, they were always at least 18 to 20 before they married. They started getting married younger in the last generation. In Laos, polygamy is common. When the war was very bad we lost a lot of men.

Choua: The custom is still present, that's my concern. Polygamy in Hmong history—it used to be because we didn't have enough manpower to work in the fields. It helps the family to have more family members. But later that process began to be something other than benefiting the family—rather it was for self-fulfillment.

The woman doesn't have a choice. But the scariest thing, women start to see that as a status symbol. Being chosen to be someone's second, third, fourth, or fifth wife. The younger you are, the more status.

Pam: If you're youngest, you're more favored by the husband, so you can play like a spoiled child. In my situation, it's different, though. Knowing that if a man comes asking for my hand in marriage, my parents can just force me to marry the man. So when my husband wanted to marry me, he just . . .

Choua: Took her.

Pam: More like kidnapping me. By then I knew that it was too late. Even if I said I don't want it, I knew that my parents would force me to marry him. But in my case, I'm very glad that I married him.

I was raised very different than Choua. Our family doesn't have boys, and Choua was raised more like a boy, and me like a girl. I was always taught, always expected, a woman role. Choua, a big difference.

Choua: I would disagree with that, but I'll get to that later. *(Laughs.)*

Pam: When my parents brought me up, I didn't argue back. Let the elders say what they want to say. Even if your point is right, you don't have the right to argue back. You just keep it to yourself.

But when I married my husband, it's very different, because he's had some education. He wants me to communicate, speak up what my feelings are. He told me, "I'm not a person that can read minds. If you don't up and talk to me what you are angry about or what's upsetting you, I will not know." He encouraged me to speak more for myself.

If I could change the time back, would I marry my husband? Yes. Because I have had 15 wonderful years. The only thing I regret is that when I was pregnant with my daughter, I got embarrassed and he didn't push me to go back to high school. So I dropped from school for quite a few years there and then catching up has been very hard.

Choua: Pam's husband was older, he was in college when they got married. It was not a force issue, but it was not a desire issue either. Her desire was not to get married, but in the Hmong practice, once a girl gets to a guy's house, she's unreturnable. Almost like, "No refund."

She got dragged . . . tricked. Pam had a cooking class with an American woman and he said, "Let me take you to your lesson." Instead of taking her there, he just rushed her off to his home. And then phoned my parents, saying, "I want to marry her." Once that phone call is in, she's totally trapped. In the Hmongs' eyes, she is legally married to him. By the time they got the marriage license, she was pregnant with Terry.

Before that, when Pam was growing up, we were in a transition period when we were constantly moving from one place to another. When we came from Laos to Thailand, she was the oldest. The first thing is family survival. You don't think about education anymore, you think about food on the table. Because she's older, she was pressured to go and find work.

Pam: No, there was no pressure. Not from my parents, from myself. The background we came from, my dad used to be a commander in the army. When I was little we had servants in the house that brought warm water in the morning for me to take a bath. We had people that cooked for us, things like that. Then suddenly when the war was over, people started hunting my dad down. When you escaped, you lost all of your belongings, you couldn't have even a single picture with you. All the money you have, you use to buy your way out. So by the time you get to Thailand, there's no money left.

During that month-and-a-half time before the aid arrived, people were starving, dying . . . I was 12, but I could see the big change. My dad used to be wealthy and suddenly he doesn't know how to survive. I was glad that my dad sent me to school when I was younger, because I could speak Thai very fluently. At that time, adults couldn't find jobs anywhere.

I felt like if there was anything I could do to get some food for the family, I'd do it. I remember this lady, she had a grocery business. I went begging for food. I said, "I can work for you, I'm very hungry, I'm just working for food." She said, "Oh, you speak Thai." Then I worked for her for a whole afternoon, for one meal for myself only. Then she said, "Why don't you work for me and I can supply food for your family." Boy, that's a great deal. I took it, and I was saving my family, for them not to die of hunger.

Choua: And not just my family. We have an uncle too, with eight children, she was supporting that family too. She supported 13 members of the family.

Pam: It was a short time there, but boy, it sure . . . My lifetime in Laos and my lifetime in this country, it's not as long as those months struggling in Thailand. Many people I knew had young babies dying daily, hundreds of people dying daily from starvation, and people going back to Laos.

Choua: Having to adjust to being a refugee, especially for the men, they had a tremendous time adapting. To beg for work so you have food for your family, that's something most men would not tolerate.

When we came to Thailand, people were dependent on the Thai government and American relief, they started getting dependent on drugs. And infidelity, because there's nothing to do in a camp, no education, boring, what do you do? Young girls get courted at a younger age, that's the only social thing they can do, why not?

When my family first came to Chicago, it was mind-blowing for me. Skyscrapers, escalators, elevators . . . I will never forget our first night on the twenty-fourth floor of a skyscraper. We went up on the elevator, I thought it was some kind of testing box. We'd been tested for so long, it was part of the regular routine for refugee people. Then we came to a long hall, with lots of doors. They said, "This is your home." My uncle was there, family reunion, great moment. The next morning, I opened the window curtains . . . *Ohhh!* So deep down! It scared the hell out of me. You're used to ground level and then you're up . . . That was my first experience in America.

When Pam got married, my role in the family suddenly changed. Now I was the person who would take on the responsibility. But now resettled in the U.S., our residence was more stable. My father took me to meetings, community gatherings, opportunities to explore my horizons. Whereas Pam jumped from Thailand, where everyone was so poor, right into marriage.

Of course those responsibilities mature you very fast. Letters, finding jobs, helping translate at clinics, hospitals, unemployment, filling out applications—you name any app, I can fill it out. *(Laughs.)* And when more Hmong refugees started to resettle in Chicago, my sympathy extended to the whole community. Always as a volunteer. I was at everybody's call.

When I was 11, I translated for women in the birth room. It scared the hell out of me, but I had to do it. I translated for Hmong women when they had physical examinations. I don't know who got embarrassed the most, me or the patient.

You learn over the years to be aggressive. One of the things my husband accuses me of is, I don't have patience. My husband accuses me of being too authoritative, giving out commands, which of course is true. That's my character. But at the same time, ever since I married my husband . . . He has a more gentle nature because of his upbringing, I adapt some of those skills from him too, so it balances.

I got married three years ago. When we met, I was in high school, and he was in college. He was doing tax preparation at that time, helping my family with their taxes. And I was providing the information, so we worked as a team. We found that we are compatible, we work well together. We got married after he graduated. Shortly after that I went back to college for a year, then I got pregnant. I'm still trying to continue my education, I have about three courses left.

After college, I got a job as executive director of the Women's Association of Hmong and Lao. At the Women's Association, we served from elderly women to young women, we had three basic programs. We served the young women who are teen parents, and other high-school students, through mentoring and tutoring. For the elderly people, we have a knitting class, gardening, and other activities. And we also have a self-sufficiency program where we find jobs for poor families.

I went into high-school classrooms to do tutoring, that was the hardest thing I ever did. I had a lot of students tutoring in basic skills,

English, math, science, history. Those students are expected to graduate within the next few months, and they have not had those basic courses nailed down. It really scares me, what will happen to these children. I raised a lot of these issues with the school district and I got no response back. I called the administration office, I wrote to the administration office, about the concerns.

A friend of mine said, "Why don't you run for the school board?" I thought he was joking at first. I actually decided to run in May, two weeks before the party convention. I had a whole printout of names of delegates I needed to contact. That whole two weeks, I'm just sitting down with the phone by my ears. I don't know these people. I have some opinions about what's going on in the schools, but I don't know whether they support my issues. The first delegate I called, she mentioned some of the things I was concerned about. I found a lot of similar needs.

I thought the concerns I had were unique to the Hmong community, but they weren't. Hispanic, black, Native American students, white students, for that matter . . . after I got done with that list, my confidence went sky-high. But then I had the convention to think of. I prepared my speech. I was pregnant so I felt awkward at that time, I was big enough. I went and bought a dress just for the convention, I came across this hot-pink magenta, I looked good in it. That became my campaign color.

I was hesitant to be talking . . . I went there not expecting to be endorsed. You're an Asian woman, you're young, you're pregnant, you have all these strikes against you. You don't have a name in the community as far as politics goes. But I thought, at least I'll raise the issues so the awareness is there.

I got endorsed. I guess I can be perceived as someone who's new to the process, naïve in a sense, but maybe that can be a positive, a fresh force. People connected to how I felt.

One of the things that hurt me the most, the Hmong community really criticized my age. They felt I was too young, not representative of the community. They wanted somebody who already was established politically, knew their own minds—they thought I didn't know my own mind. But nobody had been established! I wouldn't object, if only someone else had volunteered.

People would come up to me on the street and say, "You're not going to win." The support wasn't there. When I got elected, that really changed. The most arrogant said, "She won because she had the American people behind her." Which was a put-down. Other people would say, "Maybe we're wrong about what we said, maybe you're doing right."

I want the community to realize that some of the youth are doing very well in school now. Last year at graduation, 20 percent of the members from the top class were Hmong. We have our share of problems, but we have people who are doing excellent in the school and in the community as well.

I consider myself an advocate for women, because there are certain things happening that . . . As a woman, I feel we've been cheated. As women, we have the right to say what's on our mind.

We are a changing society, we need to keep in pace with that change. I'm not saying we need to let all the traditions go, we need to retain those important things. But to adapt to the life that we have now, the old way doesn't work anymore, the women doing all the work and the men and boys not doing anything. Equally, individually, they're going to have to be responsible. What's a better way is to share goals, to share house chores and other responsibilities. Like I always tell my husband, we have to work on this on a daily basis.

There are barriers between women of color and white women, but we have so much similarity. For example, we have children. Every woman knows about that—no matter where we come from, children are the dearest subjects in our life. Let's talk about husband and wife, we know that. (Laughs and rolls her eyes.) Let's talk about housewife, we know that. Whether you are a rich housewife or a poor housewife, there are certain limitations that the housewife can conjure up, the image they have . . . Women bonding, that's the same, we have a different understanding than men. We tend to be more sensitive. Those feelings can bring the women community together. The only barrier I see is not talking often enough.

Rocking the Boat

No single strategy characterizes the women's movement. Women set social change in motion by creating or joining organizations, doing street theater, raising money, and filing lawsuits. Diane Fass simply walked through the front door of a businessman's club.

Motivations for "rocking the boat" range from Wendy Brower's sheer enjoyment of rabble-rousing to Bev Hall's anger about the low status of clerical workers. Marianne Christianson speaks of exhilarating women's conventions and of meetings with chocolate-chip cookies. Luanne Nyberg remembers outrage at how the social-service system treats poor women. When the women's movement got underway, Marilyn Bryant was unwilling to play bridge on the sidelines. Desire for a swim team for her daughter led Charlotte Striebel to activism on behalf of girls' athletics, while Elsa Vega-Perez felt a sense of accountability to the Hispanic community. Although Kate Wulf hated public speaking, she did it because she found it necessary as a feminist organizer.

Wendy Robinson Brower

Wendy Brower speaks rapidly, laughs often, and rolls her eyes at life's in-justices. As a clerical worker, she organized Minnesota Working Women in 1980. The group is an affiliate of the national organization "9 to 5," which advocates for clerical and service workers. Wendy is 43.

One of the jobs I almost took, back in 1978, was as a classified-ad person at the St. Paul newspaper. I thought, "I'll get to work for a newspaper, it's a step in the door." *(Laughs.)* Well, it was a roomful of women, about 20 of them, lined up in rows with the supervisor on a riser behind them, behind glass. And this was for a $4.30-an-hour job. That's the way the workplace is organized. You've got these women running around out of control, you've got to keep them penned in, you've got to watch them every minute.

Instead of that, I got a clerical job at the University of Minnesota, in the vice president's office. That was when the inequities of what men and women are paid for the work they are doing became most apparent to me. In the basement of my building there were job post-ings every week: your clerical, your technical, your professional, your academic, and then you had maintenance or janitorial.

At that time there was a secretarial shortage. And there were lots of qualifications to be a secretary. Grammar and spelling, post-secondary ed-ucation, three to five years experience, type 60 words a minute—all those things. My job paid about $800 a month. And right across on the other side of the job board, they were looking for janitors. It only required an eighth grade education, and it paid $200 a month more. For starters.

Then I went to work at an art museum. I was secretary to the executive director, and this man treated me like absolute garbage. He thought of me more as his slave, I think, than as a human being with any feelings or contributions other than jumping at his every demand.

I ended up typing about 90 words a minute when I worked there, because there was so much to be done. But it was the kind of job where I would get to work, I would hear him come in, and immediately my stomach would start to churn. It was so stressful, I had to leave.

I went to work for an employment and training program. We were working with really disadvantaged low-income people. And I'm not kidding you, we had some men that were getting trained and employed, and they'd start working at about $9 an hour. These guys had just been incarcerated for 10 years, they'd battered their wives, or they'd been on the lam, and we could get them fairly high-paid jobs.

Then we'd get women who were single moms, and they'd been to technical school or something, and they had all these skills, and we couldn't get them placed at anything higher than $4.50 an hour. I thought, something's wrong with this system.

In that job, I had the opportunity to go to a lot of conferences. At one of them, someone was there from Working Women, from the national office, and that's when I learned about that organization. She was talking about how women are treated differently, the pay, all this stuff. And I thought, "You're right, this is it, this is the answer. You're speaking the language of all the things I'm feeling." So I wanted to get something like that started here.

In 1980, we organized a little group to meet one Saturday morning at the downtown YWCA. I had put a little announcement in the *Skyway News* inviting people to a meeting. About 30 people showed up. There were actually people who wanted to do something!

Soon after that, a prominent feminist sent us a check. I just started to cry when I opened up the envelope, I couldn't believe anybody was doing this. That really helped get us from day one to day two. I quit my job and started as the Working Women organizer. The Y gave us a little cubicle. Then the national organization gave us a little money. The Christian Sharing Fund gave us a little money. We never had a lot of money, we were always on a shoestring.

We had a lot of fun in that organization. When Governor Perpich was elected in 1982, we set up a meeting with him about issues affecting women in the workplace. Pay equity was first on the agenda. We dressed up one of our members as a white-out* bottle and we wrote on there, "White out low pay." At first, nobody wanted to be the white-out bottle, but we said, "Listen, nobody will know who you are." *(Giggles.)* We used a cardboard ice cream container to make the cap, with just eye holes to see out.

So I remember being in the grand reception area with the big polished table, sitting there with the governor, and there was this white-out bottle. The governor really supported pay equity, but he didn't get it about the white-out. I'm sure he didn't have a clue what white-out was. And the white-out bottle couldn't sit down—we kind of failed to think about everything *(laughs)*, there she was in this cardboard tube that didn't bend.

Another thing we did that was fun, that got a lot of media attention, was our annual Boss Award. We were getting applications from people about the crummiest thing they had to do for their boss, and we got amazing things. One woman wrote to us about her boss making her put out her hand so he could flick his cigarette ashes into it. We didn't even mention that one, because it was so atrocious.

There were women that were expected to clean up the bathrooms. One woman submitted a nomination, she was working for a law office. Her boss would come into the office on Mondays and make her go to the nearby laundromat with his clothes. She had to do his laundry. We called it the "Jockey" award.

But the best one was this executive who was having a romance. When he traveled out of the country, he would have his secretary call up his girlfriend and repeat all these love messages over the phone. The secretary found this totally obnoxious. She had gone through all the proper channels at work about getting him to stop. She talked to him directly on numerous occasions, told him she didn't like it, but he wouldn't do anything.

So she came to us. When the day arrives, here we are with these TV cameras rolling. We give him this award, and he doesn't realize this is a putdown until we're halfway through. *(Laughs.)*

On National Secretary's Day, we would try to draw attention to our situation. We were always in competition with the Professional

---

* "Wite-out" is a brand of typewriter correction fluid.

Secretaries International. They wanted to make sure people knew that *we* were the rank and file, and *they (looks down her nose)* were "executive assistants." We had a lot of things in common, but there were definitely two schools of thought here. We were the rabble-rousers. But they secretly, in their hearts, loved what we were doing.

For one Secretaries' Day, I analyzed the wages at Minneapolis City Hall. The city's head of affirmative action gave me all the information. I showed graphically the wage rates and the occupational segregation, all that horrible stuff.

The numbers were really dismal. Less than 2 percent of the females working for the city made over $30,000 a year. Dismal. And about 75 percent of the males were earning that amount of money. The men were making all the bucks. It didn't matter if they were sweeping the streets or doing management, they got themselves into high-paid positions. And the women, of course, were all clustered in the low-paid positions.

After that, the city told the affirmative-action director he couldn't ever give that kind of information to anybody, ever again.

We raised that whole issue of comparable worth/pay equity. When we started, people had no idea what we were talking about. "Are they nuts?" The other thing we were really ahead of our time on: we were talking about worker safety, the tight-building syndrome, the effects of computer terminals.

In fact we had a bill at the state legislature. Was it 1982? Just a little bill to give work breaks for people who worked at computer terminals all day. Oh, my gosh! The manufacturers' association, IBM, everybody sent out the big guns. We got a few votes in the senate employment committee, but we didn't get any votes in the house employment committee. Not a one. I was flattered that the big guns came out, though. *(Laughs.)*

We were just ahead of our time, there's no question about it. The word "ergonomic" is not so foreign to people now, they understand about chairs and positions and shields on the screens and tilting them. The computers themselves are better, they're more flexible than they used to be in the old days.

A lot of people thought we were organizing a union, but that wasn't the case. In fact, the women dealt with so much unfairness and sexism during the day that the last thing some wanted to do was to become part of another institution where sexism was just as rampant.

And they couldn't fathom paying union dues on top of the rotten wages they were already getting.

But to other members, unions made great sense. I ran into one of our former members the other day. She's a union organizer for clerical workers at the university now.

We never got much support from unions, except for the Coalition of Labor Union Women. The male-dominated unions saw us as a threat. Someone who was working at the AFL-CIO called me up one time, shortly after we started. I was working in this little cubicle all by myself. The AFL-CIO person just screamed at me, because we had the gall to put out a flyer without the union bug. Well, I didn't know what a union bug was, and the labor for the flyer was donated.

A lot of the Working Women members did not identify as feminists. For clerical workers who were not making much money, maybe had a couple of kids at home, had to pay the rent or the mortgage, maybe the husband isn't too well off either . . . you don't see yourself as part of a social movement. You see yourself as struggling to survive. You just want to do a little better.

It wasn't until I got involved with establishing Working Women that I started to understand feminism myself. Sometime in there I said to myself *(whispers)*, "I guess I *am* one!"

Diane Fass

It was black sooty diapers, in the late '60s, that led me to become political. *(Laughs.)* In Florida, I would hang out my son's diapers on the backyard clothesline, which I loved to do when it was nice and sunny. But if I left them out too long, they would get soot all over them from the crate factory a block away. All the women on the block would have to take their clothes in before the factory let its smoke out, and we'd have to close the windows. I filed a complaint with the state, and a few years later it was changed.

Diane Fass was a feminist organizer in the 1970s, a homemaker who helped establish Minnesota branches of NOW and the Women's Political Caucus. At 52, she is now an art dealer.

In 1971, I was invited to speak to a group which met at the Minneapolis Club downtown. I had been to the National Women's Political Caucus convening meeting and was now getting ready to start the state organization. The title of my address was "Opening Doors to Women." I invited my friend Kathy Olson to go with me, because I was good at writing a speech, but I was real nervous. I was tired of answering all these stupid questions, like "Do you wear a bra?"

It was a males-only club. One member was the editor of the newspaper. A woman reporter saw the announcement of the meeting on his desk and asked if she could come and report on it. But he said women weren't allowed at this meeting. She then asked if she could get a copy of the speech, and could she interview me? He said yes, so she called me the afternoon prior to the talk. I said, "Yes, I can give you a copy, I'll meet you by the gate." She said, "That's the front, aren't you going in the back?"

I knew some women had lunch there but went in the back door. I sort of knew that, but I didn't know it was an absolute ironclad rule. I hadn't paid that much attention. This reporter calls me back and says, "Women aren't allowed in the front door, no woman has ever gone in the front door. Are you going in the front door?" I said, "That's my speech, of course I'll go in the front door." When I picked up my friend she asked if we should go in the back door. I said, "No, we can't, my mother didn't raise me to go in the back door." *(Laughs.)*

So we go, meet the reporter by the gate, give her the speech. There's a photographer with her. We go in the front. Of course he takes a picture. I open the door, and standing there is a guy in a little uniform, a little hat. He says, "You can't come in here." I said, "Senator Pillsbury invited me here, I'm supposed to give a talk to his club." He said, "Well, you have to go around the back." But meanwhile, I'm in the door, and the picture's taken. I was inside. It was like, how do you even get around to the back? You have to go all the way back out to the street and all the way around. I said, "No, can't I just go in and call Senator Pillsbury?" There was a big stairway in the front hall, and he did not let me go up those stairs. I didn't know where they were meeting. So we followed him through the building, and the reporter was following with a photographer, taking pictures.

They called Senator Pillsbury and he came down the elevator, this wonderful little iron cage. And he said, "We thought something like that might happen." I actually, honestly did not plan to do that. It just happened. I had just started a new job and I was way too busy to figure out doing an action like that. I didn't think it was going to be such a big deal.

So I spoke, it was nice, and they liked my speech. The reporter had told me to call her and tell her how it went. So I called her, and then she wanted our husbands' names. Of course that was how the newspapers identified women then. She said, "We have this great story and we want to put it on the front page." I said, "Well you'll just have to use *our* names, that's all there is to it." She says, "I have to talk to the editor." Well, he had been in the meeting. She talked to the editor and he did the name-change policy. That was probably more important than walking through the front door of the Minneapolis Club. So instead of putting my name as "Mrs. David Fass," or "Mrs. David (Diane) Fass," or "Doctor Mrs. Diane David Fass," I got in as my own name.

And there was this big picture in the paper of me walking through the front door. Of course that was the early '70s, so I wore high heels and a short skirt. It's definitely a pair of legs walking in. *(Laughs.)* Actually, I was a little embarrassed about all the publicity. But from then on, they could not keep one woman out of that front door. They finally had to change the policy. That's my claim to fame—walking through the front door of the Minneapolis Club. *(Laughs again.)*

Bev Hall

Bev Hall, 39, is a bargaining agent for clerical workers at the University of Minnesota. She was president of her American Federation of State, County, and Municipal Employees (AFSCME) local, negotiating pay equity for state employees in the early 1980s.

I dropped out of college in order to pay off student loans, and I took the first job offered. It paid $2.70 an hour, a file-clerk job at the state retirement system. The guy I was working for was an amazingly cruel person and had no concept of getting along with employees. "Thou shalt be at your desk at eight o'clock," "there shall be no flex-time," "you will never get sick leave," God forbid. "If you're nice you might get a vacation." So we contacted AFSCME. There were only 20 of us. Management didn't mount much of an "anti" campaign because they didn't think we could win—which is always nice. We had the big election, and we won.

I was a steward, and one day I got a notice in the mail that the union needed somebody for negotiations. Well, none of us had a clue what that was about. (Laughs.) Somebody else was going to go, then they couldn't, so I went. It was over at the community college. First off, I couldn't find the place. I didn't know a soul. But they started talking about stuff that was kind of interesting, empowering people to do things for themselves.

There weren't a lot of women or clerical workers involved in the union at that point. It was mostly driven by the trades and technical employees, who were predominantly male. And I was 25 or 26 years old. I was on the negotiating committee—still without a clue. It was jump in with both feet.

Both the union and management negotiators were very dramatic, with a lot of yelling and screaming and table-pounding. Well, I saw some potential for me. It sure as heck wasn't there yet, for a young woman in a small agency. There were two other women on that committee of 20 people, but both of them were older than my mother. I could see things needed to happen.

I got to be president of the local that represented all the small departments. I'd been treasurer for one term, they conned me into that. There's a lot of work to being treasurer. There's this report you have to send to the national union, pages and pages of financial stuff. After that I said, "Forget it, I'm running for president—that has to be easier." (Laughs.)

After that contract was settled, the law changed so the bargaining units were organized by occupations instead of by agencies. That's when we picked up all the clerical employees. I expect the average age dropped by 10 or 15 years, and the gender balance definitely swung to women. The majority of the council has been women ever since.

There were 6,000 of us clericals. We advertised ourselves as "the largest bargaining unit in the world." So I went from president of a local with 100 or 200 people to chair of "the largest bargaining unit in the world." There hadn't been a lot of clericals involved in the bargaining process—there'd only been, like, two of us—ever. And the other woman retired. So there I was, the expert!

There were 12 or 13 of us clericals on the bargaining committee of around 80 people. There was some animosity about all these "girls" that got brought into the union. Some of us were practically uppity at that point. We wanted things. I remember discussions about significant others. There were people that couldn't figure that out for the world. "Why is this an issue?" "Why don't you people just go get married?" "Why don't you girls go have children?" That was the real message.

We had a horrible round of negotiations between AFSCME and the state for the 1979-81 contract. We tried to negotiate sexual harassment complaint procedures, we had beginning talks about pay equity,* but nobody in management was sold on that. There was a three-week statewide strike in the summer of 1981.

During the strike, we surprised everybody with our strength. There were lots of single parents, folks who were just barely making ends meet. The first thing after the union comes in, we have a strike. Management was amazed. Their attitude was, "We'll take a strike because there won't really be a strike. Or if there is, they're gonna cave-in so quickly, that'll be the end of the union."

The clericals were the most visible piece of the strike. It was scary because no one knew what was going to happen. We were doing what we could to help folks out, but it was 50 bucks here, 50 bucks there. When you're taking 17,000 people out on strike—the whole union— the strike fund doesn't go far. In my agency all the clericals were out. We had one member who was still going in, a male. So all these women were really sacrificing, then there's this guy who was making more money than any of us, and he was crossing the picket line. We talked to

* Pay increases for jobs performed mostly by women, making their salaries comparable to those for "male" jobs requiring equal skill, effort, and responsibility.

him and it didn't do any good. We had other guys talk to him, that
didn't do any good either. It was hard for people.

After the strike, somebody came to me and said, "There's never
been any female officers of this council, ever." The vice president was
leaving. They said, "You're the one who's got the guts to do it." Well, I
didn't. I never thought I wanted to be vice president of anything when
I grew up. And they talked and twisted my arms—one arm today is still
hanging by a thread. *(Laughs.)* At the convention, the guy who ran
against me was definitely running on an antiwoman thing. "Women
don't know what they're doing, they're too new, they don't know what
this is about . . ." That whole line. But people weren't buying it. I won
handily. So I was the first female officer in the council.

And then the pay equity law passed, and we went into pay equity
negotiations.

Before the strike, the women were sold on pay equity. But management said, "We can't single out a group of, God forbid, *women,* and
give them a whole pile of money. And besides, it's a stupid concept.
How are we going to compare these janitors to clerical workers?" And
a lot of our janitors didn't see how you could compare them to clerical workers either. The women had gotten studies done, but they were
sitting on a shelf collecting dust somewhere. We kept saying, "Look,
there's a problem here."

After a pay equity law passed in 1982, it was a big education
process. Mostly for the male-dominated units, explaining how in the
end everybody was going to benefit from this. The strategy was, keep
talking it. We talked it and talked it, they heard it and saw it every time
they turned around. We needed to do this, nobody was going to lose in
this. If we had to put some money into people's salaries, it was because
they had been so far behind for so long. We talked about some of the
clerical workers who were strapped, sitting out there 22 years old with
a kid or two trying to make ends meet on six bucks an hour. So the
men would see we're not joking, this is real stuff.

By now there was new management and it was all peaceably settled.
We got pay equity for everyone in four years. The ones that were in the
worst shape we bumped up faster. And actually before I left state service, I got some pay equity myself, so I even knew what it looked like.

We don't have pay equity here at the university yet. We still have
clerical workers who are eligible for public assistance. As we were ne-

gotiating the contract, we would say, "Look, you have people here working full time who have to work a second job, because they can't make ends meet on what they're being paid." I don't know why the administration has such a hard time understanding that. If they went out and tried to live on six bucks an hour I don't know how far they'd get. But the university's attitude was somehow that was okay, for people to be on public assistance while they work here.

The arrogance you run into here, the attitudes about clerical work are really sad. The class divisions are still there. You know where some of our worst problems have been? In the predominantly female departments, the places you'd think would be the most supportive. It just floors me when we have employee problems there. Pressuring women on maternity leave. The university culture is so inbred, faculty think they are above all of this. "There's this peon who may or may not be a human being and I don't care, I'll do whatever I want to my peon." It's so ingrained here.

The union is still male-driven. It's changed somewhat, nobody's going to be overtly sexist. But it's still there, nobody kids themselves that it isn't. For some folks, if the women's leadership had never risen up, that would be just fine. In the 14 years I've been involved, there still hasn't been a woman president of the council. After all these years when a majority of the members have been women.

But there are successes out there too. The women have made a difference. We can get pay equity in this state, we have lots of flextime stuff going on now. We started some good stuff.

If I'd still been in a clerical job, I couldn't have done the leave things I did with both my kids. With both of my boys, I took six months' leave. But I knew I was not cut out to be a full-time domestic goddess. It's just not in my genetic build. *(Laughs.)*

My husband stays home with them. I think he's a better parent than I am. He's got more patience than I do. He's a musician so he works evenings, weekends, odd hours, and goes to school part time. It works real well. He's the only dad in early childhood family education class—he talks about the "other moms." *(Laughs again.)*

I'm dreading the day he gets his degree and starts talking about getting a job. I think what he's doing now is more valuable than any financial stuff he could do. We're not rich, but we're okay. We can still feed and diaper our kids.

Charlotte Striebel

Minnesota's National Organization for Women presents the annual Charlotte Striebel Long Distance Runner Award to recognize a woman who has struggled long years toward a feminist goal. Charlotte, who lobbied successfully for a state law requiring equal opportunity for girls' athletics, is now in her sixties. A professor of mathematics at the University of Minnesota for almost 30 years, she is also a lawyer.

In the '50s and '60s, you had a sense that you as a woman were doing something wrong if you had a career. With our jobs, we were made to feel grateful that we were there at all. It never occurred to us that we should be treated equally, because just allowing us to be there was such a huge concession.

You lived with that second-class citizenship. Then with the beginning of the women's movement you suddenly realized you didn't have to put up with it. In the late '60s I read *The Feminine Mystique,** and that was a dividing time in my life. I had an incredible weight lifted from my shoulders, understanding things that had just confused and hurt me before.

Before, I told myself, "I don't understand what's going on, but I have to keep my head down and keep trudging on." I tried not to look on one side or the other side. There was a lot of deliberate narrowness, which was the only way to deal with the kind of rejection you had in those days. To suddenly be liberated from that by reading one book was rather astonishing.

I guess in some ways the astonishing thing was that we didn't figure it out sooner. But of course, I didn't have any women friends. I didn't have many friends at all because there weren't any women in my field and I didn't fit in with the men. I was divorced, and my personal life

* By Betty Friedan.

was just my kids, and that was all. But since becoming a feminist, it's been just one damned thing after another! *(Laughs.)* All kinds of things, most of which were lots of fun, very gratifying.

I got involved in girls' athletics in 1971, when my daughter Kathy was 12. My son had been involved in swimming for a long time, he loved it, and it was a wonderful influence in his life. We moved quite a bit at that time and swimming always gave him an instant entrée to friends and activities.

Kathy started swimming as well, but when she started junior high in St. Paul there were zero athletic teams for girls. She wanted to have a swim team and so she went to the school authorities. They said, "Fine, get enough people interested and we'll start a girls' swim team." So she got enough people that were interested and then the school said, "No, we were just fooling, girls don't do that sort of thing."

She swam with an Amateur Athletic Union team, one that was not organized through the schools, and all she really wanted to do was to be able to practice in the morning. The boys on her team had a morning practice at school. And we lived just blocks from school. It seemed far easier for her to work out with that team in the morning rather than get up at five o'clock and drive out to Bloomington for the AAU practice, which is what we had been doing. So when they wouldn't start a girls' team, she went to them and said, "Well, could I just work out with the boys' team in the morning?" They said, "Absolutely not, this is a *boys'* team."

In the meantime, through my activities with NOW I was aware that the St. Paul city ordinance on equal opportunity had been amended just that year to include a prohibition of sex discrimination in education. So I filed a grievance with the city human rights department and the upshot was that my daughter became a member of the boys' swim team at the school. It worked so quickly, it was breathtaking. Within three days she was on the team.

The human rights department had gone to the school and said, "Look, this violates the law." And then the school said to us, "Well if she's going to be on the team, she has to go to the meets." Well, that was all right, she went to the meets. And that got a lot of media attention.

It was mostly very positive. The *Minneapolis Tribune* came out and took an adorable picture of her which they put on the front page. There she was, 12 years old, looking just as cute as a button in her bathing suit, holding a trophy she had just won. Of course the coach was quoted as saying something stupid, but coaches always do that anyway. It was always the adults that were the problem, never the other kids.

Later, my daughter had been competing in St. Paul and she was doing very well for a seventh-grader. She wanted to swim in an individual medley, and the way they did it was, to have a chance to compete in a meet, you had to challenge the person in one slot on the team. She did that, and sure enough, she beat him. She was very pleased and proud, she was going to get the third slot. We went to the meet, which happened to be outside St. Paul.

She was down with the team. She was actually on the block ready to swim, when the coach from the other team came over. He protested that she was there and said she could not compete because it was outside of St. Paul and the St. Paul ruling was not in effect there.

So they pulled that little girl off the block. *(Her voice breaks.)* And it still hurts, 20 years later. The little boy that she had beaten got to swim. The cruelty of what that man did to that little 12-year-old girl! This is a man who coaches children, whose life is devoted to children. The fact that he could do something that cruel to a child gave me some sense of the depths of the problem. And of course I wanted to kill him.

Later, it was pretty clear that one of the motivations for schools to start girls' teams was the desire to get girls off the boys' teams. What we really wanted was girls' teams anyway, so that was all right. But I have always been sad that they haven't developed more genuinely sex-integrated activities, because that makes such sense in track, and tennis, and golf . . . To this day, there has never been a mixed-doubles tennis set played in Minnesota state high-school competition.

Luanne Nyberg

Around the state capitol, Luanne Nyberg is known as a savvy lobbyist. Now age 44, she has lobbied for poor women, for welfare rights, and for the Children's Defense Fund. She grew up "consciously being groomed to become an executive's wife with a liberal-arts education so that I could raise well-educated children." She became active in the politics of the Left during the 1960s.

I joined the antiwar movement with both feet. I became an active member of SDS.* I was actively involved in many demonstrations. I sold newspapers on street corners, and had people spit on me. I got arrested in Mayor Daly's home precinct in Chicago and was threatened with being shot in the back if I ever came back again. Later I stood up with bullhorns in the garment district of New York, calling for a shorter work week.

The feminist movement was beginning at this time, and there was discussion in our group about the role of women. There were some women protesting, but I was not. I truly believed the rhetoric that it's class warfare and race issues. I thought the male/female stuff should be subordinated to that.

I had friends who joined consciousness-raising groups, but I thought that was really threatening. I felt insecure about the notion that women could be with one another and not need men. It was fine for baby showers or picnics. But for doing something important, like talking about your life, I found doing that only with women very threatening.

I would say about myself at the time that I really didn't like other women. I didn't respect them very much. They were too soft, too irrelevant. Not liking women, however, didn't include my sisters. My family all lives here in Minnesota, and I'm very close to my sisters.

* Students for a Democratic Society.

I went to work for the welfare department because of the notion in the movement that people with college degrees should be labor organizers. All these oppressed women, the welfare recipients, should be united with the welfare workers against those who make the rules—the bosses, we used to call them.

At the welfare department I started to understand how terrible, how oppressive the system is for low-income women. Also for the workers. All the hierarchy there were men. Some of them were wonderful guys, but a couple of them were just horrible, and the higher they got, the more horrible they were. Up to and including some county commissioners, who were just beastly.

That was the beginning of my feminist consciousness, working in that female atmosphere. It was absolutely obvious to me, because of my political analysis . . . *(She trails off.)* Here I am, making ten dollars an hour more than this woman who's trying to raise these kids. And we're yelling at each other. She's mad at me because I'm trying to enforce these terrible laws. And I'm mad at her because she's lying. Yet, she's lying to survive.

I felt very directly, in my day-to-day work, that this is insanity. I would find myself thinking, "These women have to survive and they're going to do whatever it takes," including lying, including schmoozing, including whatever. Still, when somebody lied to me, and I knew they were lying, I'd think, "Do you think I'm a chump? Do you expect me to *believe* you?" Even though there were pressures to do the job right and to administer the laws, I just hated myself for that reaction. Blaming her, or wanting to catch her.

It was during those years that I began to understand that women, particularly low-income women, were really getting screwed. They were being told to raise their children on chicken feed, that raising children isn't work, that they should go out to work. But if they go to work they get 100-percent taxation by having their benefits cut dollar for dollar. The women were put in absolutely untenable positions.

At the same time, there was very little emphasis on child support. The women were being held responsible—prove everything about your situation, get a note from your landlord, prove what your car is worth, prove this, prove that. It was absolutely ridiculous. But the fathers weren't even being contacted. If they were, they would just come in and claim that they only earned this or that, they had all these bills.

No one ever verified it. It was so unfair, so patently unfair, so obviously unfair.

At the welfare department, my co-workers were women. Working with women allowed me to see there's another way. I've come to understand that I really like working in an all-female atmosphere. I don't think about it when I'm interviewing men now. We've had men working at the Children's Defense Fund, and I like men. I get along fine with them. But I love coming in here, and thinking, "Oh God, I don't have to deal with any of that stuff." I like having only women around. It's easier, more efficient, it's quicker, we understand each other. There's less staking-out of territory. We know how to cooperate, to find a way.

In 1974, her marriage broke up; she quit her job and went on welfare herself.

There I was, divorced, with a baby who was two and a half. I thought I'd just step back and not stay active with the welfare-rights folks. And I was certainly not going to do any of that party work, that far-Left stuff. I made a quilt, I baby-sat for my niece, and I kind of rested. I took 15 months off to try to figure out what I wanted to do with my life.

What I wanted to do, after all, was to stick with welfare rights, the low-income stuff. I was outraged about the lack of social commitment to child support, the lack of child support from men. The money angle. I've always believed that if women could have their basic needs met, could earn enough to go to the grocery store, to have decent housing, just the necessities of life, a lot of the problems we're trying to solve wouldn't be there. We could knock off about 80 percent of all that—the violence and neglect, the chemical abuse, family breakups. A lot of that is related to money.

So I've spent most of my time since then working on basic needs: minimum wage, pay policies, AFDC,* child support, food stamps, medical assistance, child care. I can remember in my earlier years being outraged that feminists were working on credit issues. I thought, "Hey, the people I'm worried about don't *have* any credit cards." I thought, "Oh, it's such an upper middle class thing. What about poor women?"

In 1978, I went back to work as the head of a welfare-rights orga-

---

* Aid to Families with Dependent Children.

nization, the Recipients Alliance. It had been around throughout the seventies, and was supposed to do grassroots organizing. But we didn't really have the staff to do it, it was so poorly funded. I don't think our whole budget was ever more than $20,000 a year. We got a monthly tabloid out and translated it into Spanish, and we helped people represent themselves. We went with them to appeals. We did some legislative work. But we couldn't do real grassroots organizing because we just didn't have the staff.

I remember one day when we went to Honeywell* to try to get a grant for the alliance. We went to see some vice president, a man with white hair, who had this lovely tie. One of these really expensive ties with little things knit into it—and it was little bombers! We explained about low-income women and their children and their need to stand up and speak for themselves. He started talking about being raised in the Depression. And if his family could do it, why couldn't we do it?

I've always felt that I haven't done justice to the anger of the women who really go through this. I was on welfare, but I knew the rules. I was in power compared to the average woman on welfare. Even though I was very poor—I would spend weeks agonizing over whether I could buy an $8 sweatshirt, and it was cold in my house—still I knew the rules and I knew the people. I was very much an insider. Because of that, I never felt that I adequately represented, or helped unleash, that anger.

I still have vestiges of the class-analysis thing. But I've learned recently that womanhood, in and of itself, makes a difference regardless of your class or your political beliefs. I didn't believe that for a long time. I used to think that conservative women, rich women, were just as bad as the guys. I now see that's not true. The experiences of womanhood, no matter what your class, changes how you see the world. How you can empathize.

I never used to be outraged when I saw women being slighted. In my early years, I thought that was irrelevant. Or I wouldn't even notice it. Now I get really mad, especially at TV commercials. I spend a lot of time yelling at the television set because I can't yell at people in my work. I feel put off when I see so many male images, or things that put women down. At least the civil rights movement has done a good job

* A corporation with military contracts.

in making that kind of thing unacceptable. There's still a lot of racism, lots of inequality and discrimination, but they've at least made the point that you can't say these jokes, these offhand comments. We haven't even gotten that far, as women.

Sometimes I feel burned out. I clearly understand I've got a strike against me as a woman in what I'm trying to do, which is to change big systems. I come in with this label—not as powerful, not as tall. She's got boobs, so cover them up. But I've found I can do hard things. I have the ability to do it, I can actually just do it. I used to think I couldn't do that, go into that guy's office and just threaten him, or whatever. *(Laughs.)* And it can succeed, sometimes. I've got the support of other women, even if they're not thinking about me at that particular moment. I have a community to come back to where I'm going to be supported and understood. I can go out and do that hard thing, and come back and be just me.

I learned that if you keep at it, things do change. What keeps me going are the victories. Lately I've been working on getting kids health insurance. It's a small thing, but in this culture it's a big thing. When we started this project five or six years ago, there were 150,000 kids in this state without health insurance. We did a survey last summer and now there are only 69,000. It's my work, and the work of others that I've joined with, that has covered all these kids. That's what keeps me going.

Marilyn Bryant

Marilyn Bryant was the first Republican chair of the state's Women's Political Caucus, a founder of the Women's Campaign Fund, and a tireless fundraiser for women's programs. She says she is "a touch over 60" and jokes, "Have white dress, will travel."

I went through a very traditional period in the early years of my marriage. You know, raising kids—I stayed home with the kids, the way we did in those days. And I did all the Junior League stuff. I never read

Betty Friedan's book, so I wasn't aware of the women's movement through that. But I became aware of articles in magazines or whatever, in the late '60s and early '70s, seeing women's issues coming more to the forefront. I think that led to my seemingly sudden, but probably not so sudden, conversion *(laughs)*, if that's what you call it.

I was completely sympathetic with the things I read. I knew a lot of women my age, of my generation, who I think were very bored and dissatisfied with their lives. And a lot of them, because they had a lot of potential . . . my gosh, you'd have graduates of private eastern colleges constantly going to play bridge or whatever they did. I'm not saying that's a waste, but after a while I think it can become very destructive. So you'd see marriages breaking up, or women drinking. There were a lot of women drinking, it seems to me. I think they realized they were missing something in their lives.

I think the women I know socially have a great deal of understanding and empathy for the women's movement, and I've always wondered if a lot of them didn't wish they could be part of it. But at this point in their lives, it's not worth it. And I understand that. I'm not saying they're unhappy 100 percent of the time. They're probably very happy generally, and feel themselves to be fortunate. But they aren't going to start, at this age, saying, "I think I'll go run for county commissioner," or "I think I'll go . . . " They just aren't going to do that.

They've become settled in a different kind of a life. I think they're sympathetic, very. And I will say, a lot of these women will give money. They don't want their name on it, a lot of them don't want their name on anything, and they aren't going to come to anything. But they'll give money, so you know they're there. A number of years ago, when I was more visible because of the Caucus, we were at a party and I was talking to the wife of a prominent man. He came up and took his wife by the arm, and steered her right away from me. He didn't want her to be contaminated. *(Laughs.)* It was the most obvious thing I've ever seen. Didn't want her to "catch it."

I never would have anticipated or set out on a course to become a fundraiser. But of course you eventually see the inequities as far as the funding for women candidates, for women's programs. For the YW, whatever. The projects or the programs for women, they're always underfunded compared to men's. You look at the figures from the foundations—the Women's Fund has figures on the percentages of corporate and foundation monies that go to women's projects, and it's quite shocking how small it is. I think it's less than 10 percent.

I only raise money for women. I only give to women candidates. And it makes it very easy when—you know all the calls—when people call me. "Thank you very much, I only give money to women." The inequities have been there for so long, I think it's terribly important to do what we can to balance that out. And I think women are much better about the whole level of giving, that's been a big adjustment. I remember years ago when we started the Caucus annual lunch. I was sick and tired of going to $15 wine-and-cheese parties, so I said, "Why don't we have a $100 lunch at the Minneapolis Club?" Well . . . there were huge gasps: "No one will come," or "It's elitist." I mean, there were all kinds of reasons. I said, "Well, let's try it, and see what happens." Actually, it was the elitist part that bothered people more than the "no one will come" part. There was a lot of soul-searching about it. I said, "Listen, we want to raise money. If people are silly enough to come and pay a hundred bucks for lunch, let's take their money and run."

That was really a watershed, a $100 luncheon in the Minneapolis Club. That was written up in the paper, and questions of "How did you happen to decide to do this thing?" And so on. Well, of course, it's a tradition that still goes on. Now, as you know, a hundred bucks—that's an entry fee. (Laughs.) People are asking for $250, people ask for a thousand. You would have never thought of doing that then.

I think women have become so much more sophisticated and knowledgeable. You have your EMILY'S List, you have your WISH List,* so they aren't so shocked at being asked for money. In fact, with the Women's Campaign Fund, when we started that . . . three of us had lunch—lunch, we had breakfast! It was about 20 degrees below that morning, and I thought, "My God, what am I doing here?" One of them said, "I think it's time. I think women are ready. We're going to start a women's campaign fund, and they're going to pay a thousand bucks each." That was another leap forward.

I think if women's projects are going to succeed and advance and grow, we have to be the ones out there raising the dough. Some of the foundations, if they give $10,000 to a women's thing, boy, that's a big

---

* EMILY'S List raises money nationally for pro-choice Democratic women candidates; the WISH List does the same for Republican women.

deal. But they'll give $50,000 or $100,000 to the men's things and think nothing of it. Women have been forced to accept the crumbs. I think if we—*when* we—have more women on corporate boards, reviewing those things, and more women in positions of importance in foundations, we'll see some of that change.

I've been very lucky. There was something in Betty Friedan's book, her newer book, *It Changed My Life*. At the end she says something like, "When I am old I will look back and think about these days, and the things we have done, and I will pity those women who have never had the chance, or dared enough, to be involved." She didn't say it exactly like that, but I feel very much that way. I wouldn't want to sit on the sidelines.

I guess that none of us goes to bed or wakes up thinking, "I'm a feminist, what am I going to do about it today?" It just becomes incorporated in the way you live your life. I think it had an influence, or an impact, when we had our first grandchild—Elizabeth. They were in California when she was born, and the next day we had a meeting at the Women's Campaign Fund. I came in and said to everybody—I put some money on the table—and I said, "Ante up, everybody. This money is going to be for the presidential campaign of Elizabeth Austin Bryant." I said, "It may be 50 years, but we're going to start saving now for Elizabeth Austin Bryant's presidential campaign."

Elsa Vega-Perez

Elsa Vega-Perez is energetic, persuasive, and a fast talker. She was director of Minnesota's Office of Equal Opportunity from 1985 to 1991 and is now director of the Hispanic Education Project. Her parents are from Puerto Rico. Elsa is 40.

I was born and raised on New York's Lower East Side. My mom played numbers and took care of everybody's kid in the neighborhood to put us kids through Catholic school. She was a very strong person, under-educated, but a fighter, a protector.

It was fun in my family, but there were so many social problems.

Right before I was born, my dad fell from the six-story building where he worked as a caretaker, and that ended his work life. Not knowing how to pursue legal issues, he lost out. There was never any compensation, so we lived a lot on relief. And as a result of the morphine at the hospital, my father became a heroin addict.

My brother also became chemically dependent at an early age. My sister was raped and got pregnant when she was 15, and my brother fathered a kid when he was 16. I saw so much of their pain, and that gave me the strength to go the other way.

Sundays when families would visit, the women would be in the kitchen and they would serve the men, who were playing dominoes. Boys and girls would play together, spin-the-bottle and kiss-cousins and all that. But the men sat back, ate these wonderful meals, and played dominoes and drank the beer. And the moms cooked, and they cleaned up, and they gossiped, and they cried about Tio beating up Tia and that kind of stuff—the indiscretions that went on in families.

My mother would say, "*El hombre es de la calle,*" the man is from the street. So he has no barriers, he can have other women, do whatever he wants, he's not going to be judged. But I couldn't date until a certain time, I couldn't wear certain things until a certain time, girls didn't do certain things. And women must be ladies, be good mothers, have good reputations.

When my brother got a girl pregnant, he didn't take responsibility. We did. My family took her in to live with us. My father took her on the bus to deliver the baby. My brother was a junkie in the street, but I bought the Pampers. We weren't going to let my brother's kid be out there.

I married my childhood sweetheart when I was 18. He was just out of Vietnam. We came to Minnesota, just to get out of that hustle and city. You know how you're taught in school, the Dick-and-Jane kind of books? You see Dad has a car and you see Mom at home. Everybody is so happy and everything is so clean and there's trees and a cat. I liked that, and I never saw that in New York.

After a year of experiencing culture shock, I moved my entire family here. The culture shock came because I had never lived in a total white environment. I had been a secretary. I was great at office work. But here I couldn't get a job. I had a thick New York accent. I was not polished enough for the Nordic life, I stuck out like a sore thumb with all the blond, blue-eyed women.

I finally found a job at an insurance company. They gave me great reviews, so I'd go in and say, "I'd really like to know how to move up in this company, be an underwriter. What's the ladder?" The man would always look at me and say, "Quite frankly, Elsa, if you're not happy here you can always go somewhere else." That hurt me, because I saw other women getting promoted. But I was the only colored girl in the place.

I decided to go back to school. Harry wasn't comfortable with that. He was trying to dominate as a husband, not as a partner. When I saw that he was trying to stop me, I decided we needed to separate. I said, "Later, bro, you gotta go." He left for New York and I stayed in Minnesota.

I took a medical secretary course, but dropped out of school maybe three weeks before finishing—Harry was gone and I needed a job. I got into a job-training program. They assigned me to the Neighborhood House, in the Hispanic community, where I dealt with problem kids, girls that were doing drugs. I was young and had street smarts, I was accepted by them. It was like teen day care, after school and at night. I got the kids to go to the technical college for free haircuts. I knew how to hustle other groups to support bake sales, candy sales, taco sales.

The training program was for a year, and then the agency you worked for was supposed to hire you. But the agency wanted someone with a degree. The woman they hired had no sensitivity. She was a social worker, a white woman. She could not get the trust factor from parents and young kids. And she didn't even stay in the agency for a year. I would have committed my whole life to this agency because my heart was in it.

Harry came back five years after he left. While we were separated, we had a long-distance relationship. There was always a real love connection there. We had so many things in common, our values are in synch. We came from the same neighborhood, same types of parents. So it was just a matter of dealing with differences and letting each other grow up.

Finally I went back and said, "Harry, it's been five years, we need to move on with our lives. I'm sure you want to fall in love with somebody, and I will too if you don't want to be my husband. I want a fam-

ily and a man." He said, "Fine, we'll try it." So we did. And now we
have two kids. I usually get my way *(laughs)*—is that feminism?

In 1982, I was one of the four founders of Casa de Esperanza, the
battered women's shelter for Hispanic women in St. Paul. Abuse is very
prevalent in my community. My sister was in a marriage for 15 years with
a man who beat her and humiliated her. And my father hit us kids—
more my sister and my brother, because I knew how to manipulate.

Hispanic women needed to feel safe by having a shelter environment that's not totally foreign, the support sessions needed to be in the
comadre system. *Comadre* is the co-mother system, the woman that bap-
tizes your kid. She's a very significant person in your life, someone that
you have to account to. I'm under the impression that white women
don't have to account to anybody other than themselves, and maybe to
their own family units. But in our community, we have to be accountable to everybody. To the mother, to the father, to the grandmother, to
the *madrina** . . .

In my community, if you are not accountable, you're ostracized.
And the male abuser benefits from that nurturing. We protect him, we
understand his problems. "He doesn't have a job, he's a minority, he's
been disadvantaged." So we enable this whole disease. When you understand that, then you're able to intervene effectively and help this
woman sort things out.

And the food things, you need a shelter where you can cook the
rice and beans, and you don't eat the meat loaf and the mashed pota-
toes *(laughs)*, you know? So you can feel comfortable putting the Latin
music on. You need somebody that is sensitive to the fact that we want
to go to the salsa dance on Saturday, not to the Orpheum.

I'm worried about the interpretation of feminism to men, and also
to women that have not looked at feminism. As we move on as feminists, I think we need to bring the brothers along. It's an issue of
power, because our men don't have power. Who's being left behind by
this movement, and do we care?

* The co-mother.

At first, I thought feminism was for white women. But other women of color would say, "We need to understand what the issues are, build commonality with white women." And then I saw so much oppression from men of color against us, women of color who were trying to build bridges. When we were starting Casa de Esperanza, the men said, "You just want to be white women." No, we just want to be safe, we don't want to be hit any more. When it was that simple, you could see the feminist agenda.

At one time, I was on a conference panel. I was new to the panel circuit, you know *(laughs)*, one black, one Hispanic, one Indian, one Asian—the four food groups. When somebody asked me a question about feminism, I said, "I don't feel part of the white woman's agenda. You don't show it from my eyes, it's hard for me to connect."

Well, the keynote speaker at that conference was Dr. Mary Frances Berry.* And she said, "It's a woman's agenda." She quoted the stats, she educated us that we are oppressed as a gender. It took a woman of color to say, "Elsa, it has nothing to do with the white girls' movement. It has everything to do with if we don't fight for choice, then white men will stop us from choosing who we are as people, as white people and as black people and as brown people." It took the voice of color to reach me.

Even if you're not a woman of color, you could talk the talk. You can attract people of color, if you put color in your speech. You need to be sensitive, to quote Maya Angelou, Lolita Lebron, Harriet Tubman, Rosa Parks. When you use that *(snaps her fingers)*, we hear you.

The song needs to be sung to the voice. When you see a person of color standing by the white woman, and both can articulate, and one can tell it in Spanish . . . when we do it together, then we're marching.

---

* An African-American scholar serving on the U.S. Civil Rights Commission.

Marianne Christianson & Kate Wulf

Marianne Christianson and Kate Wulf live together in an inner-city neighborhood of St. Paul. Their large, comfortable house has seen hundreds of meetings and fundraisers. They were active in women's groups at a time of internal strife, such as when the Socialist Workers' Party attempted to take over NOW in the 1970s.

In the '70s and '80s, Kate was president of Twin Cities NOW, state coordinator of Minnesota NOW, and a national NOW board member. Marianne was a vice president in her local union, the Minnesota Federation of Teachers, and president of the Coalition of Labor Union Women (CLUW). Marianne is 47, a teacher in an inner-city school. Kate is 40, a supervisor in the state Department of Human Services.

Marianne: In 1974, I became a high-school girls' track coach. And the pay was like $200. I had more track meets than the male coach and I had more kids out. And the men got $1,000, I think. And we noticed. Not only me, but a lot of other women in the district. Our union started a committee to work on equalizing pay. That was the major eye-opener for me. From that point on, I stopped being afraid to say and to do what was necessary.

Kate: For me, becoming a feminist was more gradual. Reading *Ms.* when I was in college. It made sense to me. It fit with the way I perceived Christianity. The oneness of humankind. "Neither Jew nor Gentile, male nor female . . ."

Marianne: In church, I was taught that "the woman is the heart, the man is the mind." I always had trouble with that. But church taught me that women are supposed to be totally subversive to men.

Kate: You mean "submissive!" *(Laughter all around at this slip.)*

Marianne: I enjoyed the time I was president of CLUW, but . . . I got in trouble. In the early '80s, I went to the national AFT* conference. I was active on the floor, working on a pro-abortion resolution, and I had initiated a women's caucus. The leadership saw me as a threat, they had already made all the decisions in committee. They sent down the troops on me, I was surrounded. I said I'd back off.

Shortly after that I was at the CLUW convention, I was running for the national board, and the AFT came to me and said, "We have picked somebody else to run representing us." I went to a few more conventions after that, but I've left the national scene. Unions are like other organizations; you can do it locally, but the larger scene, the national level, is not nice.

You just get tired. I spent years going to meetings and meetings and meetings and meetings. I have to admit one thing, when some of the perks were taken out of the meetings . . . just like Congress *(laughs)*, you just want some cookies. When they said, "We can't pay for the cookies out of union dues any more," I started thinking. Why am I doing this? Five hours a night—you want my time? I want my chocolate-chip cookie.

Still, we won things that people have fought for for many years. We got coaches' pay equalized, health benefits, parental leave. For many years in my retirement fund there's been a provision that you can designate an unmarried partner. You look back at the teachers' union, 50 years ago . . . if you were pregnant, you were gone. Now you watch TV and there are pregnant newscasters and pregnant weatherwomen. A lot of those things were union-driven and union-motivated.

Times have changed. Just the other day—I supervise a recess at lunch, sixth and seventh graders. One day last week, the boys were playing basketball. The girls wanted to be part of the game, and the boys didn't want to play with the girls. The girls said, "Fuck you then, we're not going to stand for this sexist shit." One of the boys has his shirt up, and one of the girls said, "Look at you, you don't even have breasts!" *(Laughs.)*

We've come far in many ways, because the girls are not sitting down and saying, "I guess we don't belong." And though I may not like their choice of words, the ideas are right on.

---

* American Federation of Teachers.

Kate: I'd been in NOW less than a year when I was asked to run for the chapter board. They wanted to put up a slate to block the socialists. Internal politics always, even in the very beginning.

There were years when feminist organizing was my life. I was at meetings every night of the week, and sometimes I would have three meetings a night. That was not unusual, to get off work at 5:00 and have the first meeting at 5:30 and the next one at 7:00 and the next one at 9:00. It was a crazy schedule. I can't imagine ever doing it again, but I also can't imagine where I'd be if I hadn't gone through that. I wouldn't have met Marianne—my life would have been much emptier.

It did help to shape me. Gave me a lot more confidence and taught me some things I don't ever want to do again. *(Laughs.)* Like public speaking. Lordy, I hate that. It was something that I had to do, it was a big part of the job of state coordinator. I would have five speaking engagements a week sometimes. You think you'd get used to that, but I never did. My stomach churned every time I did it.

The highlight was a debate at St. John's University. I was invited to debate a woman from the Eagle Forum* on the question, "Should the ERA be ratified?" It was 1982. They had taken a poll on campus before the event, and something like 85 percent of the student body was opposed. I took off work the day of the debate because I still hadn't written my remarks. I just drew a blank. There were snow flurries, so I called to see if maybe they had canceled it, and they hadn't. I ended up writing my speech in the car on the way, while Marianne drove. We had the debate, it went very well. I actually got some fan letters. And we won, something like 73 percent voted in support—which amazed me.

It was exciting and affirming, but I still hate that sort of thing. I believed in the stuff and I felt I had to do it.

Marianne: I met Kate in 1980 at a state Democratic-Farmer-Labor Party convention. All the feminists were getting together in one room and they were checking everyone's credentials to make sure a spy wasn't entering. I almost didn't get in because I didn't bring my proper credentials.

Kate: We didn't want the "right-to-lifers" to take over. I became more aware of her later, in NOW, when she ran for delegate to the NOW national conference. She said all the "brothers and sisters of the

* An anti-feminist organization.

union" stuff. I said, "This sounds like a Socialist Workers Party candidate." But she got up, and she was just so strong, the personality came through. I thought, "Boy, that's kind of a neat woman."

Marianne: In 1980 I also went to the national NOW convention in San Antonio. We forget about those conventions, the impact they have on a first-time goer. The incredible pride at being a woman, the power and the beauty of gathering with other women. Now we're more cynical, we know too much about the politics. But I remember just walking through an airport afterwards and realizing that I felt taller and more in control.

Kate: I was at that conference too, by that time it was my fourth national conference. And the main thing I got out of that was the political infighting, a big fight over bylaws that year. I was wearing a little button which I still have that says, "It's not burnout—I'm a victim of arson." *(Laughs.)* Which is the way a lot of folks felt within NOW. There were so many purges . . .

But I remember my first national conference too. My first big march, the ERA march in Washington. And how thrilling it was. The whole Capitol Mall filled with hundreds of thousands of people. Mostly women wearing white. A friend of mine had arranged to meet her mother "at the Washington monument." Her mother had said, "I'll be wearing white." They're still looking for each other! *(Laughs.)*

Marianne: There are things like that, that people need who have been in the movement for a number of years. We need refreshing experiences. Free of the cynicism and the political fighting.

Kate: And we need to remember that there are people still coming in for the first time, for whom these things *are* the women's movement.

The first NOW event for me was the 1976 ERA rally in Springfield, Illinois. We had 25,000 people there, which outnumbered the city population. I remember going into a restaurant, we just filled the restaurant. Some of us ended up going back in the kitchen and helping the staff. You know, setting the tables and helping get the food out.

It was my first rally, it was really exciting. But again there was controversy because a group called the Lesbian Feminist Organizing Committee (LFOC) was with our state contingent of NOW. We had cleared their coming and carrying a banner with the organizers, we thought. But when we got there, the organizers said they didn't want any of this lesbian stuff, because Springfield was a conservative community.

They finally let the LFOC carry their banner, but we were supposed to lead off the parade and we ended up being the dead-last delegation. Still, it was thrilling.

In 1977, I remember the Women's Meeting in Houston. We sang "Happy Birthday" to Margaret Mead. I think it was her 80th birthday the day she was there. Three of the First Ladies were there. All of these people you'd read about and seen on the news. In the lobby of the hotel, a group of Hispanic women started gathering. And pretty soon they had joined hands and they were singing "*Viva La Mujer*"—it was just wonderful! At the end of the convention they had Margie Adam* up there in white satin tails playing the piano. We were all singing "We Shall Go Forth" in three-part harmony. An overwhelming experience.

Marianne: How long has it been since you've had that kind of experience?

Kate: Probably when Gerry Ferraro got the nomination for vice president, that was the last time.

Marianne: We have to talk about our part in that. We consider that we were responsible for her being chosen as the vice presidential candidate. *(Both laugh.)*

We were at the NOW conference in Miami Beach. Ferraro made a speech, and we liked what she said, so we bought Mondale-Ferraro buttons. Then we went to a Mondale reception and Joan Mondale came up to me and said, "Where did you get that pin? Can I have it?" And I gave it to her. Two days later, Ferraro was announced.

Kate: You said, "I'll give it to you if you'll wear it." And she said, "I can't wear it publicly but I'll wear it on my pajamas." *(Both laugh.)*

Marianne: I remember when we hired the first state lobbyist in NOW, in 1982. I was the legislative coordinator. There had been a resolution passed to go ahead and deal with getting a lobbyist. So we did it, I thought we followed the process. But people were pissed off, because we didn't go through the process they had envisioned. They criticized us for not publishing the opening in two newsletters. For not doing affirmative action.

We should have done all that, ideally, but the legislative session was already underway. There was some critical issue we wanted to target that year. There weren't very many people with any experience lobby-

---

* A folksinger, composer, and pianist who raised funds for feminist causes.

ing. And we were only paying $400 for the whole session, give me a break. I agreed with the process concerns, but I was not willing to wait five years.

Well, we forged ahead. Time judges it. We formed the future with some of those actions. We set up a standing NOW platform so you wouldn't have to debate issues every year. And do you remember planning the first "Day at the Capitol?" That was 1982. We cut out a picture of the capitol and glued it on something to make the brochure. We met in the rotunda and had the Susan B. Anthony birthday party, the lieutenant governor came . . .

Kate: We've had struggles here in the state, but the ones that were devastating were national. They played hardball. Sometimes we had to fight for microphones, people tried to intimidate you physically. It was such a negative experience. Here we are with all of our ideals, our common agenda, and people were so mean-spirited. I didn't want to be part of it. It wasn't all like that, but there was a lot of it.

In one of our struggles on the national NOW board, the member from South Dakota said, "This makes me heartsick, the enemy is not in this room." But some of the other board members said, "Oh, yes they are." That was too much for me.

Marianne: Politically, we went national for a while, both of us, and now we're at the block level, block-club members.

Kate: Trying to change the macrocosm and the microcosm, create a more accepting, inclusive, healthy community right here.

Marianne: The community we're living in, we have the poorest of the poor here, and we also have the well-to-do. This block alone, we represent every continent. We have the Scottish Jew three houses down, we have an Arab living behind us, we have Indians, we have blacks, we're sort of a microcosm. We love that portion of it. But we don't like the shootouts, we don't like the crack houses, we don't like the gang people walking by.

Last fall I was out doing yard work, and a shootout started. It was like the OK Corral. There were 40 rounds of semiautomatic weapons fired. I started running into the house, realized I forgot the lawnmower, ran back out . . .

Kate: Can you believe that? She was going to rescue the lawnmower!

Marianne: Sometimes we say, "Let's just get out of here," because it's so scary. And yet we look at the wonderful people, really good people . . . They know we're feminists and they know we're a couple.

One of the most traumatic things for us was the murder of our next-door neighbor. Robert was a black man, a sweet man who defended us publicly against people who were harassing us because of our sexuality. There used to be a teenager across the street, she'd shout obscenities at us. Robert went out and told her to stop. He went out a couple of times. He said to me, "I hurt real bad to hear that."

A wonderful, good, loving man. That's what's so important to me, as a feminist or as a lesbian, or any of those things, to look and say, "These are good men." To recognize all humanity, whether it's by age or race or whatever. Not to exclude so many people. That's what someone like Robert meant to us.

In the Country

Living on farms or in small, rural communities shapes the lives of many women. On the one hand they find role models in the tradition of strong women who do farm work and maintain the social fabric of their communities. On the other hand, their isolation poses special challenges.

Isolation can simply mean having no car, as Norma Nuessmeier points out. It can also mean less access to first-hand information: Carol Bly first heard feminists described as vegetarians concerned with celestial rhythms. For women who challenge the status quo, social isolation is a common experience. For example, coffee-shop denizens in Cheryl Hoium's small town assumed she must be divorced when she reclaimed her maiden name.

Like activists everywhere, rural feminists rely on humor, friendship, and the satisfaction of making a difference to keep them going. Marion Fogarty laughs at the names of farm-association women's auxiliaries such as the Cow Belles and the Porkettes. Nuessmeier treasures her childhood friends. Faith Zwemke's voice is proud when she explains that her small town was far ahead of larger cities in establishing a pay equity program.

Norma Nuessmeier

Norma Nuessmeier is in her late fifties and lives on a farm in southern Minnesota where the fields stretch to the horizon in all directions. Set back from a country road, her house is reached by a long driveway. The silence is broken only by the sounds of birds or the occasional drone of a tractor. Norma grew up in a small town nearby. In 1971 she was the first woman to be elected to her township board, a position she still holds. We drink coffee at her kitchen table on a warm, sunny day.

Yes, I would consider myself a feminist. I was a charter member of NOW, back years ago when it was not considered, shall we say, the thing to do. I've been a great admirer of Gloria Steinem for years. I've subscribed, a charter subscription, to *Ms.* magazine.

In the late '60s, I was sitting out here on a farm at that time, and I was extremely isolated. With small children. No extra car. The only way I could leave this farm was to call my mother to come out to get me. I was always interested in continuing education. I was taking courses over the TV, you know, different things, so I'd take these courses that pertained to women. And maybe because I have three daughters, and I have a sister . . .

If you go back in history, women were considered chattels. But according to *my* history, in my genealogy, none of the women were chattels. Many times it was the women who were the moving force to leave. To move on. We have letters from the Civil War period from one of my ancestors to prove it. They didn't go along just for the ride. *(Laughs.)* No, they definitely had their voice. And were strong women.

But they had to have been—just to survive, they had to be strong. I'm not sure *I* would have survived before running water. *(Laughs.)* But that's me.

My husband's side of the family, now, the women walked three paces behind with their heads down. I was a real anomaly. And I caused a lot of waves. They had trouble accepting me, definitely. I think the day I really thought my marriage was on strong ground was the day my husband told his parents, "Back off . . . This is our life, you're not living it, we are." Because they *did* try to interfere. There again, his father was: The Man Ruled. That's the way he was brought up. His mother, now, she's a strong woman really, but she was also a total wimp-out. She didn't even get running water in her house. Why? Because they bought a tractor.

There are so many more opportunities out there today for young women than there were. Even for young farm women. For instance, just two weeks ago Farm Credit Services, which is a federal land bank, did a women's seminar kind of thing. And it was put on by Sister Kay and Sister Michelle, and it was talking about how to be aware of yourself, and how to be—you know—stronger within yourself. And I thought to myself, isn't this great for these young 20- and 30-year-old women? To come and hear this? To hear these things about how good it is to validate yourself? Why wasn't that there when I was that age? I needed it. How I needed to be able to go and hear someone else validate what I was feeling!

My pro-lifer neighbor over here, she will not understand . . . Hey, I'm against promiscuity. I'd just as soon no child had to be aborted. I'm with you on that. I agree with that. But do you really think that's realistic? Why in God's name are you wasting all your energy waving a sign out there in front of a clinic? Stopping girls who are making a tough decision in the first place? Making it harder for them? To me, they are not pro-life. To me, they are anti-life, because they're not thinking of the life of the person who is already living. I think that's such a shame, that they can't get past that.

I became very pro-choice when my sister became pregnant as a teenager. Ended up going to a church home and gave her child up for adoption. And there was an 11-year-old girl in this church home, in Indiana, who had been raped by an uncle and was forced to carry a baby to full term. It angered me so. This child—she was mentally defi-

cient too—but why . . . why put this child through this? That's one of
the things that really made me pro-choice. Who has the right to make
this kind of decision?

I wasn't really known in the community about being pro-choice
until I'd taken one of my daughter's friends who'd gotten pregnant . . .
She couldn't tell her mother, didn't know what to do. I paid for it. I
drove her up to Meadowbrook.* I had already joined Planned Parent-
hood, you know, I'd sent them money because I believed in it.

I ended up taking—at one point, I had three girls in the car. Two
were going up for abortions. I was driving to Meadowbrook. You have
to stop, you know, before you make that turn to go into Meadowbrook. Well, the picketers were out. I'm stopped, and this one picketer
is shoving this "Stop the Killing" card crap in front of my face. I looked
at her, and she looked at me—and it was my neighbor, from right over
there. This was how I became known.

Now, I'd always known they were . . . I was pro-choice, but it was
really, you know, a little low-key there. So she looked at me, and I
looked at her. After that, I could not be a delegate at the Democratic
convention. They came out to make sure that I was never again a delegate. They're adamantly against abortion, which is their right. But
they do not have to force their views on me. That's what really gets me.
After that, it was pretty funny, we got blackballed, we didn't get invited
to card parties, a few little things like that. But as far as my husband was
concerned, he couldn't care less.

Most of the girls that I know, that were my children's friends, were
so afraid to talk about it to their parents. Even though they were in-
dulging in sex. Hey, I came right out to them—I don't believe in it, I
don't believe in promiscuity. I'm sorry, I was a virgin when I got married and I do not regret it one bit. And I hoped and prayed all my children would be virgins when they got married. I have no way of knowing, that's their business, but . . .

The girls were so scared. They'd come out here to talk. And ask
questions. Because they couldn't ask questions at home. It wasn't because their parents weren't what we'd call educated, or good parents, or
anything like that. But they just couldn't do it. It was that great wall of
silence.

* A women's health clinic that provides abortions.

I had an aunt who was a battered woman. This was in South Dakota, and the family kept it secret. But my father went out and brought her and the children home. They lived with us. My father was in some respects a feminist. He was the one brother that his sisters knew they could rely on. Daddy was very much of a caretaker.

I guess the thing I find so startling, I found it so hard to believe, was the sexual abuse of children. When I went to college . . . you know how you sit around in the dorms and talk? I've kept a diary since I was seven, so I know this story is true. There was a group of us sitting around, when I was a freshman in college, within the first month. I don't know, we got talking, and this girl started talking about the fact that her father sexually abused her. I was so irate . . . because fathers didn't do that. Fathers were your protectors. Oh no, I called this poor girl a liar and stormed out of there and took half the people with me.

You know, I would dearly love to meet that girl today and beg her forgiveness? Because she had to have been telling the truth. You don't make that up. And I think to myself, I shouted at the poor girl. Years later, when you realize that this happened . . .

It was outside my experience, too, until my aunt called. I think I was a sophomore in high school, and they lived in Rapid City, South Dakota. We always knew they had problems in their marriage, because my uncle would go on these binges of alcoholism. But nobody ever knew he was beating her. She didn't say anything until he started beating the kids. Then she called for help. And my father and one of his brother-in-laws got in the pickup and drove straight through to Rapid City, South Dakota, and picked up her and the kids and brought them back.

Sad to say, her husband died two months after the divorce. He died of a heart attack and, because she hadn't signed something, I can't remember what it was, she hadn't signed something in the divorce decree, she couldn't collect Social Security. Which was another thing to make me a feminist. I mean, they had been married for over 20 years!

My girlfriends and I have discussed the fact that we've gone from sandbox playing to talking about investments to the deaths of our husbands. We feel we've run the gamut. I have friends that I've known for over 50 years. We're still very close even though some of them have spent 30 years not living here.

The type of friendships—even if we haven't written or spoken to each other for six months—we can pick up the phone and it's an instant connection. These are mostly high-school friends. We've grown together. We think of what we were like in high school, and we didn't talk about the important things then. I think my daughters are so lucky with their friends because they do talk about the things that took us to our thirties to really open up and discuss.

We often talk about the fact that when we were teenagers, you were taught to be competitive with other women. One thing you could not have, when we were teenagers growing up, you could not have a male as a friend. He was either a boyfriend, or you didn't talk to him. And isn't that strange? When you say you want to get married, and spend your life . . . If you can't be friends with the man you're married with, then you really have a marriage in trouble.

My girlfriends and I still get together, at least once a year. Sometimes twice a year, it depends. Do you know, when my husband died, one of my friends was on a plane going from here to Las Vegas. When she got word, she immediately turned around and came back. Another friend and her husband were in Arizona on vacation, and she immediately got on a flight and came here. Two of them drove up from Nebraska.

We've all had stretches, like when our children were young . . . But whenever there's been any sort of important event in any of our lives, we've always been there for each other.

These friends are all feminists. Very strong women. We talk about it. Now, we're not all pro-choice. Some of them would probably balk at being called a feminist. But yes, *I'd* call them feminists. They're strong women, all very much in tune with themselves.

Cheryl Hoium

Cheryl Hoium grew up in Thief River Falls in far northwestern Minnesota. Her math teacher laughed at her in the seventh grade when she signed up for football. Cheryl was an early member of NOW, and reclaimed her own name after marriage long before that became an accepted practice. At 45, she lives in northern Minnesota and commutes to St. Paul for her job with the Commission on the Economic Status of Women.

Actually, I changed my name twice. I was very uncomfortable changing my name when I got married in 1971, but I'd never heard of people not changing to their husband's name. When I was first married, for three weeks I couldn't bring myself to go to the bank and sign my new name. It was a real traumatic experience for me. We needed a checking account, though, so I finally did it.

We were living in Milwaukee at the time, so when we moved back to Minnesota I decided to go back to my original name. I just changed it back, the same way I'd changed it before. I went to get my driver's license, and never encountered any problems there or anywhere else. Except American Express. They wanted me to apply for credit, even though I already had a card. I wrote them a scathing note saying I was the same person, and they gave me a new card. *(Laughs.)*

I was our sole support. My husband was going to law school and doing just a little part-time work. I went to apply for another credit card and gave them my name. They changed it to my husband's name. I can remember having a discussion with a woman at Marshall Field. I said, "This is silly. If *I* don't pay this bill, you're out. He's not earning enough." She said, "I know it's silly, but those are the rules."

When I changed my name back, in a small town like Little Falls it was quite a traumatic experience for people. They didn't know how to deal with us. You give your check at the grocery store and they stare at it and stare at it . . . They would ask, "What are you going to name your kids?"

I was a real curiosity. When I went to open our bank account, I wrote down my name and I wrote down his name, and our address and phone number and all that. We had it all down, but the guy at the bank was still leery about this. My husband had to come in and sign the stuff anyway, so when he came in, the banker asked him if this was okay. Of course, he said it was fine. I didn't realize until recently that I'd put my name first and his name second. I don't know why, it just seemed logical to me. But that really was a clinker for the banker, that *my* name was first on the checks. I only noticed in the past few years that they always have the husband's name first and the wife's second.

We were a good subject for gossip. As you might expect, and I only get this secondhand, people in a small town talk a lot about you behind your back. There were always rumors that we were divorced, that was a frequent rumor. Once another attorney in town came and asked my husband, "Are you and your wife still married?"

People always thought I was weird, odd. I know being in church . . . I can remember the minister talking and he'd look around and see me, and he'd amend his sentence. He'd say "men," and then he'd see me and add, "and women." I always felt that I was a consciousness-raiser wherever I was. I can remember being at a local restaurant one night, and people were telling a joke. All of a sudden they stopped, and looked—because I was there. My husband used to say, "You're really a great influence, because all you have to do is be there and people change their behavior. They start thinking differently."

I got tired of it after a while. I mean, being the novelty. I always thought I was a damper, and people were always worried that they would say the wrong thing. People who were our friends wanted to be politically correct, and didn't want to be offensive. But it got a little stressful at times, I didn't enjoy it.

That's gotten to be old hat now, even in Little Falls. People have gone on to much more outrageous things than having different last names. *(Laughs.)*

Marion Fogarty

Marion Fogarty lives on a farm in Belle Plaine, Le Sueur County, about 50 miles south of the Twin Cities. She and her husband Leo have 340 acres and raise corn and soybeans. Before that, they raised cows—and six children. They have been married 42 years. Marion, 62, was the first woman to sit on the executive board of the Farmers Union.*

I was always so busy being a "good girl," through the parochial school and everything. I ended up marrying a farmer, still being the good girl. It was after the children got a little older that I started to challenge some of the good-girl ideas I'd always grown up with.

The first thing was birth control—that was closest to home. As my teenagers grew, what with dating practices and what the church was teaching, it just didn't seem to balance out. I was a catechism teacher, I was a choir director, I did many things in our church in town. But as my children got older, and as I got older, I began to challenge the birth control business and the rhythm method. The rhythm method, you can see, did not work too well for me. *(Laughs.)*

When the youngest one got into school, and I had more time, Leo and I became involved in our Farmers Union. It was very political. That was the step that took me out of the house and into the political arena.

I first started thinking of myself as a feminist when I got political, because my activities did not seem to count for anything. At Farmers Union meetings, we always had name tags. No meeting was complete without them. I would change my name tag from Mrs. No-Name Fogarty to Marion Fogarty. As the lone woman on many committees, I was always given the pen and paper—to be secretary. With a smile, I would pass it on saying, "I sing and dance nicely too." I can remember passing a petition around to be signed in a group of husbands and

* A statewide farm organization.

wives, but only the men signed. I learned a lot about sexism in the Farmers Union. *(Laughs.)*

Some of that is changed now. It used to be that the different commodity groups had women's associations. The wheat producers had a group called the "Wheat Hearts," the cattlemen's association had the "Cow Belles," and the pork producers had the "Porkettes." That really got to me. Now they're incorporated into the associations.

Every year at the state convention they would have a "ladies luncheon." I remember they had the Mother of the Year one time, and another time we had someone who grew flowers. Now, here at this convention you're all wrapped up in policies to help the family farmer and you get all worked up on this, and then they put us women down in the room to hear these "nice" things. I changed that. We now have an open luncheon and both husbands and wives are invited.

Another thing that got me was the "Good Guy" awards at this big convention. I kept saying, "You can't do that, that's not right." So one year, we had Sister Mary Something from Wisconsin, who had been active in farming. She was the "Good Guy" award winner. It didn't work very well. *(Laughs.)* The next year we had the Good Neighbor award.

That's how I started feeling my feminism. But I think it really came out when Gloria Griffin* ran for Congress in our district in 1976. I was very active in her campaign, and that's when I met the feminists from the Twin Cities. You know, the ones who had burned their bras and had horns coming out of their heads. *(Laughs.)*

I have a label. "She's a 'woman's lib.'" I don't know if they still call it that, most of them have outgrown "women's lib," but that's the idea. They will come and try anything to get me riled up—which I no longer do. I quietly dismiss their innuendoes and their smart remarks. It's funny, they don't ostracize me. I go to showers, but all I can do is smile and talk recipes, and who got the divorce. There's no hope of ever raising any conversation above the home. I do play bridge, I sub bridge, and if I get good cards, it's all right. But if I don't get good cards, I suffer. *(Laughs.)*

I think I was angry all the time, once I got started on this. Because of the latent, sexist, macho-male stuff that was rammed down our throats. And I was angry with the women for not seeing this, not even

* Her story begins on page 236.

with their children. I kept saying, "Your girls would not be able to par-
take in all the sports in high school if we hadn't fought for it." I tried
to bring it down to the personal. But they didn't buy it. I don't think
they realize it now, even.

I've put about 20 years into this and found maybe 15 feminists in
Le Sueur County. That's not so bad.

Faith Zwemke

*Some people believe that feminism reaches rural areas last. That wasn't true
for Faith Zwemke, who served as a council member and, later, mayor of a small
town with a population of 3,500. She established pay equity for the town's employees long before any big cities tackled the issue. At 42, she is the state coordinator for pay equity.*

I always feel proud that I went to one of the last country schools.
In that school, girls and boys weren't treated differently. We all had du-
ties, and everybody had to take a turn at everything. Clean the black-
board, take out the garbage, even clean the can.

Living on a farm with three girls, we all had to work outside. We all
had to drive the tractor. I certainly liked driving the tractor a lot better
than I liked doing dishes. I liked machinery and I liked bikes. It was fun
stuff.

I wanted to be a boy, I prayed that I would turn into a boy. One of
the big reasons was, I hated to wear dresses. If we played house, I
would visualize myself as the father. A good friend of mine has since
said, "What you realized is that boys had more privileges." I think that's
right. Men got to do more fun things. I would visualize myself driving
the car. I would get to go off to work.

In 1974, I was teaching high school in a small town. A couple of
my friends were teaching a social-awareness course, and they got these
audio cassettes called *The White Male Club.* The tapes got us talking
about sex roles and it all started to make sense to me.

I was coaching the speech team. The statewide topic for speech contests that year was "sex-role stereotypes." I had a brilliant student, a girl named Julie. She was tough, she took it on with this "All right, let's get 'em" attitude. This young girl would come back after these meets fit to be tied. The judges called her "antagonistic." They wouldn't have called her that, I don't think, had she been a male. She would have been "well-informed." And she was perfect in speech. She read everything, she had all her facts. So I became a support group for her.

Also at this time, I was teaching a mass-media class. One of the units was called "Sexism in the Media." My classes would be, like, 16 boys and 4 girls—mostly boys with nothing but raging hormones. They took the class so they could run the camera and so they wouldn't have to write English papers. So I taught this sexism in the media unit. Part of what I was doing, I'm sure, was teaching myself.

After teaching for eight years, I was kind of burned out. Eventually I opened my own music store. I was barely making it with my business, but I was enjoying my life. The feeling I had the whole time I owned the store was, it wasn't really work. It was fun. I never felt like I needed a vacation. Plus, I became the local women's support group. I had this green rocking chair in the back of the store. Women friends would come in and say, "Faith, I need the green chair!" They would sit there and tell me about their woes.

In 1980, I decided to run for the Princeton city council—and won. I was the second woman on the council. At some point I went to a League of Cities conference. The program listed a "Women in City Government Lunch." I thought they were *serving* the lunch. I rebelled. I thought, "You mean that's what these women do? I am *not* doing that." Somehow I went and they weren't serving the lunch, they were meeting. They were saying, "How can we get more women on the board?" They were telling horror stories about being the only woman, how the men treated you. That became an important support group for me.

Two years later, I decided to run for mayor. I lost. The person that won was a real Wyatt Earp-type guy, the ex-county sheriff. But he quit after a year, and I was appointed. I was the first female mayor there.

I was accepted even though people perceived me, certainly, as "one of those women's libbers." But that little town of 3,500 was pretty tolerant, it always amazed me. I always wore pants, but that reflects how a lot of rural women are. They look strong and straightforward, not frilly. Plus I had grown up on a farm, I fit into that setting.

As mayor, I was supposed to be the emcee for the annual Miss Princeton pageant. *(Laughs.)* Well, first of all, I would not say "Miss," I'd say "Ms. Princeton." But anyway, I didn't know what to wear. So I finally decided to rent a tuxedo. It was a navy blue tuxedo, and it came with two cummerbunds. I had a pink cummerbund for the pageant *(laughs)*, and a red one for the American Legion banquet. The previous mayor, the Wyatt Earp guy, he was a big deal in the American Legion. When he saw me walk in, you can imagine how he felt. Here I come, the mayor, in my tuxedo with my red bowtie and my red cummerbund and a big red flower!

The pageant was on Thursday, dinner on Friday, parade on Saturday. The last day, parade day, I wore the tuxedo and rode in a convertible, waving.

When I was on the city council, in 1982, that's when the pay equity stuff started. One day I was in my bathtub, reading the newsletter from the Council on the Economic Status of Women. The newsletter explained how they were going to establish pay equity for state jobs. At the time, our city administrator, who was certainly a good old boy, was concocting all this personnel stuff. I saw the link. And I pushed for the city to evaluate the jobs fairly, pay the women what they were worth. We did it before any other local government in the state.

Men have a hard time opposing pay equity. At least, they have to give lip service. They can't just say, "We don't think women are worth as much as men." They have to say, "It's too hard to fix," or "It costs too much." They don't want to come right out and say women should stay home or should get low pay.

We're checking local governments now for compliance with the pay equity law, and there are still blatant problems. There are cases where her job is valued at 400 points and his job is valued at 125 points, but she gets $1,000 and he gets $2,000. It's important in those small towns, too, because rural women are so isolated from other women. This is one way for some of those rural women to unify in some way, to find each other.

Economic empowerment is the ticket to freedom. Everybody responds to money in this capitalistic society. By telling a woman she's worth as much as a man, in the paycheck, *that* tells her she's worth something.

Carol Bly

I always wanted to be a writer. When I was eight years old, I wrote a poem which my aunt sent to the *New Yorker*. When it came back, she said, "Now you've got your first rejection slip from the *New Yorker*," and she said someday I might get published by them. I wanted to be published by them in the worst way.

Carol Bly has since been published by the New Yorker. *She has also published several books of essays and two collections of short stories. She lived on a farm in western Minnesota for 27 years before moving to the Twin Cities, where she teaches writing. The aroma of home-baked bread fills her house as we talk. She is 62.*

I've just newly started to be a feminist. Before, I let all those early people like Gloria Steinem do the soldiering for me. I just sat home and raised children. I was happy in my life.

I was interested in what they were doing, but I wasn't psychologically conscious. I saw feminism as a pile of trouble, so I stayed out of it. Much of that early stuff, if you'll remember, seemed pretty dumb for a person with an IQ over 120. It's dumb for women to say that men are related to the sun and that women are in rhythm with the earth and the moon. That was the first stuff that made its way out into the countryside. And somehow it got tied into vegetarianism, which always irritated me. *(Laughs.)*

Also, the early feminists were doing crazy things. It seemed as if straight people were coming out of marriages and becoming lesbians in order to prove something. Well, I was out there raising four kids and doing clean-cut farm work. There was no way that would seem great to me. I was very isolated. I couldn't really see what was going on.

I'm your example of a slow comer, a slow learner. A slow learner, that's what my psychotherapist said too. I had three and a half years of getting smart through psychotherapy—that's why I became a feminist. I didn't understand the relationship between American discultivation of women—that is, that women should be treated so badly psychologically—and anything that was happening for me. But after psychotherapy, I understood it.

Have you noticed the new TV ads? They're very bad in the last few years. Little girls are saying, "My mommy's towels are whiter than your mommy's towels." So we're going backwards, and the fight's on. That brings out the people like me who come in late.

In the rural area, there were no home-grown feminists. They'd get beaten. It wouldn't ever cross their minds. Women are so much the second-class citizens. They treat *themselves* as second-class citizens, with a lot of self-hatred—and each other with lots of disdain. Without meaning to, of course.

In a small town like that . . . if women are single, they aren't anything, just forget it. If they're married, they support the system. The biggest passion they have is to *keep civilization going.* To keep it civilized, so that men don't get it down to filth, dirt. In a week, if a woman doesn't watch herself, farmers will start putting parts of things in the back seat of the car. With the grease dripping. You have to watch everything.

Women keep the organizations going. They singlehandedly keep all the events, all the celebrations, the church organizations going. That's their job. They do amazingly well. Amazingly well. But they're not innovative, and they're not very brave. They're not very good about confronting the enemy, because confrontation is not a skill of a *supportive* person.

Men routinely, across the board, expect to be the ones to carry on a conversation. They get to do the talking. That's still in place—it hasn't changed. The amount of sneering at women that still goes on is unbelievable.

In a small town, nobody respects the humanities. You'd have to say the humanities are the study of invisible subjects—all the things that have to do with love and goodness. And so those conversations are never had, out in the open, except in the most brutally simple sorts of ways. It's hard for a woman, for the kinds of things that women are mostly working with, to say anything and not be sneered at.

I never realized what a nightmare that is, for women living in a small town—unless you have all your resources inside you. Rural life was fine for me. I loved it. I'd always wanted to live that way, to live on a farm. I like nature. And I liked the sweetness of the people. My town was a very sweet town.

When I'm up in the country now, if I talk to the local people too much, I lose my self-image. Because women's self-image is so low. You get treated like nothing, just nothing. So I try to stay away.

I remember when I went out to live in the country when I was first married, I couldn't believe it. My mother had been a feminist. She was outspoken, and women got their say in her family. They believed in the smartness of women, and women had conversation. So I was in shock when I moved to rural Minnesota, where women were not expected to converse on any subject.

When I was a humanities director for the American Farm Project, when we talked to the young couples, I'd say, "Lois, I want you to talk on this one. Where are you on this subject?" She would invariably turn to her husband. Then I'd say, "Nope, you don't get to go to Bill. Bill gets to talk later." She'd say, "It's just that he knows." And I'd say, "Yes, I know. He knows, and *you* know too." We'd have to do that again and again and again, because those women are not used to being a spokesperson at all, for anything.

You get invited to Thanksgiving and they'd say, "Well, are you going to Cordell's for Thanksgiving? Because Cordell's will be there, and Jim's will be there, and Bob's will be there." That means Bob and what Bob owns. Bob-apostrophe-s—Bob's wife and children, which are his property. When I first heard that, I couldn't believe it.

I'm a slack feminist, but I'm working on it.

In a Man's World

While movement pioneers broke new ground, some women managed to find footing on ground already occupied by men. They brought new faces to police cars, shoe-repair shops, judges' chambers, and many other traditionally male enclaves. Kathy Willis wielded a torque wrench in a factory, Susan Vass took the stage as a stand-up comic, and Sharon Sayles Belton supervised male parolees.

Many women dutifully began working in traditionally women's jobs—Linda Lavender Miller as a flight attendant, Nancy Evechild as a waitress, Rosalie Wahl as a volunteer for "good-government" issues. They discovered, however, that the pay was low, the opportunities were limited, and the men made most of the decisions.

Getting into a man's world, and staying there, was not always easy. Some women attribute their access to new state and federal laws. Several members of the Filipino American Women's Network point out the racism of being perceived as exotic sex objects.

Once in the door, these women felt they had to prove themselves—and often repeatedly. Many recall the sense of isolation, of being the only woman "in a man's world."

Kathy Willis

Kathy Willis, 50, is on the grievance committee for the Oil, Chemical and Atomic Workers union at her factory. She sits near the fireplace in her Minneapolis home with a cup of coffee and a cigarette.

Back in 1978, I went to this job placement service. I didn't want secretarial. So the woman said, "I got this ad, they're looking for somebody to work on their factory floor." So I went and applied, and then I went back. I hounded them for, like, a week. They needed some more women there because of some federal rules. So I went into this setting where I had to prove myself every day I walked in—that I had a right to be there, that I could do the job.

Now I've been there 15 years. At 10 years, you get a little pen set. The next time, I'll get the little quartz mantel clock. After 20 years you get a bigger clock. *(Laughs.)*

There I was in this factory. There were three other women there— they had only been there six months—and 40 men. Not really men, they were *guys. (Laughs.)* Even though the median age was close to 40, they're boys. We make plastic netting, extrusion. Some of it's that orange construction fence, plus mattresses, carpet—you name it, we do it. It's your basic factory setting, a huge warehouse. So I'm used to 25-foot ceilings and 200-foot vistas, you know? When I sit here at home I have to look out the window, otherwise I'd get claustrophobic.

There's some heavy lifting, a lot of pushing of rolls, a roll that can weigh anywhere from fifty to a thousand pounds. I get to drive a fork-lift—they're fun. The job has given me a lot of confidence with what

I can do physically, it's given me more coordination. I was really a klutz when I first started.

I liked it right away because this job was machines, which had always fascinated me. I got to get dirty, I didn't have to worry about keeping my clothes clean. I could wear jeans. I could be me. I could smoke—well, now we can only smoke in the room, but . . . we can eat on the line, we can swear if we want to, we can just kind of be.

I had to learn all the machines. They have tooling that needs to be changed, which means using lots of different wrenches. My first day on the job, one of my superiors said, "Give me a nine-sixteenths Allen." I said, "What the hell are you talking about?" He took me by the hand, over to the tool box, and said, "This is an Allen set." I didn't know what an Allen wrench was. I knew nothing. I had to learn all that really fast.

A lot of the work, being short, I'm working over my head. It's a lot of repetitive work, taking bolts out, torquing them to 150 pounds—which takes a lot of oomph, to hear that click on the torque wrench. And I'm doing it up here. I'm taking out parts that cost a thousand to fifteen hundred dollars. There ain't no way I'm gonna drop it, because I need this job. So I would start to shake. I'd have guys standing around me, laughing at me. "Come on Shorty, come on Shaky, you can do it!" I'm down there just sweating, it's all I can do to get those bolts. But I want this job, I need this job, I've gotta do it. Were they supportive? Heavens, no!

It's part of the culture in a predominantly male environment. They ride each other, they tease each other. To some extent, if you're gonna fit in, you have to take it and you have to give it back. You can set your own boundaries, but if you set them too close to yourself, you're gonna alienate everybody. So I took a whole lot of shit, a whole lot of comments that were very sexist. "Hey baby, let's go out in the warehouse." My comeback was, "Geez, I'd love to, guys, but I left my magnifying glass at home." They'd look at me . . . *(Laughs.)*

I did my 30-day trial period and the foreman gave me a challenge at the midway point of that. He said, "Kath, I don't think you're gonna make it, I just don't think you can do this job." That was all I needed. I was, "I'll show you, you bastard, I can do this fucking job just as well as any of these boys out here." And I learned it, because I wanted that job.

There was that challenge, the machinery, there was always something new. To me, it's fascinating. It's noisy, it's dirty, but it's a challenge to make something. To change the machine over, to get it into production. I still learn there.

To my face, on a one-to-one basis, everybody is wonderful. I do socially have a pretty good time there. It's when you get a bunch of guys together that they're obnoxious. They're still doing "snuggies," still doing "titty-twisters" on each other. It's just rude. Wrestling with each other because they don't know how to be close. They throw things at each other, they yell comments. One of the favorite comments is, "Eat my shorts." These guys are so homophobic. And pointing at themselves all the time.

There are times, to this day, that I still have to do twice as well. Even though I'm the only one that knows how to run the machine I'm on. If management wants to run a new product, they come to see me. "Kath, can we run this on your machine?" R & D* comes, the other guys come. So I'm working into a position of respect and some authority and power there, but . . . I mean, it's been 15 years.

If I had been born with different plumbing, I would be in management. There are people who started about the time I did who are supervisors and managers, but I don't have the right plumbing. Management through the years hasn't been willing to back a woman in that position because of what the men on the line would say. When I've confronted them, there is absolute denial. "We just didn't need anybody." Or, "That was a different management then. We're here now." And I'm like, "Well, I still don't see much difference."

It has been okay as far as a paycheck goes. It's bought me cars, it's bought me houses, it's taken me to Mexico. It's given me stability. I'd moved a lot in my life, so it gave me a place to be for eight hours a day. Something that was a challenge physically and somewhat mentally, when I'm learning a new machine or doing a new product on a machine. But other than that, it's been the stability of being able to do a job with no problem. Even though most of the guys there think I should have a problem doing it.

* Research and development.

Linda Lavender Miller

Linda Lavender Miller, 49, began her career in the traditionally female jobs of flight attendant and clerk. Since 1975, when she was hired as the result of a court order, she has been an officer in a suburban police department. She was the state coordinator for Minnesota NOW in 1977. We spoke in her living room, near her collection of antique dolls.

I went to work as a flight attendant. I was coming up against a lot of unfair stuff for women, but for some reason I wasn't able to compute it that way. We had to be unmarried, and if we got married we were without jobs. I never figured out until years later that they were using us to sell the airline, we were a commodity. What does it mean that you're unmarried? In those days, the great majority of passengers were male. The message was, "Not only do these women look good and do a nice job, but they're also available."

When I was flying, there were no women who worked in the cockpit—they had the captain and the engineer and the copilot, those people were always men. The women were flight attendants. Wherever you are overnight, the airline has a contract with the hotel. They give you your room key at the desk, you don't pay or anything. The men were each handed their own key. For the "girls," for every two of us there was one key, we shared rooms. One day it hit me. I said to the captain, "Why do you guys get your own room and we have to share?" He looked at me and said, "Because we're men!" At the time, that was all the answer I needed to hear. I just needed to be reminded. *(Laughs.)*

Another thing was, the most senior flight attendant on the flight is the boss—seniority is everything. Your flight card always designated who was senior and who was junior, based, of course, on length of service. That was without exception, there was no way around it. *Unless* there was a male flight attendant on board—even if he started yester-day, he was in charge.

We had to weigh a certain amount, and the men didn't. When we came to work, we had to step on a scale. The company decided how much you could weigh, not the doctor. If you were over the weight they had designated for you, you were laid off immediately without pay until you met your weight. Which was a boon for the diet-pill industry. *(Laughs.)*

I ended up getting married unbeknownst to the airline, like we all did, and continuing to work. You had to be in charge of the phone when you were on reserve. If there was a guy answering the phone, you might be asked why he was there in the middle of the night. So eventually the stress was too much, and I quit. That was the end of that career.

Then I worked in some typical women's jobs, and after six years I had a baby. I planned on staying home for a couple of years, but pretty much as soon as I had the baby I got a divorce. So much for that plan.

I got a job as courtroom clerk, which had always been a man's job. I was interviewed by a man who asked if I was a member of, get this, "Women's Lib"—like it was a club! I said, "No, but if I don't get this job, I'm going to join." So I got the job.

Later I heard about a job as a police dispatcher. I knew they had free parking *(laughs)*, and parking was one of the biggest items of my budget when I worked downtown. It was called a civilian dispatcher.

It did complicate my life incredibly because it required that you change shifts every two weeks, a day shift for two weeks, then four to midnight, then midnight to eight. You don't have enough room in your book for me to talk about my child-care problems. In day care, you had to pay for the whole month, even though my son only came two weeks out of every six weeks, so I was paying full-time day care all the time to hold the spot. Then I'd pay a baby sitter, so when I'd work four to midnight I'd pay day care that he wasn't going to, then I'd pay the babysitter. When I worked nights, usually we'd go to my folks and he'd go to bed there, so it was a really screwy situation.

The way it was set up, there were two dispatchers on duty at all times. One was a police officer, and one was a civilian. The police officers were always male, because that's the only kind they had. The civilians were always female, with one exception. They hired one man who wanted to be a police officer, and he did become one. But the jobs were identical. We had identical consoles in front of us, identical telephones, we both dispatched cars, we both answered telephones. The only difference was, the civilians had to type. When there was quiet time on "dog watch," midnight to eight, *they* would read magazines and *we* would be typing, we had that extra duty. And of course the male police officers were making about double what we were making.

There was just a door between the jail's booking room and the dispatch room. Occasionally a female was arrested, and they didn't have a good way of doing routine searches of them, because they didn't have any women. So we were asked to begin searching women prisoners. I objected. It might sound simple, but there are things to learn about doing searches, for your own safety and for thoroughness, and we didn't know those things. None of us came there with the idea of being police officers, so it was completely foreign. We didn't have the training, and we weren't being paid for this.

It wasn't long after I started getting a closeup look at police work that I started having this little thought that I could do this job. It got so I would dispatch calls and then I would think about what I would do if I was on the call. And I would compare that with what happened. More and more I started thinking, "Not only could I do this job, but this place needs to have women doing this job, too."

The supervisor of the dispatchers was a police guy, he wanted us to wear uniforms. I didn't object, because it's a financial savings. But the part that did bother me was, he went out and bought some bolts of blue material and brought them in—he thought we should *make* our uniforms because we were women. That was abandoned, but the thing with the prisoners was still troublesome.

By this time I was saying out loud, "This isn't fair, we should be making much more money, and, furthermore, why don't you think about hiring women officers?" Other things were going on, too. Secretaries were occasionally used in undercover assignments because they didn't have women to do that kind of thing. Undercover assignments can be real dangerous even for police officers. But to take secretaries who don't have the training . . . It seemed like as long as they were allowed to do those things, women would never be hired as officers.

So, eventually, a few of us went to the state human rights department and filed a complaint on the pay issue. That was 1974. It escalated

from there. Obviously it caused a lot of conversation in the police department. *(Laughs.)* A supervisor told me one night that, in all honesty,
he realized that women were going to come into this job. But they were
not going to be normal women, women like you'd marry, women like
we all are used to. I guess he thought they'd be from another planet.

Ultimately, in 1975, the human rights department found in our
favor. We were ecstatic. But a few hours later, we were miserable because they laid us all off. They picked two police officers to be the dispatchers. So we were all without jobs, and some people were real unhappy with me because it was my big idea to start all this. I felt really
awful. So we got back in the car and went over to St. Paul and filed another complaint for retaliation.

The original settlement said the people who were working there
would be allowed to test for the job of police officer. Only me and one
other nut wanted to be police officers, so the other women dispatchers
lost their jobs. That was real sad.

It got worse, though. There are a couple parts to testing for police
officer, a written exam and a physical agility test. Everybody knew
what was on the agility test, you had to run a quarter of a mile in 90
seconds, you had to push a squad car so many feet, carry a resuscitator
out of a car, up a couple of flights in a building, walk a balance beam.
Those of us that were going to test were out running and doing all
these things to prepare. Running was the only big challenge. But what
we didn't count on was that they would change the test—and the com-
ponents, for the first time, would be a major secret.

We took the written test and we passed with flying colors. The
agility test came and they added a component that had never been in
there before, which was to climb a smooth-board six-foot fence. Go
over a fence with no place for a toehold, pull yourself up by your arms.
It's a test that will cut out about 90 percent of untrained women. So of
course we failed that portion miserably. We filed a different case, discrimination in testing, and there was a lengthy court trial a long time
later.

At any rate, we were all now without jobs. Nine months went by.
Then the human rights department got an injunction ordering the police department to hire us in spite of the fact we failed the fence test.
By that time, I was the only one left who was willing to go. So I went,
and it felt like I was walking the plank, it was really scary.

People in the department were polarized. There were very few coming down on our side, although there were some real courageous guys I have always been grateful to. There was a petition signed by the vast majority of the department that was emanating out of the watch commander's office. Men were called into the office off patrol to sign it. There were some men that *didn't* sign it, and that took a lot of guts.

I was pretty much not spoken to. After the injunction was issued, I called the supervisor and asked, "What time do I go to work?" He said, "Well, the judge told you what day to come to work, I guess the judge can tell you what time to report."

When I went in the lunchroom I sat by myself, there was not much desire to be seen talking to me. You have to have a field training officer, you ride with this person for a number of weeks and they show you the ropes. Well, there was a problem getting anyone to take me. There were some wives who didn't want their husbands to ride with me. One guy said he would take me, but he got pressure.

I was dating an officer there who happened to be president of their union. He ended up taking a ton of heat but he stood up for me. His fellow union members held a special meeting to impeach him from office for defending this horrible plot to get women in.

About this time, I got connected with NOW. I went to a workshop and I was just overwhelmed with information and with the people I met. I ended up being state coordinator three years later. Those were good days for me, I got a lot of support. Part of that was this newfound strength I got when I thought maybe the police were right, I couldn't do this, women didn't belong here, I was just going against nature to even suggest such a thing. I got strength from thinking, "Wait a minute, there's a lot of other people who understand the world the way I do, and this is okay." So it helped me.

NOW was a credential that seemed to cause a great deal of concern among my colleagues. (Laughs.) I'm not active now. I became pretty overwhelmed with the job of police officer, raising kids, working shift work for years—it pretty much took up my time.

It was a lonely time, but I had support from my friends and the people I met through NOW. I had the support of my family and the man I was living with. I don't want to say, "I couldn't have done this without some man," but the truth is, he helped me a lot. When the fighting gets over with, and you get in the squad car for the first time by yourself, and you drive out of the parking lot . . . I can still remember looking around at the shotgun and the uniform and thinking, "Do I know what I've done? I've been talking big now for a long time, and this is it."

But then I began a fascinating career. Financially, it's been wonderful for me, somebody with my background and education, which wasn't extensive—I've been able to do what I wanted to do. I've raised my son, I've had a decent living, I had a job I thought most of the time was real important, I felt like a contributor.

My enemies were all older than I was. *(Laughs.)* They didn't die, but they retired. I did patrol for a long time, but I did other things, too. I've never had an assignment in the police department that I didn't like. You're so involved with people right where they're living. That can be intense and burnout stuff, but it's doing good, at least on a little scale. I carried a sense that I was doing something for women. In my own little sphere I think I've had some impact on policing, I've changed some attitudes. There's 8 women now out of 100 officers—not a lot, but 8 is a lot more than 1.

My biggest fears in my career have not been on patrol, they've been at the department. Some of it was funny, like the whole issue with what women officers wear. I figured, of course, I would wear what the men did. The chief wanted me to wear those little ties like women in the military, but I didn't want to wear something special . . . And the hat thing. Well, the truth is, I've never had my hat on except at funerals. But uniforms weren't cut for women. So I had men's pants, with no hips, you have to buy them big enough to fit the hips and then you have this huge waist. The shirts buttoned on the other side, that was no big problem. But the men's shoes felt like cement, they were too wide, you couldn't run and chase the "bad guys." I used to feel like a kid dressed up in her dad's clothes.

It's been an adventure. I wouldn't say a police department is particularly a warm and fuzzy environment anyway. It wouldn't have been for the first woman coming in, but coming in on an injunction was really not . . . Especially in those beginning years, there was pornography in the mailbox, that kind of stuff. And of course I've never gotten over that reputation. I haven't filed a complaint in 17 years, but they think I'm still likely to any second. In a way, that's put me in a protected spot.

I still get angry, but it's not as intense or long-lasting. Maybe I feel like I righted some wrongs, and some justice was had, and I don't have that need anymore. Part of that anger grew out of the sheer frustration that no matter how fair this is, how right it is, they're gonna win—and they didn't, for once. I won. By the way, I won a lot of money, too. That helped my anger a whole lot. *(Laughs.)*

I had a new officer walk into my office a few years ago, and he said, "Can I ask you something? Is it true that you sued the department?" I said, "Yeah, that's true." He said, "Why did you do that?" I said, "It had to do with hiring women." He said, "Didn't they want women? How come?" I said, "I don't think I can explain it to you." So that's a long way.

Sharon Sayles Belton

I was in college between '69 and '73, at the height of the black power movement and the Vietnam War. Because the black power movement was going on, I became strongly attached to the positive elements of black pride. I spent a lot of my time affirming my racial identity. We did art, we did poetry, we did plays. I was in an African dancing troupe and I danced at colleges and universities across the country. It was a strong cultural experience, and it helped me feel good about myself as an African-American woman.

Sharon Sayles Belton is the first woman and the first African American to be elected mayor of Minneapolis. She was on the city council for 10 years. Previously, she spent 10 years with the state's Department of Corrections, first as a parole officer for male offenders and then as the assistant director of the program for victims of sexual assault. She is in her early forties.

At college I picked a writing course, and the writing course took me to the prison, to Stillwater, where we had a small group of guys who wanted to write. We were teaching them the skills we were learning in our classroom. It was through that experience that I learned that most of the people who are in prison are of color. And nobody was working with them who knew anything about the African-American community.

I got drawn into that like who knows what. It prompted me to make an application to the governor's internship program, and to try to do something, to make a change. My obsession became, "You've got to be out there trying to help people who want to help themselves." There's nobody there to advocate for them. That has probably been my whole life, it's something I've done my whole life.

When I first sought a job after school, I took a civil service test and did very well. My recollection is that I had the highest score for the position I was tested for. It was for a job as corrections agent, and I really wanted to do that. I wanted to work with male offenders—not with women, not with juveniles—but with male offenders.

When a position became open, it was in a unit supervising men. They had never let women supervise adult males because they didn't think we could do that. It made me angry, because I knew I was qualified. I knew I got the best score in the state, I had an excellent interview—and the reason they wanted to keep me from this was because they didn't believe women were capable of supervising men.

I remember I was constantly calling. I was calling the central office, saying, "What's going on?" I was calling Personnel. It came back to me that one of the people in Personnel had said to the supervisor, "Why do you want to hire her? She's one of those pushy women." And that really made me angry.

I ended up getting into the unit, and it was an interesting experience, because half the guys there were—"Oh, she's just there for affirmative action. She's not qualified." I had to constantly say to these guys, "Look. I took the test. I had the best score. I know this job. I did this job for free while I was a student, for almost two years. Give me a break. I know parole, I've worked with women, I've worked with men. I know the human-service system. Give me a break."

Taking into consideration that you're working with offenders—and okay, so whatever your beliefs or stereotypes are about blacks and crime, it was, is she going to be tough? Is she going to be lenient? Is she going to give breaks to black people because of her race? Because she's a woman, is she going to be able to command the respect?

I think I proved to them that they ought not to make snap judgments about us just because we're women, or black—and how we might treat a client. I was tough, I was fair, I was knowledgeable, and I was able to do the job. After a while, after proving myself for a number of years, they finally got the message. *(Laughs.)* There were a couple of guys who were really very good and very supportive all along, and they made it easy for me. But I was the first woman, I was the first African American. There had never been any African-American women working as parole agents with adults. I felt like I was breaking new ground.

When I was an agent, part of the work I did in my field office, on the side, was to talk about sexual assault. I was in the community, doing some organizing, doing some public education. I got involved in victims' services while I was still an agent, and that gave me the training and expertise to move into management over at the state sexual assault program.

Part of my goal in going there was to try to help make the sexual assault programs meet the needs of ... I don't want to say non-traditional victims, but *women of color* who were victims. The programs were not doing that. We knew there was a significant number of women of color who were victims of sexual assault. And we knew that some of the myths around sexual assault had other implications when you introduce the subject of race.

So we spent an inordinate amount of time—probably justified—trying to figure out how to talk about the unique issues associated with sexual assault when you talk about black victims. You have to start talking about black perpetrators, and the historical context of black perpetrators and who their victims were. As well as issues that are part of our community. You know, not only who is raping the black woman, but what are the myths about *her?* Are they all hookers? Are they oversexed? All the other negative things.

There's a tension that exists in the African-American community when you talk about rape, because we think about it historically. About the fact that black men have been wrongly accused, they were killed and lynched and put in prison because of false accusations. So when you start talking to an African-American community about rallying around victims, you can understand it is—and was—a very tense experience. It was difficult to garner support. It was full of mythology. I think it was that work that started me strongly identifying with feminism, and starting to experience the repercussions of having done so.

There was not a whole lot of support within the African-American community for women who were identifying with feminism.

I might also mention, being a single mom out there struggling by myself with a disabled child—looking for housing, looking for special-ized day care—also helped me link with women who are out there struggling, too. It helped me know that nobody's paying attention to our needs. For the most part they don't pay attention to anybody who doesn't have the status of white males of privilege. It was a very hard lesson to learn, and it's still very painful when I look back on it.

There were times in the snow and the rain, you're pushing the stroller up to the bus stop, and collapsing it, and taking this baby and getting on a bus. Get to a sitter, and then get to work. It was a struggle. Remember, my baby was not healthy, she had seizures and other prob-lems like that to worry me.

There's another experience I had when we were trying to start a program in Minneapolis. It happened to be with Harriet Tubman, a shelter for battered women. My name got thrown out there as a person who ought to be drawn in, because there were some very good people who wanted to have diversity—although it wasn't called diversity then—to have affirmative action.

But once I got there, it really didn't feel like the door was wide open. There was a real undercurrent of, "Well, we're glad you're here, and we're opening our arms for you to be involved, but don't look for any leadership opportunities here because you guys are new to this thing and you haven't paid your dues." Somehow I had to prove my-self, earn my stripes or whatever, as if I didn't come in the door with the same experiences that some of these other women had had. Well, maybe we hadn't been on the same line in the battlefield with them, but certainly we'd been in the same war.

People, quite frankly, want you to choose. Are you black or are you a woman? I mean, how can I choose one over the other? Because I work on feminist issues, or on issues that are important to women, doesn't mean that I'm not concerned about the discrimination I expe-rience because of my race. I have to do both.

It's not either/or. I think that's the wrong question. There are people who don't believe there's any value in the feminist movement as it relates to women of color, because they think it dilutes our strength as people of color. They're skeptical of the feminist movement because they think it's just an opportunity for white women to seek the privileges of white males.

I don't think so. I think women of color have gotten some gains, too. But we have special needs that other women need to understand, and they need to join us in that fight, in *our* fight. I'm not going to get equality with white women unless white women understand racial discrimination and decide to band with me on that. As we struggle with issues of race, we've got to have *all* women speaking up.

Otherwise, white men won't do it. They won't. I don't want them to do it out of fear, because when you do public policy out of fear it's never long term. It's a quick-fix band-aid: "How can I make you feel better so you'll go away?" We're at a critical juncture, and I think the feminist movement and the civil rights movement have to have another kind of wedding. I tell you, it's got to happen.

One of the things I'm really interested in is how do we get over this dilemma, the hostility over race and feminism. That's something that's certainly been haunting me as a member of the feminist movement. I don't want to feel that I'm a "black feminist" and you're a "white feminist," and that somehow that means something different. We haven't talked about that enough.

Nancy Evechild

A hippie in the '60s, Nancy Evechild quickly became a radical feminist. She is now a teacher, a psychic healer, and a lesbian mother. She is 44.

I tried to commit suicide when I was 18. At the time, the only reason I could see was my fear of ending up in a dead-end job like my mother's. Soon after that, I moved to Denver. I got involved in an SDS group, Students for a Democratic Society. Later, I was in this collective cadre of revolutionaries, living in the mountains like a back-to-the-land hippie.

At the same time, I worked waiting tables. I worked at the only topless bar in town where you didn't have to prostitute. You could if you wanted to. I don't know what kept me from it, I guess I didn't really need the money.

Another place I worked, we wore these little matador tutus because it was called the Matador Lounge. The men who came there wanted to touch our legs and our butts and stuff. I worked with a woman who let them. But I wouldn't. These were white businessmen, these were the class enemy. We'd work the same shift—and I'd make $10 in tips, and she'd make $85 in tips.

I drove down from the mountains to work every day. I'd stop at a friend's house and put electric rollers in my hair and put on my eye makeup and go to work. I could feel my transformation from one person to the next. I remember one day walking from my locker to the bar and realizing that I hadn't shifted from "Nancy" to "waitress" yet. It was awful. I didn't want to be Nancy and be in that place.

At that time, I was living with three men. One day, I read a magazine article about women doing more than their share. Then I saw someone had made a sandwich and left the bread out on the table. So I just unconsciously put the bread away . . . and stopped dead in my tracks, seeing what I did. So I gathered the men together that night and said, "I just had a revelation, and it's about sexism."

Later, I found some women and we started doing feminist organizing. That was a time in my life that I never went anyplace without a permanent magic marker. (Laughs.) Because I was always writing on something, the sidewalk, everyplace—like, "If men got pregnant, abortion would be a sacrament." We'd spray paint, "Kill Rapists."

I was by then living in a women's collective, and we started a newspaper, Big Mama Rag. Meeting one another was like meeting ourselves so often. The ease of being just with women, it was awesome to see the energy that women could create. We believed that we were dedicated enough, rageful enough, that we could move mountains. I believe now that our rage is pretty ancient, and that's why it's so deep.

That year I changed my last name to Evechild. Why should I have my father's name? I never liked my father, although I didn't know why until I started to have incest memories. My mother's name is Evelyn, which is where I got the Eve. And of course from Adam and Eve.

And I was born in the evening, so I'm a child of the evening. I feel close to my name at twilight.

Now when I hear young women get married and they change their names, I'm just dumbfounded. Why are they doing that? It's sad. Your name is not trivial.

By 1973, the war was pretty much over, there wasn't so much of a movement anymore. Women in Denver weren't organizing much yet. And I missed the green of Minneapolis. I longed for water, snow, rain, green trees, lakes. So when the collective broke up, I came back to Minnesota.

By that time, I had come to the belief that people are by nature bisexual, and that sleeping only with men was silly. Ever since then I've called myself a lesbian, even though I've had long-term relationships with men. So I went to the Lesbian Resource Center to try to connect up. I was very disappointed.

Somebody had just given them a lot of money and they figured they'd buy U.S. savings bonds. I couldn't believe it. I had just spent the last four years fighting the government tooth and nail, and now these women were gonna buy savings bonds!

Part of who I was all this time, I was a hard-drinking, tough woman. I moved from Denver with two pieces of clothing: my leather jeans and a T-shirt. I shot pool. But I was working at a food co-op for only $25 a week and couldn't make enough money to keep myself in beer.

In Denver I'd learned bricklaying, so I went to the bricklayers' union here. They wouldn't have me, though. They'd never had a woman, and they weren't going to have a woman. So I went to school and learned shoe repair.

I loved shoe repair and I had a good reputation. Most of the women who worked in shops just sewed the uppers, the "women's work" where they didn't put soles on, but I did all of it. Then I got a job teaching shoe repair at a technical institute. It's a male-dominated place, so I was a natural attraction for women students. I encouraged them to talk to me and to the administration about sexual harassment. I confronted male teachers who said awful things to them.

I worked with the sex-equity coordinator there. She had been out in front for so long, and had been so battered by it. I said, "I can step out in front for a while," and she said, "That's good, I can support you." We worked really well together, even though she's a lot older than me and very conservative looking. We liked each other's energy.

Most of my students were men my age. One fellow older than me was going to do some orthopedic work on somebody's shoes. I asked for the prescription, and he said, "We don't need one." I pointed out that you can't do orthopedic work without a prescription. He said, "No bitch is ever gonna teach me anything." Well, the whole class was in a circle around us. But I just said, "*This* bitch is the only teacher you've got, so take it or leave it." And he turned out to be one of my best students.

In 1985, I started living with my partner Vicky and her three kids. At one point we were on TV, on a show about lesbian couples. Shortly after that the state decided to close the shoe-repair program. We had full enrollment and a waiting list, and they'd never closed a program like that before. I believed that part of the reason was, I was a lesbian and a feminist troublemaker.

It took me a long time to heal from the closing of the shoe-repair program. I was unemployed. Then I developed a training program on sexual harassment in the workplace, and now I'm training staff at auto dealerships. I can relate to car salesmen, these are working-class guys. In doing the training, I realized how much of men's identity is tied in with being "not-women." Their intent isn't always to hurt, it's to define themselves.

Rosalie Wahl

Rosalie Wahl, 68, is the first woman to be appointed to the Minnesota Supreme Court. She grew up in rural Kansas and attended a one-room country school. She went to law school at age 38 when she had four children, with a fifth child born soon afterward. In 1977 her appointment to the supreme court was announced at the Minnesota Women's Meeting in St. Cloud. The crowd of 4,500 went wild.

I grew up without really knowing what a woman's place was, which is quite an advantage. If you don't know where it is, you don't have to be in it. *(Laughs.)* But I think there was always a double standard, even in our family. Their expectations of the women were always higher. I don't know if this was just my grandmother. She was a wonderful old Scotch-Irish woman with high moral values, a Methodist.

After I moved to St. Paul, I went to this big old Salvation Army bookstore down on the island in the Mississippi River. They had wonderful books. I found Vera Brittain, and through her I found Virginia Woolf, and then Olive Schreiner—that whole generation of women. I suppose they were feminists, although I don't know if they called themselves that.

That's where I got my grounding, the whole idea of feminism. There was a generation back there that I was reading in the late 1950s. I feel that I've always been walking along in the same direction. I like the historical view. I feel very connected with women, not just horizontally but through the generations.

I went to law school because I'd been involved in all these community activities—school-board elections, DFL* politics, a lot of things. We worked for years trying to establish a county library system, and I was tired of the effort that was necessary to get people aroused about an issue. Aroused enough to go to the courthouse, or to city hall, or to the legislature. And then we'd sit there, and we'd wait, while the men on the inside made the decisions.

When I went to law school in 1962, there were just two women in my class. I went to night school because I needed to be there when my kids came home from school. I still had a big foot in the nest. It was easier, I thought, to go at night. So there I was at quarter to six all those years—put supper on the table, and out the door.

In the late '60s and early '70s there was all this foment . . . in the political parties, in the DFL. I can remember the DFL women slugging it out to get the woman chairperson paid. The man had been earning $18,000 a year, while the woman was doing as much or more work, and getting paid nothing. And the women out there on the line were saying, "We don't make coffee if we don't make policy." They were refusing to ring the doorbells.

* Democratic-Farmer-Labor Party.

I'd been asked to put in my name for the supreme court, but I wasn't sure. All the judges I knew were men. They seemed to me to be poured from a mold. They seemed so formalistic. I didn't know if it was possible to be yourself and still be a judge. But there were some who were different. There was one who was a very good judge, but he was also himself. He'd create an atmosphere in the courtroom where he'd greet people coming in. "Hello, Mr. Smith, how are you today?" And there were a few others that I saw, so I knew it was possible. I also knew that when you're urging the appointment of women, you've either got to put up or shut up. *(Laughs.)*

I remember the meeting in St. Cloud, after that huge explosion that evening, when someone came up to me afterwards and said, "I used to wonder why I would drive on those winter nights, 50 miles in the cold, to talk to five or six people. And now I know." It was exactly that. It was the women in the Democratic Party who said to the governor that they wanted a woman on the supreme court, that nine-zip just wouldn't do it.

The first thing that women bring to the court is their experience of growing up female in this society, which is very different from growing up male. Your experiences are different, the way you may react, what you think is important. How you weigh, for example, violence against a person. Or how you view certain issues in the area of family relations.

I think one of the things men have trouble understanding is the experience of a midlife woman who is being divorced. Most men in their fifties are at their prime, at the peak of their earning capacity. They just don't understand that a woman who's been out of the labor market, who has played by the old rules—I see in so many of these long-term marriages, even if she had a profession or vocation when she was married, 20 years later there's nothing much left. Many of the things she might have done, she can no longer do. Her earning capacity is permanently impaired. Maybe she can sell lamps at a department store—if she's lucky—but what does she earn? So what is reasonable?

In the whole area of sexual assault, and assaults on children, so many men don't understand. They don't understand the harm that's done to children, or the harm that's been done to young women. They don't really understand the effect on their whole lives, on their sexual lives. So much that goes on is real damage. They think, "Oh well, it's not that big a deal." That's a gap, that's an immense gap, that sometimes seems hard to overcome.

On the court, we try to listen to each other. I think we learn from each other. As time goes on, there's greater understanding. Besides, women are as different from each other as men are. We have differences of opinion on just about any matter you can think of.

I was on the court five years before Jeanne Coyne was appointed. I had thought that it didn't really matter that I was the only woman there. The day she was sworn in in the morning, we heard cases in the afternoon. At about 5:00 or 5:30, as we were going out of the conference room, I said something inconsequential as I went by her. It was something I probably wouldn't have said to one of the men, although I'm sure they say little things like that to each other. I realized at that point that I had been lonely in a way that I hadn't even realized.

But it wasn't until later in that year that all of a sudden I thought, "Well, I don't have to be *everything* a woman could be on this court. Jeanne can be part of it." At that point I realized there had been this burden, this tremendous pressure that I was, in a sense, the representative of women there. If I made mistakes, anything I did would be held against all my gender. I wasn't consciously thinking of it, it wasn't until I . . .

One of the things I'd always admired about my male colleagues, when I got there, the men all seemed like there was so much elbow room, the men were just who they were. That's one of the big advantages now that there are more women on the court. You can be just who you are. You don't have to be *all* women.

Filipino American Women's Network (FAWN)

Five members of the Filipino American Women's Network (FAWN) relax around a conference table at the Minnesota Women's Building in St. Paul. They discuss their definitions of feminism, their connections as Filipinas, and their interactions with white women.

Fredilyn Sison, 30, is an attorney working as a public defender. Elsa J. Batica, 42, is a YWCA director of social action. Jocelyn Ancheta, 33, is a government safety-program coordinator. Sharon Marie Apolonio Ramirez, 34, is a program-evaluation consultant. Corazon Cris Brizuela, 43, is a scientist at Minnesota Mining and Manufacturing (3M).

Fredilyn: Is there a word for feminism in Tagalog?

Elsa: There is a word that would be the adjective for what a feminist is. There is no literal word.

Jocelyn: All I can think of is the word for tomboy *(laughs)*, which isn't . . .

Fredilyn: Well, I consider myself a feminist, but at the same time I like the term "humanist" because it's so inclusive of everybody else. That's what I'm working toward. Obviously I'm working towards the rights of women, but I could never separate myself from my color. I don't feel very comfortable in the feminist movement. You don't see a lot of black men marching in the feminist movement, and you have to wonder why. I'm not blaming feminists, I'm blaming the patriarchal system.

Elsa: It doesn't bother me any more to call myself a feminist. How other people define it, that's their problem. But if you ask me my definition, it's looking at a vision for the future and acting out for it. We're looking for ways we can improve ourselves, including our men and all of us.

Sharon: I always was a feminist, I am a strong feminist. The thing that's run through my career is my focus on women's issues, issues around oppressed people, and poverty issues. The source has been my anger about these injustices—that's been motivating.

For example, I've always been aware that Asian women are seen as sex objects. Once upon a time I was thin and cute *(laughs)*, and I was sexually harassed by a lot of men as this exotic Asian woman. This guy, freshman year in college, I thought he was a friend. And he told me he was hanging around with me because he thought I was exotic. I was an Asian, and I would go to bed with him because I wasn't white!—those were his words.

I've been involved with lots and lots of women's organizations, and FAWN is the first one where I feel like I've come home. I was on the board of one women's group, and it fell on *me* to bring up issues of race. There was a feeling that people didn't always take you as seriously, as a person of color. You couldn't be as honest, or if you were honest . . . (*She shrugs.*)

Elsa: A lot of other organizations, that's why I've shied away, because I'm not allowed to come to terms on my own terms. FAWN is open, everybody can come, we have diverse backgrounds.

Cris: So when are we going to have a meeting on Goddess worship? (*All laugh.*)

Elsa: What we're trying to model in FAWN is that everybody can grow at their own pace. The rule is you have to speak from your own experience. Your experience is the greatest thing in the world.

When white women ask me, "How can we attract women of color," I think, there is no sign here that says, "This is for white women only." So why is it that I don't come, or if I come I'm the only one? First, there has been no trust built that you would listen to what I say. Would you give me time and space to grow? You're running, you're jumping . . . and I'm just catching on.

The train is running, the women's movement is running. It's running so fast, and they haven't slowed down. What we have in FAWN is, "Who cares where this train is going? Let's just make sure that everybody knows where the end is. There is this huge train, it's okay if you're in car 12 and others are in car 1. That's fine. But you are on board."

Cris: FAWN is working towards this issue of class. All of us are educated, but there is a whole class of Filipino women who are uneducated, who are exploited. They are forced into being single parents, or into relationships that they need to get out of. A majority of the immigrants, many are mail-order brides. Whatever we are accusing the white feminist group of, we are practicing it within our group. We need to reach to those other women, they need us.

Elsa: I wouldn't play down the work we *have* done. They may not come to our meetings, they may not feel comfortable. We don't have the energies to be everywhere. But FAWN has done a great deal for the mail-order brides. I have housed homeless Filipino women in my house.

The mail-order brides problem starts with white men who don't like American women because they're so "aggressive." So they look to the third-world countries. We have a saying back home, "Those who are pressed to the wall would hang on to even the sharpest blade." There are women who advertise, "I am available to be a wife." So a marriage is arranged, and the woman comes to the U.S.

Later the men are surprised—"Oh my God, they have brains." They're supposed to be quiet and subservient and—lo and behold—they have brains. Then the men become abusive. In 1989, January alone, I had nine women calling me. Trying to get out of those marriages, and not knowing what to do.

Cris: With the mail-order brides, there's the issue of the green cards. See, they have three years, they can't just get out of the marriage, or they will get deported. But it's physical abuse, their life is in danger.

Elsa: Because of poverty, the way the families have coped is to sacrifice a child. There was an article in the paper here about child prostitution. They asked the father of a 10-year-old girl, who brought her in totally lacerated, "Why did you do that?" And he said, "She was young, and we needed the money for the other children. Now we have $400, and she doesn't have to do that anymore." And mail-order brides is the quickest way for any woman to pay up any debt.

Jocelyn: That presentation I did recently, the women's center asked me to talk about mail-order brides, but the majority of my presentation was on the historical context. To give them the framework. I think they wanted ... *(she searches for words)* ... more like blaming the victim. "Why would those families sell their daughters?" So my presentation was all on colonial history.

Elsa: Most often, I know more about white women than they know themselves. But do you know me? Do you know how many languages there are in my country? How many islands? Do you know my history? If people say, "I know a little bit," then I'm more interested. I'll tell them, "First read two books: *America Is in the Heart** and *Strangers to These Shores.*** Then we'll talk."

Cris: Boy, are you tough! *(Laughs.)*

Susan Baumbach Vass

Susan Vass is a "star," a well-known comedian both locally and nationally. We meet in her home in suburban St. Paul. The conversation is punctuated with her rich—and contagious—laugh. She is 45.

I come from a very traditional family. My father was a pharmacist in a small resort town, a very '50s town. My mother was a full-time housewife and substitute teacher. She worked off and on to buy him birthday presents or things like that. In that era, many women could only *get* money from husbands to buy them birthday presents—something I always found odd, even as a child.

I was different, my attitudes were different, from most girls of my generation. Almost from birth. I wasn't interested in girl things. I was a tomboy, I was an athlete, I was a debater, I was valedictorian of my high-school class, I was a scholar. I liked hanging out with boys more than I liked hanging out with girls. Girls wanted to talk about hair and fingernails and bride dolls and weddings, things I was not even remotely interested in.

At the same time, I had enormously strong maternal feelings. I knew for sure that I wanted to be a mother. I played with dolls at a very advanced age, until probably 13 or 14. I think I got my last doll for Christmas at the age of 13. When 14 came around and I didn't get one, but got a hairdryer or some such thing which indicated that I should be

* By Carlos Bulosan (1946; reprint 1973).
** By Vincent N. Parrillo (1980).

moving along, I was bitterly disappointed. I always wanted a family, at least five or six kids.

In many ways I had an odd combination of a very traditional up-bringing, yet with some pretty non-stereotypical attitudes. My mother was an athlete, and she was a funny person. I thought women were supposed to be funny, and not just laugh at the men's jokes.

The Vietnam War colored our whole generation. When I went to college and met my husband there, we had that ax hanging over our heads at all times—the draft. You were going to have to fight in this awful war. That was the motor force of our life, how to avoid that. We never got into drugs, which lots and lots of people in our generation did. And we were married, so we never did the free-love thing. The counter-culture thing just passed us by, and we became political as a way to deal with that feeling of impotence.

I joined the Socialist Workers Party. Some women have claimed of the movement, not just the party but the Left in general, that women were doing all the shitwork, and running the mimeos, and were never the leaders. That was simply not the case with me. I was elected to everything possible within the party, and within the radical movement.

But I was always a reader, and started reading the early feminist stuff—Kate Millett, Robin Morgan, Simone de Beauvoir, of course, Gloria Steinem. I really came to feminism more from an intellectual standpoint than from a feeling of personal oppression.

As I was doing the reading in the early days, the first thing I felt was a shock of recognition. My God! I've been all alone thinking these things—and here's someone else who thinks them. I'm not insane. And there was a lot of anger. The first year, I went around just an angry lit-tle bundle of energy. *(Laughs.)* I whacked my hair off, for that horrible Joan of Arc look. I wore jeans and sandals and ugly clothes and no makeup, and I didn't even want to see men or have them in my world. Except my husband, whom I loved.

There was a whole lot of anger. Especially when Susan Brown-miller's book on rape* came out. I basically couldn't even read it. I could only skim it because it was so disturbing. It's the same with battering

* *Against Our Will: Men, Women, and Rape* (1975).

stuff nowadays . . . my eye will sort of fall on the page and then just trail off. I think, "I don't want to know, I don't want to hear about it."

After a while I realized I had to let go or I wouldn't be able to function. I would just burn out like a little firecracker. I still get angry, though, particularly over things which should be settled, questions that are forever open. Like the choice issue. It just won't die. They keep chipping and chipping away at this right.

From feminism, I got a wonderful network of women friends. I got to see other women as role models, not only in government or business, but role models for living. I had often felt more out of touch with other women than out of touch with society. I paid a heavy price for being so different as a young girl. A lot of other girls didn't like me and didn't think I fit in. Part of my radicalization process was in becoming close to women, in learning to trust them.

I've succeeded in comedy, a very male-dominated profession. For the most part, I hit the market running at a really opportune time. I can't whine. I got tons of publicity for being a woman. I got put in a show in 1982, long before I was ready. There were others who were readier than I was who were male, but because I was different, and because I was the token, I got a leg up. The guys were pretty resentful about it, and had a right to be. But, hey, that's the way the ball bounces sometimes. They've benefited plenty from the other side.

When I was put in that first show, there were all these guys in it. It was the Comedy All-Stars and me. They would do things in the green room downstairs, like hawk up huge hunks of phlegm and spit them across the room. That kind of male thing, trying to gross me out. They didn't want me there, I was spoiling the party.

And I know many women who came after me have had a real hard time. Women tell me on the road . . . they go to East Overshoe, Iowa, and play a comedy club there, and people still consider a female comic kind of a specialty act, like a trained bear or something. You know, "We had a magician last week, and now we've got a woman." Or "No, we can't book you, we had a woman last month."

Luckily, I haven't experienced that kind of thing because I don't tour in the clubs. I do strictly private stuff, in fact almost always for women. I've been on the circuit doing these women's health meetings—and they're just dream audiences. You know, diet and exercise, diet and exercise. *(Laughs.)*

I make jokes about women's lives. I don't believe I poke fun at women. I make jokes about my own life particularly, and about the fact that we're all supposed to conform to some cookie-cutter *Vogue* cut-out. I think weight is one of those issues. I find even among the most liberated women I know, this issue still cuts very deep.

Humor is a very visceral thing. You're going to strike a chord that some people can't handle. You know, I'm full-figured, and I have some stuff about large breasts. My favorite line is about Marie Antoinette and the standard champagne glass—the original model for that shape was Marie Antoinette's breast. And then I say, "I hate to brag, but my breast was the model for the Tupperware lettuce keeper." I think it's pretty funny, but there're some people who might be offended. And I'm not sorry. *(Laughs.)*

In my career, I've been fortunate because being a woman has been a plus. But, heavens, that's not been the case for most women. I just feel for those executive women where everything they do is wrong. I mean, if you're too assertive, you're an aggressive bitch, and if you're too meek, you aren't executive material. If you wear the severe suits, you're probably some kind of dyke. If you wear something frilly, then you're not serious. There's just no way to be right.

Nowadays, I mostly write checks. I still march. But I'm not in an ongoing political organization like NOW. I'm a member, but I'm not an activist member. There's so little time for women now. The struggle of trying to balance work and children and family, and your own career, and any kind of alone time—and still get your ironing done. *(Laughs.)*

I can be supportive, I can try to be some kind of historical memory of the early days. But as far as 24 hours a day, or 12 hours a day, I simply don't have room in my life for it. I feel bad about that, and I miss it. I miss activism, but I simply have to pass that torch on to the younger women.

When I was growing up—and this was before Title IX*—I was an excellent athlete. Even though I was small, I was a really good basket-

---

* Federal law passed in 1972 prohibiting sex discrimination in education, including athletics.

ball player. I used to score 25 to 30 points in games and that kind of thing. After Title IX, the first girls' basketball tournament that I ever watched was on television. I sat in my apartment, I watched the girls play . . . and I wept and I wept and I wept. It's a small thing, hardly earth-shattering compared to grinding kinds of oppression. But on a personal level, that hurt so much. I cried with happiness for the girls now, but also with this great sense of loss that I never had a chance to compete.

PART TWO

SISTERHOODS

The Muse &
the Media

In the early days of feminism, women's voices were often absent or ignored in the arts and the media. Artist Sandra Menefee Taylor found no visual images that reflected her experience, and poet-to-be Carol Connolly realized she had never spoken into a microphone. Carol Robertshaw noted that radio, like other mainstream media, did not reflect the burgeoning presence of the women's movement.

When women began to challenge the status quo, reactions varied. One of Marcia Fluer's first experiences as a television reporter was far from positive: an unwelcome kiss from comedian George Jessel. Martha Boesing found that women flocked to see feminist theater. Mary Ann Grossmann helped transform a newspaper's "women's pages" in the 1970s—but then saw them disappear. Publisher Mollie Hoben's women's newspaper succeeded in attracting advertisers who originally considered it a small "minority" paper.

Mary Ann Grossmann

Mary Ann Grossmann claims to have been born in the city room of the
St. Paul Pioneer Press. *At 53, she has been a newspaperwoman all her life.*
She first worked the "night side" of the paper, and later was editor of the
women's pages. She has covered the women's movement from the beginning, slip-
ping serious coverage into the women's pages along with recipes and fashions.
She was the first member of her family to graduate from college.

My father has emphysema. He has emphysema because he was a
metal finisher and spent years holding this stuff against him with the
grinding wheel, putting all this dust into his lungs. I mention this because it gives me a real connection to midwestern populism, and the
whole idea of an underclass. I have great sympathy for "out" groups.
That's probably one of the reasons I instinctively understood feminism.

When I read *The Feminine Mystique* and interviewed Betty Friedan,
when all the stuff came out about feminism—"women's lib," we called
it then—it never occurred to me to question it. I instinctively understood it. I had been in the job market long enough to know what she
was saying. It was never a problem for me. The minute I heard it, I said,
"Yes." The click of recognition came real early for me.

When I came here to the paper in 1960, I was the first woman—
since World War II, I think—to join the night reporting staff. There was
real paternalism, which of course I didn't recognize at the time. When
I'd go out in a company car, the old city editor, and I mean "old" in every
sense of the word, would make me put the car keys back in his hand because he wanted to be sure that little Mary Ann was in for the night.

Otherwise, I was treated just like the men. I was chewed out like them, I was held to the same standards. It was not a bad experience. I was a general-assignment reporter, doing everything.

In 1961 I was assigned to the women's department. Actually it was the society pages at the time. I didn't want to go there because there was a feeling that the women's department was something else, the toy department. But I grew up in the '50s, and was taught to obey. So I did what I was told. I was glad to have a job in my home town.

At that time it was still very much a society section. We called women "Mrs.," and we wrote yards of copy about wedding dresses. Long descriptions about punch and teas and volunteer activities. But there were also movers and shakers: the head of Business and Professional Women, the president of the Degree of Honor. There were women's organizations with long histories, where the women were treated with respect.

I later discovered that, in a sense, women's organizations really built this town. They were the ones—the Junior League, Hadassah, the Guild of Catholic Women—who did the majority of private charity work. In the '20s, the '30s, even back to the turn of the century. These women had proud traditions, and I hate to see them mocked now.

In fact, the more I think about it, the more unfair it is. That section's chronicle, the documenting of women's lives at the time, was extremely important to the community. I think we now look back and blame—or laugh at—the paper, when in fact a newspaper is simply a mirror of its times.

I came to the department with a group of younger women who saw that things were changing. We cut back on the descriptions, and started to put in more people. We tried to bring in more women's lives. But we still very carefully straddled the line so it didn't look as though we were moving too fast.

At the time, there were about eight women in the department. The click came early for all of us. Two of the women were pregnant, and we came up with the first union-approved job-share in the country. That was in the '60s, and that was revolutionary then. Women having babies had just not come up before. We were trying to develop some kind of democratic arrangement where we were all working together. Everything was new and uncharted, and I'd have to go back and defend this to the bosses. Outside the department, I still had to find my way in the old boys' traditional newspaper hierarchy.

By that time, we were allowed to go out and actually report what was going on in the community. From '65 onward, the protests and the marches, and the whole exploration of the women's movement. We documented that.

It was hard for the men. It was hard for the editor of the paper. You know, a whole lot of people were threatened, a whole lot of people hated this. A whole lot of people thought it was morally wrong. The editors didn't like readers calling up and saying, "What are these uppity women doing?"

I had a column then. I think I was one of the first women in the state to write about feminism. I wrote all kinds of columns about it, and it was hard because women had never been allowed a voice in the newspaper before—except in book reviews or art reviews. There were no women columnists, no syndicated columnists, certainly no political columnists that I remember. So even a woman having her voice . . .

The most difficult problem, of course, was abortion. The abortion fight was first fought on the women's pages. I used to feel almost every day that I was run over by armies. First one side would run over me, and then the other side would run over me. That was before there were enough organizations so that it could be institutionalized. It was very personal. There were personal attacks on me, there were personal attacks on one another. It was cruel. It was cruel on both sides.

We didn't need consciousness-raising groups, because every day at the paper was consciousness-raising. That was what was amazing about this group of women. We had to think this stuff through every day. It was marvelous for us because we had to decide where we stood on these issues, every time we came back from covering a story.

At that time, women were paid little attention by the men. By "the men" I mean all the power-structure men, including my bosses. They paid hardly any attention to the women's pages, and they were also paying hardly any attention to this new movement of loud-mouthed women. We were able to do what we did because it was considered so inconsequential.

In the early days, when the lines were just forming, it was much simpler. You were or you weren't. You were a women's libber or not. It also became easier when this stuff started to be in the national press.

We had been writing about it for about six years before the national press started to cover it. I always thought that we—by that, I mean the movement—arrived when one of the guys from the city desk wandered in, almost with his toe poked in the ground, and asked me for the phone number of the NOW president.

I remember covering the first birthday party for the Women's Political Caucus in 1972. I remember saying, almost editorially, that the movement had arrived. That story got what we call good play. I mean, it was taken seriously, it was covered as a news event. It was covered not in a column, where they couldn't do anything about it, or as a feature. It was a news event—where you go to something, you write it down, and you talk about the fact that it happened. It got a four-column head.

There was a progression about the women's pages. First it was the society section, and then it was the women's pages. Then there was a feeling that we should not be ghettoized. So it became "Family Life," and we tried very hard to bring in the male point of view. Then in the late '70s, several sections were put together into one big features section. The women's section was closed out. That happened all over the country.

By this time some readers were saying, "Good, we don't want to be ghettoized." And the men, the bosses, patted us on the head—"us" meaning the former women's editors. They said, "Things are going to be fine, we're still going to cover women's issues, but it will be in the mainstream of the paper, and they'll be judged on their news value like anything else." In fact, of course, that didn't happen. It didn't happen here, and it didn't happen anyplace in the country until about five years ago when newspapers realized they were losing women readers.

At the time I was real uneasy. I just thought, this is too early. This is too soon. If you figure from '64 to '77—from *The Feminine Mystique* to the Houston conference*—those are what I call the golden days. They were the golden days of feminism, and they were the golden days of women's reporting. If newspapers are a reflection of society, which I believe they are, that's where society was at that point.

* The 1977 National Women's Conference.

Marcia Fluer

Marcia Fluer, 55, describes her career as "teacher, housewife, teacher, chanteuse, reporter, public relations." She was the first woman anchor on local television in the Twin Cities. Marcia now heads the public-relations program for the university, where her office seems like a newsroom, with phones ringing and frequent interruptions. She speaks in rapid tones.

My mother's an Irish Catholic and my father's a Hungarian Jew, so that's a good place to start. I grew up with a Jewish name, Edellstein, and was educated in Catholic schools. At college I majored in theater, but I got married in 1959, as many people did at that time because they were afraid to do anything else.

My parents didn't encourage me to get married right out of college. They supported me when I quit my perfectly fine teaching job and went on the road to sing in nightclubs. They were flappers in the '20s, my dad in his spats and my mom with her cigarettes and short skirts. Otherwise they were very traditional, very Republican.

In traveling around the country I often saw movie and play reviewers on television, so when my husband and I settled here, I called Channel 5 and asked if they'd ever thought of having a movie or play reviewer. They said, "As a matter of fact, the news department has been looking for someone, they're auditioning people." So I contacted the news director and was hired.

I went in as a reviewer and reporter trainee. Fortunately, '72 was the year of Watergate and the election, and I was sent as a reporter to cover the VFW* convention . . . in a room of 5,000 men, no women allowed, except reporters. Later Georgie Jessel said if Jane Fonda walked

---

* Veterans of Foreign Wars.

in they would hang her from the highest rafters.* He got a standing ovation, and then came down and kissed me on the mouth. *(Shudders.)* I just wanted to murder him. But I had to remain a lady.

So I learned a lot very fast. It was obvious that I was good at politics, and they switched me over right away to politics. I was the first woman anchor, if you count those early morning hours. I had to fight for that, though. The man who had been doing the early morning cut-ins was fired from his job, so they started rotating among the male reporters. By that time, the director who had hired me had been fired, and they had somebody new in there.

I went in and said, "I notice you're rotating this position among the reporters. Why is the rotation skipping over the letter F? I mean, is that a problem?" He said, "Oh, well, our research has shown the Twin Cities is not ready to accept a woman as an anchor." And I said, "Who says?" Well, he put me into the rotation. He expected a call from the station owner, and he got one. It was, "She's sensational. Get her there permanently." It was lovely for my ego, but after a year and a half of getting up at four o'clock in the morning, I started to wonder why I was still there at 10 o'clock at night.

I first thought of myself as a feminist probably during my early years as a reporter. I wasn't a kid when I entered the field. I was 34 years old. I was already almost as old as Christine Kraft** was when she was told she was too old and not deferential enough. And I lasted until I was 50. But I'm not sure now if I thought of myself as a feminist, or whether I just started to act like a feminist.

I was always being given assignments, groundbreaking stories like Here's a Woman Truck Driver, or Here's a Woman Who Can Actually Pick Up a Hammer and Hit a Nail Without Ruining Her Manicure. Story after story like that, to the point where one day I was assigned one of these gems and went to the assignment editor and said, "Excuse me, is this a real story?" He said, "What do you mean?" And I said, "If I weren't here, would a man be assigned this story?" At which point, he switched my assignments. So it was a level of awareness on my part. I

---

* George Jessel, a comedian, was the emcee; film star Jane Fonda publicly opposed the Vietnam War.

** A national television newswoman who was laid off at age 35.

was never waving banners or standing at rallies. As a reporter, I really couldn't anyway.

I became a weekend anchor in '82. Two years later I found out that my sports anchor was making more money than I was, although he'd only been there 20 minutes. I'd been with the station for 10 years. I went in and asked the news director, "Surely, this is a mistake?" And he said, "Some people are just paid more than others, because of market forces." Or some stupid thing like that. I said, "Then that means the anchor you just hired for the five o'clock show is paid a lot more, too?"

I told him, "I have one of the more recognizable faces in the market, if you want to put numbers on it." He looked stunned. I went, "It's true, isn't it?" And I said, "I think there needs to be some discussion of pay equity issues here." After hearing no answer for a long time, I was informally told it was simply dismissed as "we don't do that."

It was before Christmas. I took a Christmas vacation. I was going back to work on a Wednesday, because I worked Wednesday through Sunday, and sat up in bed on Monday and thought, "I'm going to be fired. Or they're going to take my show away." I went in on Wednesday and kept waiting for the phone to ring. At the end of the day, I started to put on my coat, and they called me in and said, "You no longer have the show, it's the ratings." I went, "Right." I found an attorney, a good attorney, a good *Republican* attorney *(laughs)*—someone they'd be impressed by. The day after I let them know I was talking to an attorney, they called me in and fired me.

My mother was just horrified when I told her why I'd been fired. After all, I was making a lot of money, and I should have been happy with that. I said that wasn't the issue. She said, "Marcia, if you keep this up, you're going to end up as anchorwoman in Angola, Indiana." *(Laughs.)*

I think even the failures of getting fired turned out to be positive for me. There were wonderful articles written. It embarrassed me. I became a cause célèbre. It was very uncomfortable. I was interviewed for five hours by a newspaper reporter, and I picked up the paper Monday morning and the picture was *that big.* I mean the whole page. It was biography, philosophy. I read it, and read it again, and I said, "Do I like this person?" It was very flattering, but I don't know if that was me, or me showing off, or me as . . .

But it helped me. It helped me personally. It helped establish me probably as more of a feminist than I am. There isn't any way in which I'm not a feminist, but if you talk about a card-carrying, banner-waving feminist—I've never been that.

You're working a tough business, with tough ownership that doesn't give a damn about what happens to you, regardless of whether they like you personally or not. You are a commodity, and if you are no longer adding to the bottom line, you're no longer relevant. It's more true for women than for men. The bottom line is defined differently for women. Is there a woman on television today who is as homely as Charles Kuralt? Or as old as those guys on *Sixty Minutes?*

An early producer—a very large, balding, beige man—said, when I asked him for a tape recorder, he didn't know if he ought to give me one. He didn't know if I was going to last, and he wouldn't have hired me anyway, if he'd been there. I thought that was fair because when I started I really didn't have any experience on television or in reporting. I knew I was a token. I was told I was going to be a token. But that was fine because I was going to prove myself. But he said the reason he wouldn't have hired me was because I have a funny mouth. Not a dirty mouth, or a big mouth—but the shape of my mouth. And this from a man who looks like a turnip!

You do get nervous about whether you're getting in the way of the message. Now, men don't get in the way of the message, but women tend to. No matter how good the story, there would be calls from women. "Where did you buy your sweater?" Now, how can you take yourself seriously?

I knew I had to get out. Or, as someone once said, to "repot" myself. It was going to be scary out there after 17 years in the business. But I didn't want to go back on the street, I didn't want to work for nine-year-old boys, I didn't want to take orders anymore. It was a steady stream of young producers. One of them had said, "Be sure to get plenty of cover footage, we don't want just talking heads." I was so angry about being treated like a beginner, I almost walked across desks to get at him. You get to a point where it's a highwire act. No matter how many nets there are, you just don't want to be up there any more.

In 1984, when a lot of those articles came out, I became something of a role model, a feminist role model. I was told that by women. One of the reasons it embarrassed me was because I didn't think I'd done enough. There's kind of an imposter complex going there. Could I have networked more? A lot of it's an excuse: "I didn't have time," or "I was busy paying bills." But there are other women who do the same thing, and *do* find the time.

If I had it to do over, if I'd done something different, I would have showed up more. I would have showed up to be counted. You can be counted in lots of different ways. With all the publicity, everybody knew where I stood . . . But you have to show up, too.

Carol Connolly

Carol Connolly, a DFL activist, was an early chair of the Minnesota Women's Political Caucus, served for nine years on St. Paul's human rights commission, and at age 40 started to write poetry. Her book of poems, Payments Due, *was first published in 1985. Born, raised, and educated in an Irish-Catholic neighborhood of St. Paul, she is 57.*

I was married in the '50s, when I was 23. That was late, very late, for that time. I was rebellious, even then. I knew that marrying was kind of the end, but really there were no other career choices. I can remember arguing years later with a guy who said, "That's ridiculous. You could have gone to law school, you could have gone to medical school." Well, maybe, but you would have chosen to be a freak. You would have been the outsider.

So I got married. I married a lawyer, and had a lot of kids. "If you can't be a lawyer, marry a lawyer." *(Laughs.)* I had twins after nine months and three weeks of marriage. Then went on to have four children within two and a half years, five children in four years, and ended up having a total of eight children in eleven years. Seven are living.

At some point along the way I realized: this is nuts, this is crazy. But, you know, there wasn't much you could do about it. You couldn't get the Pill, it hadn't been invented. And I was still a practicing Catholic. I remember going to the priest to ask permission to practice rhythm *(laughs ruefully)*—for goodness sake—I mean, can you imagine? He didn't give me permission.

Of course, I was overworked, overburdened. I don't know anyone who is realistic about those big families. It's not respected at all. "What do you do?" "Well, I have seven children." "Oh, so you don't work."

At some point, you realize you can't be a victim forever. You have to get it sorted out and do something. During the peace movement, I became very active because my then-husband was one of the first people to sign on with Eugene McCarthy.* It was during that time that I realized women were doing all the work, but weren't being heard. In about 1970, I stood up to say something at a meeting, and I realized I had never spoken into a microphone before. Any thoughts I'd ever had, I'd say to some man next to me, most likely my husband. I'd say to him, I'd whisper, "Someone should say X or Y or Z," and then he would say it himself.

Several of us started a consciousness-raising group. And I remember vividly reading the first issue of *Ms.* magazine on an airplane coming back from the Democratic convention in Florida. That must have been in '72. And just being thrilled, overjoyed, that someone was finally telling the truth for us. That was a huge turning point for me.

I took a class at the university, a class in women's history. That's when I knew my marriage was in trouble. I can remember leaving the house with all these children . . . We had a live-in, what is now called an *au pair*, but what we then called a live-in baby-sitter. *(Laughs.)* And my then-husband saying that if I left to go to the consciousness-raising group or to the class, he would lock me out. I wouldn't be able to get back in the house.

I stood there and argued with him. If you can believe it, I actually argued with him. And my daughter Annie, who was in the first grade, came down the stairs and said, "Mom, if he locks you out, ring the doorbell! *I'll* let you in." It was empowering, coming from my child, but I didn't stay in the class very long—I think because of all that. But I did stay in the consciousness-raising group. I refused to give that up.

I started keeping a journal in 1972. I took a course in therapeutic journal keeping, and it underlined, shored up, my feminism in many

---

* U.S. senator from Minnesota who ran for president in 1968 in opposition to the Vietnam War.

ways. You cannot lie to yourself in a journal. You have to be truthful. I
kept a journal because my life was so chaotic. I became devoted to
keeping my journal, I tried to write every day, half an hour every
morning. Then I decided I wanted to do something more with my
writing. I wanted to take a fiction class, but it was full, so I took a poetry class. I didn't start writing poetry until I was 40.

I think we all want to be understood. At least those of us who are
trying to write, we write because we want to be understood. I hated
being misunderstood. In some way, at some gut level, I knew that no
matter what I said, or how loud I said it, I wouldn't be heard. They
couldn't hear me. Which is really why I started to write, I believe. That's
why I started to write poetry, because you can say whatever you want.

My book of poems was published in 1985. It later was picked up by
the Inner City Cultural Center in Los Angeles, and was staged there
this winter. It was the most fabulous experience of my life. Everyone,
from the top to the bottom of the production, was someone of color,
except for one actor and me.

It changed my thinking in so many ways. First of all, because those
women are fierce feminists. I remember the director, who is a brilliant,
beautiful young black woman, saying to me, "I have trouble with the
women's movement, okay? I have some problems with the women's
movement, okay?"

Of course I was very defensive about it. I said to her, "*This* is the
women's movement. What do you think this is?" She said, "Fine, I accept this part, but I have some problems with the women's movement."
They were, I now believe, class based. All these women, in spite of
their enormous talent and their accomplishments, they all have financial problems. Because they're women, and because they're of color.
Black, Chinese, or Latina.

I came back to the Twin Cities, and I went to a fundraiser for the
Women's Campaign Fund, a $100 lunch at the Minikahda Country
Club. And this enormous curtain opened in my mind, and I thought,
"Now I get it. Now I know what they're talking about." I'm not saying
there's anything wrong with wealthy women being involved, because I
think at the beginning we had the freedom, we had the time, and we
could do it. But in many ways we do not understand the struggle completely, of our sisters of color, much as we'd like to.

It's just not the same. I recently had lunch with three of my feminist friends, and the big topic of conversation was . . . *(rolls her eyes)* the most ongoing topic of conversation was that the straight skirts at the Oval Room were too hard to walk in!

My book of poetry, which is surely feminist, has taken me all over the country. And to Ireland. Much of the impetus has come from men. The person at the Inner City Cultural Center who discovered my book was a man, a black male. He brought it to the stage in L.A. The book was also staged here, and the person who got it going is a white male. Men buy the book to give to women. But I've also had a lot of men who've come up to me at readings and have said, "I hate you." I just say, "Thank you so much." *(Laughs.)*

Martha Boesing

Playwright Martha Boesing grew up in New Hampshire and attended schools in Massachusetts, Connecticut, and Wisconsin. In Minneapolis in 1974, she was one of the founders of the longest-running professional women's theater in the country, At the Foot of the Mountain. At age 57, Martha laughingly describes herself as a "tragic romantic" who is working at becoming calmer and more meditative.

In the '50s, the black *film noir* had gone, and now we had June Allyson movies. Everything was this cheery, wonderful, perfect American life. Well, I was tall for my age, I was smart, and I wasn't Audrey Hepburn. I wasn't unattractive, but I wasn't a beauty. So you know, less than a beauty is zero, right? *(Laughs.)* It's an all-or-nothing situation. Eventually, something in me was strong enough to rebel. I didn't become a mouse, I became a lion. But I felt like a mouse most of the time. *(Laughs.)*

In college I was bohemian. Everybody else went off to the Yale weekends in their little Peter Pan collars. I was part of a group that went around campus in rolled-up blue jeans and men's shirts not tucked in. On the weekends we would sit up in these smoke-filled college rooms, crowd into these little tiny rooms and listen to Lotte Lenya read T.S. Eliot, drink whiskey we had snuck into the dorm in medicine bottles. *(Laughs.)* We didn't want anything to do with boys.

After college, I taught during the day at the Brearley School for Girls in New York. And at night I let down my hair, put on my black turtleneck and my black stockings and a straight skirt, took my guitar under my wing, became a beatnik, and went down to the Seven Arts Coffee Shop. It was in Hell's Kitchen, it was the new hangout for Ginsberg and Corso and Orlovsky. Every once in a while Kerouac would appear.* And I sang and played the guitar, songs I had written. I set a lot of Yeats and other poems to music, in between their sets of readings. I found that wonderfully glamorous, it was terrific.

When I got married and moved to Minneapolis—that was 1961—I worked at several different theaters. I really got my wings at the Firehouse Theater in the mid-'60s. I was in the company we started, acted in the shows, and did fundraising. We were taking LSD to find out about mind expansion, reading R.D. Laing, Timothy Leary, Ram Dass—and making our theater be about that. First we took old plays like Pinter's and broke them open. Then we began working with new writers. Then finally we got into more work of our own. There started to be a style called transformational theater where we were all playing different parts and the plays would be layered in mosaic style rather than one story that goes through. We were exploring this, playing 15 different characters in one show.

We were also involved politically in that time, very involved in the antiwar movement, I was arrested at a protest . . . It was all part of the revolution. The energy was so intense, it was like, "Better not go to sleep, you might miss it!" *(Laughs.)* So we were up all night, we were afraid we'd miss the revolution if we slept longer than three or four hours.

And it was crazy. We played emotional chicken. You know where you take two cars and see who can stay the longest before the car goes off the cliff? It was like that, but emotionally. Who can go through the most changes and not break? And there were people who did break. A lot of us were moving out of one relationship into another. My first husband and I broke up because I got in a relationship with Paul, who was the leading actor in the company.

Nobody stopped to pick up the pieces if you fell apart. There was

* Well-known writers of the 1960s.

no sense of sharing feelings, they were in the way of the work. If you said, "God, this really scares me that everybody's breaking up," the answer would be, "Well, life is change, that's what it's about. You have to learn to go with it." That was the times.

The women had power through the bedroom, and they didn't have any other power. I tended to be outspoken and give my opinion a lot and argue with the director, and he didn't like it. I didn't know that I was being rejected because I was a loudmouth female. I thought I was being rejected because I wasn't good enough. Of course, that's the burden we all carry. I'm not good enough, I'm not good enough.

Paul and I left the Firehouse Theater when they moved to California, and then he and I wrote an opera together. I had written plays before, but they hadn't been produced. This was our first piece together and of course I put everything but the kitchen sink into it. Might be my last one, who knows? It was called *The Wanderer,* it was about the war, the generation gap, LSD, it was about getting your mind blown, changing your life, joining a commune. *(Laughs.)* It was a big hit, because it was timely.

Then the Quakers sent us touring around with a group of people doing a piece called *Earthsong.* It had Kent State stuff in it.* We all fell in love with each other and the project and decided to live communally, give up everything.

I sold the house. I had this fantastic library of books from my college days, but I decided one shouldn't have things, one should just be able to carry what you have. I remember vividly taking all my books down in cardboard boxes to a secondhand store and selling the whole library for $20. Looking back, I just cringe. And going through old scrapbooks, my college yearbook, my high-school yearbook, all that out the window and into the garbage. We weren't supposed to be attached to it, right? To this day, I regret it. Poetry I had written as a child, first stories I had written. Gone, out.

So we had this old van, packed what remained and our three kids, went and lived in this commune in New England, and went on tour there. Became ardent vegetarians, did the whole thing. Oh, God! *(Deep breath.)* Communal life was very interesting, it began to uncover a lot of

---

* In 1970, four students at Kent State University in Ohio were shot and killed by the National Guard during an antiwar protest.

masks. When you live as a family unit inside a commune, it's like you marry everybody and everybody sees your garbage.

That year, 1970, we went to see Bobbie Ausubel's play, *How to Make a Woman*. It knocked my socks off. It was my first encounter with ardent, radical feminists. After that play they had discussion groups, the men went off and talked together and the women went off and talked together. You went around and all the women were saying "Oh, men blah blah blah, oh, husbands blah blah blah," and I was saying "Oh, wellll . . . I have the exception." Bobbie just looked at me, and went, "That's such bullshit." I went, "No, what do you mean? I've never been oppressed as a woman."

But Paul, in the men's groups, began to get into his gayness. We started looking for therapy. Now, being rebels, did we go find a therapist who would meet with us once a week? Nooo, we went into primal therapy, LSD therapy, scream therapy, Sufi and Buddhist religion, we were involved in those radical therapies emerging at that time. For the first time, I was really having my feelings. Oh! I had feelings. At the Firehouse they weren't allowed.

In 1973 I wrote my first really feminist piece, *Pimp*. I had read an article about a woman who sold her daughter to a man and took the money, $40,000, and went off with her male lover. So I wrote this piece about a woman and her daughter and the wife of the man she sold the daughter to. The three women trying to understand each other. It was called *Pimp* on the theory that all women pimp for their daughters in some way, and we pimp for the daughter within us, we become pimps to our own prostitution to men. So I was by now really getting into feminism.

Then I wrote a companion piece to *Pimp*, called *The Gelding*. It was based on a newspaper article about a man who had castrated his own son. I made the boy a rapist, and the father so thrown by that, he castrated the son. We put them on in tandem. Paul directed both of them.

In '74, Paul and I came back to the Midwest to start our own theater. We called the theater "At the Foot of the Mountain" because that's what we got when we threw the I Ching. Everybody said, "That's not a name for a theater!" But we started a fad. Now all theaters are called "In the Heart of the Beast," "In the Eye of the Storm" . . . We started it with three couples, but by the end of the year the men split. Paul realized he needed to go find out about his gayness, another man realized he didn't want to do theater, and the other marriage broke up. So the three women were left.

I wrote a play called *River Journal,* about women being asked to wear the mask. This woman has two sisters, one is the coquette and one is the mom. It was about her being forced into one of those roles. Her rebellion against that, going into a kind of madness. She reads from her journal as she gets crazier and crazier, she can't do either of these roles. Turns out her sisters aren't real, they're just figments of her own imagination. The city was just hungry for this. Women came out of the woodwork to see this play, it was like the first big feminist play.

We decided to become a women's theater in 1976. We found Brecht's *The Exception and the Rule,* and we decided to use it as the basis for a play about rape. We were now an extremely popular theater. We just could not do enough performances to get everybody in. People were lining up around the block to get in. We toured *Raped* to huge crowds. We opened it up to the audience, let the audience stand up and give testimony in the middle of it. That was the first of what we began to call "ritual drama." There would be points in the plays where the audience would take part, or something would begin to happen. We developed this whole form of theater which nobody else has done. There's a lot of interactive theater, but not this kind of ritualized testimony that comes from audiences.

By the late '70s there were at least 180 feminist theaters. It was the largest grassroots theater movement in the history of this country. And it's virtually been erased. People don't know about it any more. There were women's theater events all over the country, and these theaters were thriving. Some of them were very good, like Lilith in San Francisco, Split Britches, which still exists in New York, in Providence there was one called the Rhode Island Feminist Theatre—four or five that were kind of big on the map and then all these other little ones.

We entered every play with such intensity. We instituted what we called the "feeling circle," began every single rehearsal with a circle where we said what was going on with our feelings. That was such a unique, powerful tool. Sometimes they became two-hour-long sessions before we finally got into rehearsal *(laughs),* and that became central to our work. We kept it over the years as long as I was there, 10 years.

It was so intense, seven days a week, all day, putting these plays on, getting money, finding places to perform, making a people's center into a theater, putting out newsletters, holding classes, every year we toured. And the plays were so intense. The work we did was just phenomenal.

We believed the personal is political. What that meant was, you don't work on a rape play about everyone else's rape. You find out how you've been raped. We began that play thinking none of us had been raped, that we were the lucky ones. And by the time we opened that play, every single one of us had rape stories. By lovers—which we didn't think counted. Incest—which we didn't think counted. Mindfucking —which we didn't think counted. One of mine was, I had been raped by a man I had been engaged to. When I broke the engagement he raped me in response to that. Also I had a professor in college who said to me, "The truth is that no woman can be a good writer, so give it up." And I did—for 10 years after he said that, I gave up writing.

Of course, the theater developed into a dysfunctional family. That sprang out of the fact that we were women in a misogynist culture. Even reviewers were still saying, in effect, "Gosh, these plays are good, given that they're women." We never could shake that. To this day, I am remembered as a playwright who wrote for a woman's theater, and therefore I am not a real playwright.

I left in '84 to do some freelance work. I was beginning to calm down. It took me a long time to see the wholeness of my experience with the Foot, to forgive myself for the intensity with which I went through it. For not being a perfect person. We did wonderful work. And brave. God, we were a brave group of women! We just plowed through the most godawful stuff, hard things with the culture, with ourselves, trying to understand. A lot of women's groups were going through the same kind of heat, women's bookstores, women's therapy groups. Shoot-the-leader games all over the place. In retrospect, I got very little of that.

Some people say now, "Didn't there used to be a woman's theater?" and some of the young women say, "Yeah, but we're not angry like that. We don't hate men the way they hated men." We didn't hate men! Men built signs for us, Paul taught for us. When we needed a man in a play, Paul came and acted in it. Our audience was probably 70 percent women, but the men who came were very appreciative. We never did a single male-hater play there. I mean, we'd sit around and say things like, "God, men are assholes," but all women say that! That's just facts. *(Laughs.)* We were not separatists. We were separatists in the sense that we were a women's theater, for women, by women, about women—ardently separatist in that sense. But not in our personal lives. Many of us had very close friends who were men, we talked to men. *(Laughs.)*

It may be that everyone in this culture thinks we died, but I'd like you to know that we haven't. I don't know a single feminist from that time who isn't still an ardent feminist. And working. But now a lot of us are working quieter—there's no way I could write a play that didn't have a feminist plot.

The great, incredible miracle of my life is that my three children—having gone through all this intensity and craziness, sometimes real madness from the burnout and the heat—have turned into three magnificent human beings who give me tremendous hope for the future of this country. They were here at Christmas and I again felt, "My god, how did this happen?"

All my friends, who all went through what by normal standards would look like very messed-up home lives, divorces, dealing with gayness, dealing with artists who are on the fringe, a kind of poverty . . . all their children have turned into magnificent human beings. They have not, knock on wood, been the druggies, they have not been the depressed ones, not suicidal. They have gone off into the world with energy, ready to tackle the world, ready for adventures.

I don't mean they're perfect, they've got their own fuckups, they've got problems. But they're so much wiser than I was at that age. If I had any wonderful news to tell, it would be about the children of our generation of fighters. The children of the civil rights workers, of the feminists, of the people who were out on the front lines. I see it in all my friends who are my age, I love spending time with their children. So all the talk about how the kids are going down the drain is bullshit.

Right now I'm involved in a new project—a one-woman show about the second wave of the '70s. It's based on interviews of the women who made it happen. Nine women gathered at a dinner party—I play all the parts. It's called *These Are My Sisters*. So I find myself circling once again back to women. I see the backlash going on in the mainstream, the Nazi movement and the Ku Klux Klan, the vio-

lence, the drugs, it's very scary. But at the same time, I believe this
stream of awareness is happening among people. It's like the women
who used to sit and make quilts while the men were out shooting people
and animals. The women just continuing, stitch after stitch . . . and I
think that's still going on.

Carol M. Robertshaw

*Carol Robertshaw's voice is familiar to many radio listeners in the Twin
Cities, not only by the distinctive tone but because hers was one of the few female
voices heard on the radio for many years. In the early 1970s, she had a show on the
university station, KUOM: five minutes of women's news, twice a week. Later
she had a daily one-hour show interviewing women, "Equal Voice." She is 44.*

I didn't become a feminist until about a year after my marriage. Up
until then I did not hold women in high regard. I knew that *I* was
equal to any man, but I didn't think all women were. I thought most
other women were empty-headed, only interested in having kids, not
capable of . . . They tended to be manipulative, to live vicariously. I
wanted to identify with men because it seemed they got a better shake
in life. I did not want to be thought of as an insignificant human being.
I wanted men to think I was more like *them* than like those . . . *(heavy
sarcasm)* . . . *women.*

In 1971, my husband and I had a roommate who was a feminist.
Actually I thought it was kind of a silly thing to be involved in. At that
time I did not take it seriously, I really pooh-poohed it. But it was during that time for some reason I read *The Female Eunuch.** That was the
first time it ever occurred to me . . . I wasn't alone. I honestly can't remember what it was in that book that triggered this recognition, that I
had really cut myself off from half the population by ignoring and de-
valuing women.

From that experience I began to become involved with some con-

* By Germaine Greer (1970).

sciousness-raising groups. I became involved with Women's Clearinghouse, which was doing a women's news broadcast on the university's
radio station. I found out that indeed the other half of the world had a
great deal to offer me.

Do you remember feeling part of a larger movement?

Oh, yes, very much so. At that time there was a huge march for
abortion rights. College women, older women, women from—I don't
know where they all came from. I can remember feeling the power of
this mass movement as we marched down Summit Avenue toward the
capitol. I can remember walking past the St. Paul cathedral, and of
course I'd been raised Catholic, so *(laughs)* . . . this would be a significant moment for me.

I also remember the first Take Back the Night march* here in
1979. How powerful I felt. Just the idea that we could walk right down
the middle of the red-light district, down Hennepin Avenue, and just
glare into these men's eyes. Just feel so—I can only think of negative
emotions. A sense of "getting back" at them, or spiting them. That to
me was really cathartic, to be able to say, "We are powerful, and there
isn't a damn thing you guys can do about it."

I was active in Women's Clearinghouse, a radical feminist organization tied to the leftist group in the Twin Cities, Bread and Roses. But I
never totally identified with them. They were too radical. They defined themselves as a collective, but it was not a very effective structure.
After a time, *I* became Women's Clearinghouse. I had gotten a stu-
dent-announcer position at KUOM, and the collective had more or
less fallen apart. I still believed in the notion of women's news, so I
continued to do it.

It was a women's newscast twice a week, a five-minute newscast.
We felt that the broadcast industry at that time was not representing
this burgeoning women's movement. By and large, if the media dealt
with it at all, they dealt with it in one of two ways. Either as silly little
bra-burning "libbers," or as having something to do with the sexual
revolution—which they took much more seriously because mostly
they were *men. (Laughs.)*

There were few models for me. I do remember seeing the first female anchor on local TV. She was anchoring a noontime newscast. I

---

* An annual march to protest violence against women.

can remember the first time I saw that . . . and it was such a powerful image. What that did to me personally . . .

I think one of the largest disservices that the media have done is to create a situation where issues always have to have a "pro" and a "con." The result has been that the women's movement, in order to get the word out, has had to define the world in those terms, too. To a certain extent, of course, we have a dualistic world. There are men, and there are women. And that was at the heart of the movement, the idea that we divided ourselves in that fashion. So it was "us" against "them," to a certain degree.

I've always had difficulty with that. I think the biggest disservice the women's movement did to women was to foster that polarization. Was to fail to get at the core and find the common ground. To recognize that the common ground is children. Or motherhood. I feel that now. I don't think I felt it before because I wasn't a mother. Nobody in the women's movement early on ever told me that motherhood could be such a positive thing.

I don't know if there's a women's movement left now. It's hard to find these days. The movement pointed out certain needs, and those needs began to be addressed. They began to be taken seriously. As a result, certain agencies were created, certain institutions were created. That has resulted in a kind of falling out of popular culture of the women's movement.

The women who identified with feminism continue to be involved, but I don't see the kind of passion that was part of the movement in the '70s. I miss the excitement, the sheer momentum of people getting together and doing mass actions . . . I'm real sad that's gone. That was so powerful.

Mollie Hoben

Mollie Hoben, age 49, is the co-founder and editor of the Minnesota Women's Press, *a biweekly newspaper with a circulation of 40,000. We meet in the basement of the paper's office, surrounded by books, magazines, and other evidence of the frequent salons and book-club meetings sponsored by the* press.

It took me a while, those first years of feminism. I thought, "Oh, come on, what are these women doing?" I mean, I wasn't actively against it, but it didn't seem to speak to me. But by the early to mid-'70s, I was reading. I started to read Friedan and the stuff that was coming out. It really made a lot of sense. I was thinking a lot about women's words and women's silences.

So it was the reading and learning and talking to people that by the early '80s I said, "I'm not reading any more men. I've read too many men in my life." *(Laughs.)* "It's time to read women and find out what they're saying."

We spent about a year planning the *Women's Press.* The first publication was in 1985, April of '85. One of the first questions we wrestled with, that we had to think through, was whether to form ourselves as a nonprofit effort or to become a for-profit business. Most of the people we talked to in those planning days assumed we would be nonprofit because we were a women's thing. There was always that sort of, "Oh, you're doing this little women's newsletter, so of course you're non-profit." And we also didn't want to get caught in that cycle of always counting on other people to get funding, and spending half our energy writing grants and stuff. So we decided to be a for-profit business and put together what I think was a very impressive business plan.

We hoped, and hope, to be a place, a publication, a place of print where women's experiences and ideas and values are taken seriously, and given credit. And we hoped in that process to be changing the def-

inition of what news is, making our own definition of newsworthi-
ness. We hoped, and hope, to be able to give a sense of the diversity of
women and what they're doing. To reaffirm that every individual
woman's story is important and can have power. Along with the power
of organizations—which is why from the very beginning we've always
had a personal profile on the front page along with a news story. We're
trying to say both these things are equally newsworthy and important.

We looked at women's publications around the country, and that
helped us realize that we didn't want to be a women's fluff publication,
fashions and recipes. We also didn't want to be an insider ideological
paper. Those papers were succeeding, but to very small audiences. We
wanted to find a way to have the content, to be pushing the ideas, but
not to scare people away by being too . . . being too . . .

Strident?

Yes, yes. Shrill? Pushy? *(Laughs.)* Many women we wanted to reach
worried when they looked at the other papers, they seemed so closed
and angry. "It's not like I can be part of that." *We* wanted to produce
something where we could be building a sense of community, people
being part of something. I think we've done pretty well in finding that
middle ground.

In the early days, there was a real combination of the highs and the
excitement of actually doing it. And a lot of doubts, and some stum-
bling around and being unsure of our footing and of our voice. Certainly we had a hard time selling ads in the beginning. People would
say, either directly or indirectly, they'd say, "You know, this woman's
paper, people don't read that stuff any more." Or, "Your audience is
just a bunch of man-hating lesbians." Or they'd say, "You deal with
controversial things, and that makes us uncomfortable." Mostly they
wouldn't say it that directly, but that was the message.

Or, "You're just another one of the small minority papers." We
were often called a minority paper, and people didn't want to advertise
in a minority publication. So there was a real sense of not being taken
seriously, and a real sense of pressure from a lot of places to change the
tone or the content or the direction of what we were doing. A lot of
advertisers said, "If you were more lifestyle-oriented . . ." And there
were times when we started being seduced just a little bit that way because of the economic pressures. We were working for peanuts, and we
were working really hard.

The first year I remember we did a special insert on weddings. *(Laughs.)* But it was so awful, it just wasn't us. It's not that it's not important, but it's not us. There was a lot of questioning, and having to reaffirm what we were about—just having to hang on. We were very tenacious.

I think one of the main messages and truths of the women's movement has been the reaffirming of the power and the necessity of being able to name in our own words. To not let others name us or our experiences, because they don't name them the way we would. So language, and being able to claim your own words, is really one of the bases of feminism and individual empowerment. That's the basic premise behind the *Women's Press,* that we need to increase the ways each of us individually and as a community do our own naming and use our own words.

At the paper, we've learned to look at words themselves, and their assumed meanings, and not necessarily buy them. To make language more inclusive. It's also important just to claim using the words that anybody uses, but to select them yourself and describe your own experience. Think of all the books, and the words that did not get put down, the experiences that didn't get shared, because women didn't feel they could use language in a public way about themselves.

When Gerda Lerner* was in town with her new book, she was saying that part of why it's been hard for women over the centuries to progress is that women have not had control of their own stories and their own history. So each new generation of women has spent all its energy recreating and refinding . . . and then that's lost in the next generation. It's a very powerful and disturbing image.

It's very easy to say all that, but it's harder when you're cranking out words all the time to remain aware of what you're doing. I'll look back and say, "Oh, my God, did we do that?"—using a word in a very male, put-down way. But it's so common that we didn't even think about it. That's very important, making our own language. Yet having to be able to speak the mainstream language, which is the male language . . . If we're going to function, we have to become almost bilingual.

The mainstream media is starting to take notice. Every year we do this survey of how often women are mentioned in the daily papers.

* Historian and author of *The Creation of Feminist Consciousness* (1993).

Two issues ago we published it and, again, only 18 percent of the names in the daily papers are women's names. It ranges from 4 to 5 percent in the sports section to 30-some percent in the variety section. I got a postcard from a woman writer for the St. Paul paper the other day saying, "Keep up your survey, it's starting to get under their skin." *(Laughs.)* Which I was very pleased to hear. Last year when we did it, somebody we know who works at the Minneapolis paper said our article was on all the bulletin boards in the newsroom.

Now, obviously a lot of change that's happening at papers is not just because of us. But we're one factor in the pressure for change. The big pressure for the dailies is economic, though, because they're losing women readers. They have been for years, and they're trying to figure out how to change that. That's a big topic in journalism circles, and when the publishers meet. Their reader share is going down, and women especially. So it's real bottom-line stuff for them.

Every publication is biased. The mainstream media just think they aren't, because they get to name what's the standard—and then everything else is different.

Sandra Menefee Taylor

Sandra Taylor, an artist and sculptor, was a founder of the Women's Art Registry of Minnesota (WARM) in 1976. WARM promotes women artists through exhibitions, education, and mutual support. We meet in Sandra's sunny studio in an old, refurbished warehouse building in St. Paul. She is 53.

I grew up on a farm and went to school in a small town. When I got out of high school, I went to beauty school. I always wanted to be an artist, but I could never get an image of what that was. Never having been around somebody who was, it wasn't easy to form pictures. So I decided the best I could do—I knew what a hairdresser was, and of course that's very much like sculpture *(laughs)*—so that's what I did.

When I was about 32, after I was married and had three kids, I decided the artist was still waiting and it was up to me to find her. I went to the College of Art and Design in 1972 and got a degree in fine arts. There was a lot of feminist art activity going on around the country then, and I went to art school thinking that's where the big thinkers were. I went with the expectation of a new way of thinking. I went with the thought I was fulfilling my dream.

But I found the opposite. The art-school teachers were all men, approximately my own age. The last thing they wanted to talk about, obviously, was . . . *(laughs)* women. I had friends who were going "back to school," that's what we called it, but nobody went to *art* school. At that age you should be seriously thinking about earning money. I certainly didn't encounter anyone with three small children at home. The teachers were all men, and the women were 18 or 19 and—*they* didn't want to hear about it. It was an awful experience.

When I was in school and it was time to do a report on an artist, I wanted to find the women who had gone before me—but they weren't there. They absolutely were not there, forget it. Even to ask was heresy. So, you had no history. There were virtually no images that were a reflection of yourself and your experience. If your heart's desire is to be part of a continuum, and you have to think of yourself as an exception, there's a separation there. It doesn't work.

At the time the women's movement began, the arts were heavily into minimalism, which is to take the personal out completely. It's about idea, it's not about human considerations . . . like raising children. I think, perhaps more to the point, women were not reflected anywhere in the art world. Well, there were nudes—but that's not what I'd call reflected. That's about being the model, the other, the support person, the muse. That's not a doer. That's being objectified.

I started thinking about the missing information from my life, in visual ways. I grew up with mothers and grandmothers who made everything. That's probably why I'm an artist. Not because I had any education when I was a kid, but I just knew I could make anything I wanted to. So I started this character called the "missing woman." I did a whole group of drawings which supposedly were "found." Just found. These were meant as drawings from her desk when she left. We don't know what she looked like, or what she was like. But . . . we do know what she was concerned about. These are renderings of body, clothing. I call them "official documents," because the information contained in them is *unofficial*. We only get to know about things when they're deemed official and are recorded.

I did a lot of official documents. Then I started moving into installation work. Now, I'm using my own experience of growing up rural. I'm hoping to do a large project called *In Her Own Image,* putting women and land back into the picture. For women, and now landscape, it's been objectified. The viewer stands outside of what they see and what they're experiencing. That goes for both women and landscape. As we get further and further removed from our experience of the land, we objectify it more and more.

Photography and artists' books are new forms in the history of art. Therefore there's an ability and a freedom for women to move into something that doesn't have a history, with a long tradition of confirmation. Women can step in and begin to make the images because . . . they're not saddled with the patriarchal eye. *(Laughs.)* So artists' books and photography are two places where women have done wonders, in my opinion. I've chosen artists' books as one of the ways I work.

This is called *Housedress.* It's out of that tradition of no tradition. As an artist I have no tradition to bring forward. I do, however, have a tradition of women who "didn't work." So I set out to make this book called *Housedress,* which, of course, is a pejorative word. We've all made fun of housedresses and the women who wear them. So this is a house, and as you open it, you get the idea that it turns into a dress, and in the pockets—on recipe cards—are messages from other artists. I asked other women artists to write to me what they're going to bring into their art from the women in their lives who "didn't work."

Here's one of the messages: "My mother made by hand most all of the food and clothing that I knew as a child. She said she did that because we couldn't afford to buy it. As a child, I instinctively knew there was more to it. As an adult I see her reality of needing to provide, but I also learned her need to make and create. She always had a sewing room. I have a studio."

Here's part of another message: "My mother had two teachers who authored a book, *Art in Everyday Life.* It describes how the homemaker can use principles of art in her selection of furniture, table settings, vases, flower arrangements on the mantel, or even lace-making, and appreciate qualities in daily life that offer creative sustenance."

I also make books like this. Do you remember the woman who

got one of the first artificial hearts? I was teaching a class at the time, and I came across this line in the paper that said, "Artificial hearts are too big to fit into the chest cavity of the average-sized woman." Which to me was, how could you even write something like that? Doesn't anybody think there's anything wrong with this? So I made this book which repeats that phrase, and asked some women to make their own self-portraits. They made their own self-portraits and I just repeated the phrase, "Artificial hearts are too big to . . ." That's one form of feminist art.

I think the women's movement has been incredibly important to those of us who identify with it. Even for those who don't, they can't help but be taken along with what's been done. Incredible things have been done. And it's also been helpful to men, whether they can admit that or not. It's opened up the art world in ways that never were before. There had always been an image of the artist as an heroic figure—a romantic version—the artist as recluse, the artist who drinks, the bohemian outsider. Women artists have said that you can make the personal political, they have blurred the lines.

Women artists have made speaking about their lives—putting in the personal, saying that there are different voices to be heard and that art is a valid way to hear those voices and see those images—so, yes, the women's movement and women artists have really done wonders in getting new images out there and getting us to think in new ways that haven't been done before.

I'm not very big on the distinction between craft and art, because that's been a divisive argument. I would say the greatest difference between art and craft is in intention. Craft is strongly identified with technical skill. In my definition, art is more closely tied to the idea, and the skill serves the idea.

It gets fuzzy, though, when you bring up things like quilts. Because quilts are color studies, quilts are dexterity with the manipulation of a needle, a tool. So how is that different from the famous color-field paintings which hang in museums? So then you get into the issue of who made them. The color-field painters were almost all men, and they stayed in the tradition of the museum.

Is women's art different from men's? Well, that's also subject to great debate. I'll say the way women have challenged that, in the feminist art movement, is to put your experience forward, directly make

work about that. It's different today, because it's okay now for artists to
be more direct, to make work about their personal experience. But at
that point, early in the movement, women stepped forward and said,
"Enough. We're going to make cunt art, we're going to purify that
word, we're going to take that word back and deal with our own sexuality." Today, if you asked that question about how women artists are
different, you'd get a thousand different answers.

You have to keep in mind, too, that art in general is not very important. So art is disposable, dispensable. I mean, what does it *do?* And
the women's movement has not treated art as well as I wished it had.
For example, a number of years ago there was an ERA rally at the capitol. A couple of us were called because we were identified as artists
who were willing to work in the political realm. We thought our work
was very political, anyway, so they called to ask us if we would work
with this rally. We of course said yes, "But . . . we're not making the
banners." That's like the overall view: artists are like women, they're to
bring the cookies to the revolution. Well, we were very clear that we
weren't just going to bring cookies to the revolution.

My art has changed and grown, but it's still driven by the belief
that the personal is political. I feel very centered in what I'm doing
now. I get . . . diverted *(laughs)* when I think I'm not being accepted or
heard, so I try not to think about that. What I'm doing now is who I
am. I mean, the price is really high if you need acceptance. And, of
course, everyone needs to make a living. But I believe the best lives are
those you make up as you go along. Artists really know how to do that.
I think other people are only beginning to figure it out. It's difficult,
and you have to continue to believe in yourself.

Getting reinforced from the outside . . . it's certainly helpful, it's certainly wonderful, we love it when it comes! But I continue to be an
artist because that's what I do best, that's who I am. I've tried to be
other people, but it wasn't good. The essence of being an artist—and
for women in particular—is learning how to live without being attached to an outcome.

The Campaign Trail
& Beyond

The movement brought many women into politics for the first time. Some ran for elected office; others maintained the political infrastructure as party workers, lobbyists, and members of appointed boards. Many found with Gloria Griffin that women need to "cut deals" and compromise. Some risked controversy when it really mattered, as when Koryne Horbal defied her party over abortion rights.

Several women began their careers not by seeking public office but by marrying men who did. Eventually they learned that it could be fun to do it themselves, overcoming barriers great and small. Mary Pattock was ridiculed for being an advocate for women, Ann Wynia wondered what colors to use on her campaign brochure, and Joan Anderson Growe proved that women can raise money. They all shared Kay Taylor's pride about making a difference on their own.

Koryne Kaneski Horbal

Koryne Horbal was the Minnesota Democratic-Farmer-Labor Party's state chairwoman from 1968 to 1972, founder of the DFL Feminist Caucus, lobbyist, party reformer, strategist for the ERA, and Democratic national committeewoman for 12 years. Now in her fifties, she says, "No wonder I was so exhausted all the time." She is from a working-class family, and she regrets that she never went to college.

Politics came first, before my feminism. I liked politics even in school—races for the student council, homecoming queen, who becomes cheerleader. *(Laughs.)* It's all political. Even in my own family, I knew who did the dishes was political.

Politics meant opening up a whole world for me, back in the '50s. It made it possible to look beyond being a mother and a housewife. I had a lot of feelings then, about not wanting to be controlled, to be able to blossom, to think about things in a different way. But it wasn't until politics that I started to feel secure in those feelings. I kept silent for a long time, in the DFL Party, because I felt insecure. Because of my education, I felt I had to sit there and learn.

When I started out as a precinct captain, I followed through. I did the things you're supposed to do. At that time, the political parties were very strong. They had issues. They had issue conferences. I mean, they stood for something, they stood for a philosophy. You could learn a lot.

I would say I went up the ranks because I worked very hard and my work was noticeable. At that time, if you were a good volunteer, a good woman volunteer, you moved up the ranks. It was a way that I could have my own life, where I could be Koryne Horbal . . . not just someone's mother, or someone's wife, or someone's daughter.

During that time, while I was playing that role, I would still get irritated when I couldn't sit in on meetings. After I'd helped raise the funds, I wasn't part of how they chose candidates. I was curious about all that. When I wanted to learn more, the doors were closed.

The male structures were so dominant. To get power and to be in the places I wanted to be, I had used the male structure. I got there by hard work. Most of the men in the party didn't want to do all that stuff, the background stuff, the hard work that had to be done. They just wanted to run the meetings. I'd write the agenda—and then the chairman would come in, grab my agenda, and run with it. The function of the chairwoman was to have women organized as volunteers, to do the campaigns, to do all the work. We played that support role, like we play it in our lives. Then the men would go off behind closed doors and make all the decisions. They'd cut the pie, and we weren't in on cutting the pie.

When I was state chairwoman . . . *(she searches for words)* . . . I mean, I just had to become an incredible kind of bitchy woman just to know what was going on. I had to read things on the chairman's desk. I had to open the door and see what meetings were going on. Even when I traveled around, I couldn't go in the same car as him. He thought it would look bad.

The state chairman was paid, but the state chairwoman was not. I worked almost full-time, traveling around the state. It was hard for me to say to my husband, "I'm going to . . . ," wherever. He just could not understand *hiring* a baby-sitter so I could go do something for free. My support was my father. He felt very bad that I couldn't go on to college, with my mother getting so ill. He did all the baby-sitting I needed. If I hadn't had that kind of support, I wouldn't have been able to get out.

I felt I paid my dues. I mean, you only need to know how to stuff envelopes or start a phone bank for so long. You want to move into the other areas. I really resented that, I wanted to participate at all levels. I'd say my feminism came from feelings about myself and what I saw in the political system. Most women came to feminism first, and then became political. I did it just the opposite. I became political first, and then became a feminist.

At that time, the DFL had a women's federation. Each year we'd have a federation meeting, and the male legislators would come and talk to us, to get us ready to be the volunteers again. I thought that was ridiculous. A number of other women were also dissatisfied. If you were going to be a state delegate, you had to know the men. They more or less hand-picked those who could be delegates. As for going on to the national convention, that was very rare for a woman. So a group of women and myself said we've got to change this. That was when we did the study, in 1971.

A number of key women sat down and said, "Let's do a real study. We need to show other women what's happening. Even the women won't believe it if we don't have something in black and white." It was very radical to do because, before that, I was really considered . . . *(She trails off.)* I could probably have gone anywhere in the party. They would have taken care of me. The guys would have let me be in certain places, if I'd kept quiet. And I know the chairman was getting a little irritated with me because I was getting more than curious—I was getting uppity.

When we did the study, I couldn't believe it, how it opened the eyes of the party women. The statistics were staggering. We studied every level of the party, and showed how few women there were. It had nothing to do with issues, so women really came together on it. We did a road show, a panel, from one county to another. These statistics were powerful. It was something women were glad to see, and they wanted to know how we could turn it around.

We changed the women's federation to a woman's caucus. The federation in the past had been like an auxiliary, like the American Legion auxiliary. I had no idea that this would be so controversial. But at that time, even talking about women's rights was considered controversial. You didn't have to put a feminist label on it.

All the way through, I believed it was important to function within a political party. I felt strongly that in order to get some of the things we needed, I had to function within the DFL. I didn't actively participate in the Women's Political Caucus, although I was in full support. I thought it was great to have a women's organization not affiliated with a political party, because you need all those things at the same time.

I also supported the more direct actions, such as the campaign on want ads, and the demonstrations. I had an understanding that we need all of it, that women need to be in all different places to make this work. I didn't think anything they did was too radical or too controversial. I just didn't feel *I* could be that radical.

At the time I was doing some lobbying. Mostly DFL issues, because as state chairwoman I worked on the Democratic agenda. In those days, they actually had an agenda. *(Laughs.)* A number of us would get together informally and watch issues. The Equal Rights Amendment was talked about in the party, but when we started talking about it to the legislature, they weren't as comfortable as they said they were.

And then of course we were talking about abortion. I knew where I was—I believed in choice—but being a woman who couldn't have children myself, I was a little uncomfortable talking about it. I mean, I had wanted children so badly and we had adopted children—so it was hard for me to sort that out.

"Feminism" was a word that more and more people were starting to use. It wasn't the way it is now—not that it wasn't controversial— but it wasn't derogatory. It had a definite meaning to it. My definition has always been that we create a society where men and women can blossom and grow, no matter what sex you are. I also believe that feminism is not a philosophy you just adopt. You become a feminist, all the way through. I mean, I can't separate my feminism and who I am. I *am* a feminist, that's who I am.

When the ERA passed Congress, the Republican chairwoman and I formed a group. At that time both parties were for the ERA. I became chief lobbyist because I'd had more experience lobbying. I also loved organizing things. We brought together the two political parties and these other organizations, and we brought together a steering committee. I did the same kind of organizing for the ERA that I'd been doing for a long time for the party.

We organized each day of lobbying. The first day of that legislative session, in 1973, we were at the capitol with our handouts. My belief was that we've got to move fast, we can't wait. I was at odds with the national people because they were taking their time. I said, "You've got to get in those legislatures right away and get it through before the opposition realizes what we're doing."

And I was right. If we hadn't moved fast ... *(She rolls her eyes.)* That year was the first time we had a majority for the DFL in the legislature. Working as hard as I did, I was visible to a lot of the men in the legislature. They felt their election was through the help of the DFL Party. They felt they owed me. So what were they going to give me? They weren't going to give me a delegate spot, or the national committee, or let me run for office. So this was sort of, this is what we'll give Koryne.

At the same time, the whole change in abortion came about, the Supreme Court decision. In fact, when we were waiting for the final decision from the court, that's when many legislators said, "Don't mix these issues. Don't mix ERA and abortion. We'll be right with you."

But what actually happened was that when the abortion decision came down, those same legislators who said they'd be fine almost broke their legs running to get a constitutional amendment bill prohibiting abortion. That was absolutely part of the motivation for the DFL Feminist Caucus. We had to be quiet until the ERA passed, but then we all went crazy. I went after some of the legislators for introducing the constitutional amendment. I mean, I was state chairwoman. I was attacking DFLers. I don't think that's ever been done before.

It was on the front page, and I can remember from that moment I became incredibly controversial. I can remember one legislator, he begged me not to say anything to the press. He said, "You are the most effective lobbyist here on behalf of women, and if you take on that issue, you'll never be that effective again." He pleaded with me before I went to the press.

But I really blasted the DFL on the issue of abortion. Of course I made sure the ERA passed before I went crazy. (Laughs.) I went down to the pressroom and just let it all hang out. I showed my incredible despair about the DFL legislators I helped elect, who then turned around and did just the opposite of what they always said on abortion.

That was the turning point in my head. From then on, I was a feminist first, and my party was second.

Joan Anderson Growe

Joan Growe is probably the best-known woman in public life in Minnesota. She has been Minnesota's secretary of state since 1974, after serving two years in the state legislature. She grew up in a small town west of the Twin Cities where her father owned a hardware store and was mayor. She has been married and divorced twice, was on AFDC* one summer when she had small children, but later lived a comfortable suburban life. She is 56, and her four children are grown.

I really fit into small-town culture. I think my goals were to get married, to have a family, and to live happily ever after. I didn't know anything else. And that was just fine with me. You'd think that I might have identified with feminism in those two or three years when I was single and trying to raise my kids alone. But I was working so hard and struggling just to exist, I didn't identify as anything. Other than poor.

I first felt a sense of myself as a person when I moved to the suburbs and got involved with the League of Women Voters. I mean, it was like . . . finally I wasn't pregnant. And finally there was enough money so that once in a while I could hire a baby-sitter. I started doing some things on my own, and realized, "Gee, I can be in charge of this finance drive," or, "My word, I'm quite capable. I can stand up in front of a group and talk about something." I got involved in some controversy and actually liked it.

It was only then that I started thinking about inequities. But it wasn't feminism, it wasn't about men and women. I didn't rush to the charge because women were being treated badly. I rushed to the charge because we were in a war we shouldn't be in, and because there was no housing for poor people in my community.

I didn't have any trouble getting endorsed for the legislature. I had

---

* Aid to Families with Dependent Children.

trouble getting elected, but it had nothing to do with my sex. That might have actually been a plus. I had trouble because I was a Democrat in a district that was 75 percent Republican.

The year I was elected, 1972, there were six women in the house. Five of us got elected that year and joined Helen McMillan, who had been all alone. We were a variety of ages. The headlines in the paper said, "The Women Are Taking Over." I mean, we didn't even know each other, and there were just the six of us.

Since then we have talked among ourselves, the women legislators, that each of us, on our own, wanted to do well, really well. Of course any freshman does. But each of us felt an additional burden. We didn't share these feelings at the time because we didn't know if we were the only ones with these doubts. I felt that if I'd done badly in presenting a bill, or called the wrong witnesses, or had the wrong information, or couldn't answer the questions, the comments would have been, "Gosh, those *women* can't do anything right." But if Joe Smith had done badly, they would have said, "Gee, *Joe Smith* can't do anything right."

We all felt that burden, that none of us could ask the dumb questions. You had to ask them quietly, you didn't dare ask in the open. When we got up to talk on the house floor . . . silence. Just silence. The chamber was unaccustomed to a woman's voice. The first time I spoke up, I spoke on the Equal Rights Amendment. My God, there was this hush. I was terrified.

Phyllis Kahn* and I soon learned something. Phyllis had the reputation of a radical from the university, and I was this suburban woman from a Republican district with a kind of pouf-pouf hairdo . . . so Phyllis and I learned that we could garner more votes if she stood up and spoke against something I wanted. Or if I was against something, Phyllis would stand up and speak for it. We used each other in ways that we knew would help each other. And they never caught on. *(Laughs.)*

Lobbyists at that time were a little unsure about how to approach us. And God forbid that they'd ask you out for dinner. They were even more nervous about lunch. We're talking about an era when the attorney general wouldn't ride in a car alone with a woman.

In 1974, when I ran for secretary of state, I was treated differently from the other candidates. All people were interested in was, "What is

---

* One of the women elected to the house in 1972. Her story begins on page 45.

a woman doing running?" I had to constantly answer questions about, "What were my children doing without me?" "How did my husband feel about it?" Rumors about me. "Who do you think she's sleeping with?"

But after being in office a while, I found acceptance with the voters and in the party. They didn't view me as just a female any more. But it all came back again in '84 when I ran for the U.S. Senate. When you're running for an office few women have run for before, you might as well be a green-headed toad. The press was almost worse than the public. It was subtle discrimination by then, which I think is more difficult to deal with than overt discrimination.

I can deal with people who say, "I don't think women should be in public office." I say, "Wonderful, sir, you're entitled to your opinion." And you move on. But when you're constantly asked, "What's it like to be a woman?" And you're asked that question in newspapers, and on radio . . . you're set up. The public says, "Ohhh, she *is* a woman. Hmmm, we must *think* about that."

The test of running for the U.S. Senate is, can you raise any money? That's the test, whoever you are. I was constantly asked if I could raise enough money, even though I consistently raised more money than my three male opponents for the endorsement. At one time, Wendell Anderson* had raised $30,000, and I had raised something like $150,000. No one asked Wendell if he could raise money. They asked me if I could raise money. I outraised Oberstar**, who had all the Washington money, and they still asked *me* if I could raise money.

If you are female, you have to raise more money. If I had only raised $30,000, I would have been written out of the race. If I had been at the state convention, had raised $30,000, and been defeated for my last position—as Anderson was—I would have been written right out of the race. I led on every ballot, but *I* was the one they asked to withdraw.

The sexism was pervasive there, the rules were different because a woman was ahead . . . *(She controls her anger.)* The questions the reporters asked me, and the tests that I had to go through to be knowledgeable on the issues, were unbelievable.

* A former governor running for the endorsement for the Senate.
** James L. Oberstar, a congressman seeking the endorsement.

I was always asked the question, "Are you really strong enough for this race? Are you tough enough?" People thinking, "Will she be able to hold her own?" Then there was the dilemma: when we got too strong, we turned people off; but if we weren't strong, they thought you were weak. We had a terrible time finding the balance.

Sometimes I have a good sense of humor, at least once in a while. I can quip. But I didn't dare use it, particularly with the press. It would have been regarded as flippant. We were afraid I wouldn't be taken seriously. This was in '84, when you would have thought we'd have been through with all that.

I was surprised by it. I suppose the shock for me was not being prepared for sexism. Absolutely not prepared for it. I should have known better, but you see I had not been treated differently as secretary of state. I'd been there a long time, I'd established myself. My pluses and minuses were not on the male/female, they were on other things. But in the Senate race, it was back to ground zero. I thought, "My God, I can't believe this."

I'd have these experiences where I'd go out and talk about arms control, and they'd say, "How old are your children?" I didn't know how you deal with that. I've said since, in retrospect—if I were to do it again, I'd gather every reporter in my office and I'd say, "This is off the record. You now get to ask all your insane, asinine, stupid questions—about my health, my body, my bra size, who I'm sleeping with, anything else you want to ask me. And after this, no more sexist questions."

My son worked in my campaign and got so he was a pretty good spokesman. The last week, he'd done this lengthy call-in radio show out in a small town in western Minnesota, and he'd done a really nice job. As the show was winding down, the announcer said, "It's so nice to have David Growe here. His mother, Joan Growe, our secretary of state, is a candidate for the United States Senate. The election is in three days. It's been nice to have David Growe here representing his mother and speaking for her . . . and, Dave, tell me now, you've got a long drive home—is your mom going to have a nice, hot meal waiting for you when you get home?"

Mary Pattock

I never belonged to a consciousness-raising group. I guess the DFL Feminist Caucus was that for me. We used to have these retreats up at Koryne's* cabin. She had this place up north, and we would periodically go up there and spend the whole weekend.

I remember sitting around her living room, on the floor, and we introduced ourselves in depth. I remember that most of us were the eldest children, or at least the eldest daughter, in our families. And many of us had come from Catholic backgrounds. We didn't know it was consciousness-raising at the time, but that's what it was. And we were together all the time. We talked to each other daily on the telephone. "What went on at the capitol today?" "And is your husband still . . . ?" *(Laughs.)*

*Mary Pattock, 48, entered politics working for the peace movement in 1968 and was one of the founders of Women in State Employment (WISE). She was one of the six founding mothers of the DFL Feminist Caucus. As a single mother and full-time worker, she dropped out of activism for a while after her divorce in 1977. She is now the communications director for Minneapolis's mayor, Sharon Sayles Belton.***

I went to Holy Family grade school, and St. Margaret's Academy for girls, and then St. Catherine's College. By the time I left St. Kate's, I was very well educated, taught to think for myself, and those nuns had given me the very tools I needed to find my way out of that Catholic bag. *(Laughs.)* They have their ways.

In 1973 we were focused on the ERA. I was the person who did all

---

* Koryne Kaneski Horbal, a founder of the DFL Feminist Caucus. Her story begins on page 222.

** Her story begins on page 169.

the writing for that. Every time there was some literature, some information piece to give to the legislature—I did that. Press releases and so forth. I had learned the electoral part somewhat before, but now I learned the strategy, how you deal with the legislature, and what lobbying is all about.

In addition to being the person who did the writing, I was also the "apostle" to the Catholic Church. I was the "apostle" to the archbishop for the ERA because I had all these Catholic connections, and I could speak their language. I would come back, week after week, and report on the church. "What's happening?" "Well, here's what they . . ." After much negotiation, we concluded they were contained, they were not going to do anything. Everything would be fine.

At one point there was going to be a floor vote in the house or the senate, I don't remember which, except it was going to be a big vote. I remember the phone rang the night before. I was about to go out the door with my dad, and the phone rang. It was this guy from the chancery, and he wanted to know somebody's address so he could send a copy of a letter the bishop was writing. I gave him the information he wanted, and then my curiosity just got ahead of me and I said, "Would you mind reading me the letter?"

He read it to me. I was just appalled. The bishop had decided to take no stand at all on the ERA. He said the reason he was taking no stand was because two groups—he claimed it was the labor women and the Jewish women—had decided to take no position on this. He was going to be cautious. I think his letter really damned with faint praise.

I was just furious with this guy. I told him so on the telephone. I said, "This isn't what you've told me. Now, at the last minute, the day before the vote, you're going to send out this damaging letter!" I really blasted him.

Well, this was very important to me. I found out that the women's groups he mentioned had not even considered it. It hadn't come up. That was why they had taken no position. And he represented that they had. The bishop lied. My leader . . . lied. Not only had he lied, he had lied about *me*. About my interests, about my daughter's interests. All of a sudden the scales fell down and I could see that this group claiming to be the church was just a bunch of guys in politics. It totally changed my relationship with the church. It wasn't too long before I dropped out. It just didn't interest me anymore.

Well, there we were, working for the ERA. I remember lobbying one of the very conservative house members, I have a photograph of that someplace. There I am with my hair down the middle of my back, my thin straggly hair parted down the middle, so earnestly engaging this guy. I also remember being up on the balcony when one of the rural senators made his famous speech, the one about the women who wanted this bill are the ones whose husbands come home and find bastard children under the beds. We sat up there. We had to sit there and be insulted by this man.

It wasn't at all a foregone conclusion that Minnesota would pass the ERA. No, not at all. We *fought* for the ERA. We fought hard for it. We worked. I was there, Koryne was there, Jeri was there, I think Peggy was there—every day!* Every single day. Seeing people, having lunch, I don't even remember what all we did. We met weekly. It was a really concentrated campaign, and we managed to get it passed pretty early in the session.

Later on, it became clear to us that if we hadn't passed it right away in the first blush of excitement, other events would have taken over and we would have lost. We were by then dealing with the abortion issue. And we always bloody lost in those abortion hearings. That experience should give women courage to go on in the face of adversity, because there was not a bat's chance in hell that we could have done anything on abortion during those years. But if we hadn't done it then, we wouldn't be where we are now either.

I also remember another legislator, poor little guy, not too bright. I remember being at an abortion hearing when somebody was testifying against contraception, and saying contraceptives can hurt a woman's body, which of course they can, but we didn't know that back then. Anyhow, somebody else stood up and said, "Everything has side effects. Even aspirin has side effects." And this poor little guy who was on the committee, he said in all earnestness, "Mr. Chairman, are we here learning that aspirin is a contraceptive?" Everybody kind of groaned. Not too bright, that's for sure.

So the ERA passed, and I remember after that . . . I remember testifying, and introducing the concept of marital rape. I was scared to do it. It was one of those rooms on the first floor of the capitol, it was one of

* Koryne Horbal, Jeri Rasmussen (whose story begins on page 329), Peggy Specktor.

the small hearing rooms with just enough room for a table. I was standing by the door, and all these guys were in front of me, and I said this
thing—and they laughed at me. Here they were, all older men, and I was
a young woman, and I managed to get up my courage and say this. And
they laughed at me. I was humiliated, but I was also angry. Really angry.
I'm sure that was the first time that concept had been discussed.

We were also lobbying for gun control. And then we began to see
patterns . . . I mean, the same people were against gun control, they
were against abortion, they were against the ERA. We really began to
see . . . we didn't use the word "patriarchy" then, we really didn't understand that concept, but we were beginning to see its tentacles.

There was so much going on in the DFL Party. I remember one
particular day when we were in Koryne's office in the DFL headquar-
ters, and it was, "Do we dare touch it?" And "it" was the word "feminist." In fact, when I was looking in my journal notes the other day, the
abbreviation I used was the DFL-WC. For Women's Caucus. And then
I remembered this discussion, what about the word "feminist"? Is it
too strong? You know, it wasn't in currency then, the word "feminist."
It was new, it was a little harsh, it was a little bruising, it was a little mil-
itant. We didn't take the decision to call it that lightly. But we went
ahead, and we did it.

We wrote up the principles. A newspaper reporter interviewed
several of us, and he asked, "Does this mean that you're not going to
support all Democrats?" Because it had been assumed that if you were
a DFL woman, and especially if, like Koryne, you were the state party
chairwoman, you were going to support the whole team. And we were
saying, "Well, no, not necessarily all Democrats." That was heresy back
then. Very controversial. Those were the days when we were supposed
to make "helpful coffee." *(Laughs.)*

The next thing we did was to recruit members. We had small meetings, I had several in my home. I called women who had worked on
campaigns in my district. We had little orange sign-up cards. And we
had some fundraisers. I think our first fundraiser was a style show! We
understood fully what the implications of that were. But I think we felt
in those days some pressure to—we couldn't totally alienate ourselves,
because if the whole purpose was to gain power, we couldn't be too out
of it. We used a woman designer, and her clothes were woman-
designed. I mean, they weren't men trying to make women over.

We raised funds. And we met and figured out criteria to present to candidates. For the first time it occurred to us that we could do stuff like the old-time labor bosses. We had a fundraiser, we called it a "thin cats" fundraiser. And an artist who was one of us drew this skinny cat, an almost snake-like cat. And we had to develop all these things—bylaws, and all this stuff, and think it through politically. Learn all that strategy. Apply what we'd been doing for the men to ourselves.

By the time 1976 came around, there were people asking me, "Well, would you be interested in running for the legislature from this district? Or for county commissioner?" I think both those seats were open at that time. I considered it, but decided not to. For the very reason that this is not a way to live. My marriage was shaky, my house was a mess, my life was out of control. And I learned that politics can really be addicting, I mean in just a devastating way. It can come in and tell you suddenly you have to go to a meeting tonight, and you hadn't planned to do it, but you have to do it.

I decided not to run, and it was a painful decision. I was up and down, and people were asking, and then I finally said no. And what do you think happened, but my husband decided to run instead. That pissed me off. So I made my break with politics at that time. I remember one night—I took up dance, I had danced in college—so I came home from a dance class at nine o'clock one night, and my house was full of people who'd been out door-knocking for my husband. They didn't like the fact that I was coming home in leotard and tights, when *they* had been out dropping literature for *my* husband.

I had a very difficult time being the wife of the candidate. It was very hard for me. My husband's campaign manager had a hard time with me, I knew a lot more about politics than he did, and he didn't like the influence I had on the campaign. It was a miserable deal, totally miserable. The next year we got divorced, and I didn't have time for politics anymore.

Gloria Griffin

Before moving to Minnesota in 1967, Gloria Griffin led the fast-track life on Madison Avenue in New York. She worked in advertising and on slick women's magazines—Good Housekeeping *and* Harper's Bazaar. *Active in the Women's Political Caucus, she ran for Congress in 1976. The following year she became appointments director for Governor Rudy Perpich, and for the last 12 years she has been director of the Minnesota Women's Consortium. She is in her late sixties.*

I didn't think of myself as a feminist until well into the '70s. I was interested in the women's movement and what women were doing, but I don't think I thought of *myself* as a feminist. One day I saw a notice in the paper about a convention in Houston and I called up the chair of the Hennepin County Women's Political Caucus. I don't know what moved me, I just read about it and called her up. I asked if I could go to Houston for the first national convention of the caucus. I asked if I could go along just as an observer, and she said, "Oh, no, we need the votes. Come on."

I'd always been politically active, but I'd never, ever seen politics from a woman's point of view until that trip. Then I saw *everything.* It wasn't just a new view of politics—it was a new view of the party, my life, my work. Everything in the world became part of my feminist point of view. That weekend was a real turning point. I realized I was seeing the same system, but from a different perspective. I couldn't believe how blind I'd been.

I joined the Women's Political Caucus, I joined NOW. I joined a lot of the feminist organizations, and they all seemed to have their own point of view. There wasn't a group I joined I didn't like. I joined everything in sight.

One of the things which struck me at that time was who runs for political office. I thought, "How come there aren't any women running?" I suppose that's why I became a candidate for Congress in 1976. I ran not so much because I thought I could win. I don't think there was ever a Democrat in that rural district.* And because no Democrat had ever won, the DFL endorsement had become an old-boys' toy. It just got passed around between the good old boys. I was really furious about that.

We worked hard and got the endorsement, leaving a lot of folks open-mouthed. We learned a lot. You really can do these crazy things if you keep your wits about you, know what you're getting into, and take a good look at the system.

At some point the whole party knew I was going to get that endorsement. There wasn't much they could do about it. I had one last deal—we learned how to cut deals—one last deal to cut with this old guy. I'll never forget it. My campaign manager was really tough. She stood there by the phone and said, "You call him up, you call him up and say it." So we did things that even a year before I would have said, "Oh gosh, we can't do that kind of thing." News like that travels in a district, and people understood. They said, "Well, you know, she can cut a deal just like anyone else can, well, okay."

I found incredible support from women. I still have people who say, "I remember you at Mankato, don't you remember me?" And I just . . . After all these years! All kinds of women responded to nothing but the fact that I was a female candidate. I met some wonderful people. It was such fun for all of us when the biggies like Mondale came into the district. Carter was there, Carter and Mondale were both campaigning. I remember being squashed up there on a platform with Wendell Anderson, who was still governor—even though innumerable people told me that his chief of staff had said, "She couldn't win down there if she were the Virgin Mary herself."

Rudy Perpich, who was lieutenant governor, came down and campaigned with me. He and his wife Lola had come down, and we'd become friendly. Then he became governor, quite suddenly in 1977. My campaign was over, and I had about five women on my staff who'd been just super, wonderful. As long as I had known politics, which was most of my life, the young men who worked on campaigns were taken

* The Second District in southwestern Minnesota.

care of. Given a start in a profession, or given a place where they could be visible.

I couldn't find anyone to take care of my five women, so I went to visit the new governor. We had a nice chat. I told him I wanted jobs or positions for the women from my campaign. And he said, "Oh, but Gloria, you know I don't believe in the spoils system. You know that." I said, "Yes, I know that, and neither do I. But it's always been that way. Since it works for them, why doesn't it work for me?" He said, "I *am* going to have women in my administration." I just looked at him. He said, "I see you've heard that before." I said, "Yeah, I've heard that before."

So he asked me to head up a commission and help him find his first woman, someone for the Pollution Control Agency. He said, "Just don't tell anyone it has to be a woman." I chaired that commission, and it was a wonderful experience. After I found a woman for the PCA, he wanted me to continue with other boards and commissions and agencies.

His first order was that he wanted women in as many places as possible, but he soon decided that minorities belonged there too. Then it became seniors, and also the disabled. He truly was looking for a way to put more real citizens, people more reflective of the population, on those boards. The group we got together for the commission—one from each congressional district—just happened to work together really well. We were all willing to skip the party differences and try to find a woman. People would come into a meeting, "I found one! I found one!" *(Laughs.)* We weren't stumped too often.

In the early days of the consortium, I was dimly aware that some women were talking about starting an organization, but I wasn't part of those discussions. I do remember the first meeting, and I remember a number of women saying, "I just know something exciting is going on, I just know that this is something big. I've got to get there."

I remember being struck at that first meeting by someone saying, "Can you imagine what a feminist newsletter out of the capitol would do?" Right away I thought, "Gosh, that's a wonderful idea." So I was concentrating on that right from the very beginning, getting that done. We used to have to borrow the use of a mimeograph. We did all kinds of things to get that sheet out.

Others were more concerned with signing up members. Getting a committee to run things was also important. I don't think I was a run-everything person in those days, not near as much as I am now. I remember then a hundred and one policy questions would keep coming up—everything that came up would be a policy question.

I thought getting an office was exciting. One of our members just wheeled around, did a U turn on University Avenue, because she saw a "for rent" sign on a building. I learned in just a few weeks, once we moved into there, how much a telephone and a roof can do. I still tell new organizations that. What a roof and a phone does for you—it gives you professionalism, you belong to the rest of the world, you're accepted by the world. It makes all the difference.

We didn't have a dime. We were blithely out looking for space, and we didn't have one dime. *(Laughs.)* But nothing ever stepped in our way. I really was impressed, and am still impressed, by the number of women in other worlds . . . like Women in Foundations. I didn't know any of those women, I didn't know they had their own networks. I was so impressed by their willingness to help the consortium. That happened again and again and again. The groups of women who truly had goodwill for us.

I remember the evening of the first celebration, in 1980. We made $4,000. I found it incredible that we could raise that much in one evening. It's been great working for the consortium. The one really essential ingredient, I think, is the success. It was successful, right from the beginning. That's very seductive. Although there are little disappointments and stumbling blocks to everything, when you have that kind of success, you just love it.

It's like the success of the Women's Building. In the Twin Cities, there was a plan for a big shopping mall, the Mall of America, the Megamall. That's how it all began. That mall was going to be the biggest thing in the world, and it really began to annoy me. The newspapers were full of it, it was almost as bad as the Super Bowl. All you could read about was the Megamall.

So in exasperation I wrote a little piece for our bulletin that said, "I'm sick of the Megamall. What we need is a Mega-center for women." I laughed about it, but a couple of people called me and said, "Why not?" I said, "You know why not. We can't do anything like that." Someone from the nurses' association said, "Come on, Gloria,

you've got women in real estate, you've got women in property management, women in housing. Don't tell me you couldn't do anything
you wanted."

I started to think about it, and it sounded right. The way she said it.
I talked to some people and they agreed. We had a development team,
and determined what was possible. Financially and in every other way.
We all learned a helluva lot.

The first thing I learned was about raising money. Raising money
for women's *programs* is like pulling teeth. It's really difficult, you have
to explain everything all the time. Raising money for bricks and mortar—there's absolutely nothing to it. If I'd known just that little piece,
I would have made the building twice as big.

The men don't even argue. They check with the rest of the community, they check with the foundations, and it's all settled. That's true
where men do the decision-making and the funding. They're so familiar with bricks and mortar, you don't have to tell them anything.
They're so unfamiliar with women's programs, children's programs, you
have to explain absolutely everything. And even then they're not sure.

So here we are in our own building with lots of other women's
groups. This was an old porn house, a boarded-up porn house. We
think this should happen to *all* the porn places!

Ann Wynia

*Ann Wynia, 49, was the first woman to be elected majority leader of the
Democratic-Farmer-Labor Party in Minnesota's House of Representatives. After
serving in the legislature for 12 years, she was commissioner of human services
and a regent of the University of Minnesota. She is soft-spoken, with a trace of
the South in her voice.*

I was born in Texas. I come from a family that is very traditional.
We were very religious, Southern Baptist. There were two important
things in our family outside of the family and work, and that was the
church and politics. I remember once getting in trouble at church

when I was a small child. The teacher was trying to teach us about traditional family structures, and she asked who was the boss of the family. I chirped up, "My mother!" and, of course, that was repeated to my mother who vehemently denied it.

We kids always understood that our mother *was* the boss of the family. She deferred in traditional female ways to my father, but we knew where the real power was. She was a very strong person, even though she would never describe herself as a feminist. I mean, she was not afraid of controversy. In this little town in Texas she got in a lot of trouble when she integrated the Girl Scouts. That was back in the '50s, and that was quite a thing. So there was always a model to me of a woman who says there's nothing more important than family and children, and yet was involved in public affairs and felt pretty deeply about social justice.

One thing I recall from college was wanting to go to law school. But I knew a woman who was going to law school and the only goal she had was to become a legal secretary. I mean, this is Texas in the early '60s, and this is how women defined the limits of what they could do. I was interested in politics in college, and active in college politics. Again I remember thinking about my own political aspirations, thinking that I would like to marry a politician. This is how women thought about their options.

I went up to Wisconsin for graduate school and met my husband in my first year there. We were married after about a year and, maybe because of the marriage, at that point I started defining my life in very traditional ways, even though we were both in graduate school. I cooked, I shopped, I did all those things a wife does. My husband did very well and was one of the top graduate students, and I just plodded along and was not sure of what I was doing.

I attended my first precinct caucus within six months of moving to Minnesota. I loved it, and went to the convention, and gosh, I just thought it was the greatest thing in the world. So I continued to be politically active, in our neighborhood and working in the campaigns of our state representative. I remember thinking back in the early '70s how I'd like to run for the legislature. Then I looked at our state rep, and at our state senator, and both of those guys were younger than me. I can remember thinking, "Well, I missed my chance. Those guys will be there forever, they're wonderful legislators, they'll be in office twenty years, and I've just missed my chance."

Suddenly, in 1974, one announced he was not going to seek reelection, and the other announced he was going to run for the senate. I was really, really interested. But I had some difficulty just jumping out and asserting myself. The critical thing was a phone call from a friend who said she thought I should run, that it's time we elected a woman, and that she would help me. Immediately I said, "Okay."

When I informed my husband, he was just . . . I don't think he had thought I would ever do something like that. He was just kind of shocked. He wasn't upset about it, it was just that it was different from what he'd always thought of me, of what I was going to do with my life. Anyway, I ran. We had a wonderful campaign with a lot of active support from women.

Wonderful volunteers, good men and women who worked on the campaign. But I think back now of the agony we had over issues related to gender. You know, how is a woman supposed to dress when she door-knocks? We spent hours debating that stuff, we wasted endless hours debating things that in the end were just trivial. But you don't know it at the time.

One of the things we debated was what colors to use on campaign brochures. I liked red, but somehow a woman can't use red because of the association with red lights. You know, the whole thing about morality. *(Laughs.)* The scarlet letter. Well, ultimately, we did use red. But with lots of black in it because we didn't want it to be *too* scarlet.

But the thing that really pleased and surprised me in that campaign was the positive reaction to having a woman run. So many women expressed pleasure that they could vote for a woman. Even guys would say, yes, women were more honest, even though I'd feel a little uncomfortable with those generalizations. At least it translated into votes, and that was helpful.

There were also moments when I realized that in many people's minds the idea of a woman running was not so great. I remember one time I was door-knocking at a duplex. I had knocked first at the door of the upper duplex, the guy had come down, taken my brochure and turned around. I knocked at the second door. As he went upstairs, I heard somebody yell, "Who is that?" And he says, "Just some broad who's running for the legislature."

On the whole, though, it was a positive experience. I think all of us felt enormous excitement that a woman had been elected. We really did see that as a gender victory, not just an individual victory.

When I got to the legislature, I was really conscious of the fact that there were very few women. The women who had preceded us were really helpful in the socialization of the new women members. I remember Linda Berglin* in particular would stop by my office every week to see how I was doing. You had a consciousness that there were other women like you, women who expected that you were going to have some concerns for women.

My first term was very much a learning term. I don't recall it as being particularly distinguished. Even though I felt I had to represent women, I felt that I *did* represent women. I mean, that was what I was. It wasn't something I had to do, it was just something that was part of me. I remember the advice I was given about committee assignments. I was told, "Don't let them put you on Health and Human Services, that's where they always want to stick the women. You should ask for Taxes." I think one of the reasons I asked for Financial Institutions was because it sounded so unfemale. I didn't want to be typecast.

By my second term, I realized how much I was interested in human services. By that time I had enough confidence to say, "I don't care if they're women's issues, they're important to me, that's what I want to spend my time on."

In that term I worked on a bill that dealt with discrimination on the basis of pregnancy. That was a wonderful bill. I felt strongly about it because when I first applied for a teaching job, the only important question I was asked was whether I was going to get pregnant during the school year. I had realized then that my tenure, whether I got the job, was going to depend on that answer. And at the time I was desperate for a job.

I remember thinking, "My God, I don't have a right to be pregnant?" When I think back about that and I hear women today being subjected to that . . . It's so representative of the second-class status of women. Penalize women because they have kids.

---

* State representative elected in 1972, later a state senator.

Eventually I became majority leader. In some ways, I regard myself as very fortunate. Very fortunate in being asked to be speaker pro tem. I hadn't lobbied for it. It hadn't occurred to me that I would be asked to do that. The speaker just came up one day and told me I had better start learning the rules. He was going to call me up there one of these days.

I remember the first time I did it, I think I was the first woman to ever preside over the house for a session. I remember the stunned reaction from some of the people that a woman was up there. But it legitimized the notion that a woman could do a leadership job. Certainly there were other women in leadership. Linda Berglin would be the prime example. She was the first woman elected by my caucus to a leadership post. She was elected assistant majority leader during my first term. She was the woman who had really gone through fire in terms of getting the caucus to vote for a woman. That was an important breakthrough because after it's been done once, it's always easier the second time.

After presiding a few times, some of the rural males in particular were surprised I could do it. I remember one saying to me, "For a woman, you do a real good job up there." And he meant it totally as a compliment. I was very fond of him, he was a fine person. But he was so shocked that a woman could do a good job.

In 1984 I decided I would be a candidate for speaker. I was pretty brash. When you think of it, I had the least seniority, and you add that to my sex. I mean, it was very untypical of me to be so presumptuous, that I could jump over all these guys. But I think in part because I'd been speaker pro tem, and people had been so positive, I was encouraged to think it was possible.

I lost, and that was a painful political experience for me. That's politics, that's like . . . *(she searches for words)* . . . that's like being in a small room with a bunch of very skillful fighters, all of whom have long knives. You're sharp, but you begin to try to sharpen your knife. It's a very different kind of politics from just running for office.

The other thing about that election that was painful was that although a lot of the women supported me, it wasn't unanimous. It made me realize just how important the support of the women was, the moral support. I learned an awful lot in that election. In retrospect, it was good that I did it, even though it was embarrassing, humiliating, disappointing. But at least I managed to lose with some grace. After it was over I was a team player for the caucus, just tried to be a loyal member of the caucus. I was reelected to a job as assistant minority leader, but really didn't expect that another big chance would come around.

I had reached the point where I knew that losing an election would not end my life, but running for majority leader later was in some ways the election I felt best about. That was in the '89 session and I had really strong support from the women.

I don't know if there's any downside to being a feminist, not one that's immediately apparent to me. I guess you could say that the traditional ways that women live their lives were a lot less stressful. Well, I don't know about that either. Sometimes I think about that year of my life when I was unemployed. I was enormously stressed . . . I didn't feel self-worth, I was miserable, and hated myself because of the predicament I was in. So you start balancing that off against the stress of getting beat up on the house floor.

There were some stressful votes—whenever abortion would come up—but the stress was not the disappointment when you didn't win, because you never expected to win. The stress was listening to some of the horrible things men say that show they haven't the faintest clue about women's lives, and that they can feel so sanctimonious in saying those things. If they would just vote and shut up, it wouldn't be so bad.

I actually remember crying in the '89 session when the bill having to do with fetal viability was on the house floor. It was a real bad time late in the session, conference committees were going, and I was just so tired. But I remember going up there on the floor because I felt I just had to sit and be present for that entire debate. It was so terrible, I felt so alienated.

So the down side of feminism is that you expose yourself to some of that hurt and pain. But to me it's better than the alternative—not feeling anything, not knowing anything. When a woman legislator gets up and rails against an AFDC mom as lazy and no good and having too much money, that's the time I just want to scream. That just seems to me so, so . . . false to women.

When I was first elected to the legislature, we went through a period that was a real adjustment in our marriage. All of a sudden I wasn't . . . because I'd been so traditional, I just can't believe it. I was this typical southern girl who thought it was my responsibility to cook all the meals, and take care of everything at the house, and his career was the important career, and our friends were defined as his friends. The entertaining we did was for his friends and the things that would be helpful and useful to him—just the classic kind of stuff.

Well, on second thought, it's probably not even southern. And so when I first went into the legislature, and I'd been there a few years, and the time commitments got heavier and heavier . . . it was a real adjustment on his part. But we've worked out an arrangement that works. We have a lot of respect for one another, and I can do what I want as long as he doesn't have to do it too. And he does what he wants, and I don't have to go with him. And if either of us is doing something that the other thinks would be interesting . . .

For the longest time I tried to drag him to my political things, and he hated it. It took me the longest time to figure it out. It was hard to make that break, and say, "Well, okay, I'll go by myself." Women alone are, well, not the acceptable thing. And I must admit, sometimes I wish he wanted to go to some of this stuff. But at the same time I no longer feel obligated to prepare lavish dinners unless it's something I want to do.

I would like sometimes to share a little bit more of this, but I also have to say that I don't have the right. I just feel thankful that we've worked something out that lets me do what I want to do.

Kay Taylor

Kay Taylor is in her sixties, has been married for 42 years, and has a daughter and two grandchildren. A Republican activist, she is a long-time pro-choice lobbyist and a staff member of the Minnesota Women's Consortium. She has never been afraid to be different, whether speaking out for abortion rights or leading her one-woman Stamp Out Pay Toilets crusade.

My mother never said the word "sex," never. No one ever got pregnant, they were "that way" or "in trouble." Once, a neighbor woman was talking about someone who got "in trouble," and my mother said, "I never talk about things like that, I have three unmarried daughters."

I resented it when a friend of mine was kicked out of high school for being pregnant. And I resented it more that the boy who made her pregnant was not kicked out. That's the only feminist thought I had growing up. Well, no, there was another. Do you remember Amelia Earhart? Amelia Earhart failed, and that was traumatic for me. She was doing this wonderful thing, and she didn't make it. I felt betrayed.

When I was in high school, I was on the state debate championship team. I remember our coach saying what the debate team needed was a very bright boy and a pretty girl. At the time, I thought, "Yes, that's right." I thought I would like to be a lawyer. Somebody pointed out that women weren't lawyers. Okay, I understood that, so I decided I'd marry one. Which I did.

In 1964, I headed up the Goldwater efforts in our congressional district. I was almost pathological about John Kennedy. My daughter was taught to dive under a desk when an atomic bomb came, and I put all that blame on Kennedy and Johnson. The Republican Workshop dropped me because I was too conservative, supporting Goldwater. The Republican Women's Club did not want me in because I was too liberal. I was a Republican without a party.

Goldwater lost, but I did stay in the party. I was a candidate for national delegate in those years, I held office at most levels at different times. I've never switched to being a Democrat, I never will. But the Republican Party left me about 1968. They became Neanderthals.

When the party platform opposed the ERA, I was up there screaming and hollering, and after that I never could get elected outside of my precinct. I still convene the caucuses, they keep asking me and I keep doing it. I keep thinking there's going to be hope, but I'm not going to sit around and wait for it. I have been contributing to candidates for years, but we gave up giving to the Republican National Committee years ago.

Sometime in the 1960s, I heard a woman on the radio who was president of the Minnesota Council for the Legal Termination of Pregnancy. I had read a book about abortion, and I called that woman. She invited me to a meeting, and all of a sudden I was involved.

We had a bill on the floor of the legislature. It would simply have allowed abortion in cases of rape, incest, and death of the mother, or some crazy thing like that. A group of young women from the university came to the capitol. They had a long banner and it said, "Don't

mess with women's bodies." My first thought was, "That's pretty vul-
gar." But my second thought was, "That's right." That was one of the
first times I realized that the reason I was interested in abortion rights
was, it was granting autonomy to women.

I was president of the Council for the Legal Termination of Pregnancy in 1969 and 1970, and later I lobbied for the Abortion Rights
Council. I was invited out to speak frequently. It was a topic that was a
little shocking, a little racy, at that time, not perhaps quite proper. A little scary to even attend. And everybody was very attentive, they gasped
at all the right places. It was a fun thing to do, so I did that for years.

During those early years I got some nasty letters, including a
threatening letter once about my daughter. That's what scares me
now—there are so many crazies out there. The abortion issue is somehow sexy, and the crazies seem to be obsessed with sex. I'm glad they
never got to the point of picketing my house.

People I knew would call and ask me how to get an abortion.
Some of those calls just kind of ripped me up. I hadn't met the reality
of it until somebody asked me to raise money for some little girl to go
to South Dakota. So I did it by charging two dollars to everybody who
called me up on the telephone.

She didn't need much, $80 or something like that. I took it over to
her apartment. The whole place was full of diapers hanging, drying diapers everywhere. She did not wash the diapers before she dried them
for another use. She had a couple of little babies. I thought, "Well, this
is just awful, but on the other hand I'm glad she is not going to have
another child."

I'm proud of the passage of the Stamp Out Pay Toilets bill. That
was my bill all the way, I was it. Pay toilets had always bothered me. It
was 1973, and I was going through a little burnout on the abortion
issue. Everybody was gearing up for the ERA, and I decided I had to
get down to the legislature, at least be part of the crowd. So I decided
to take this bill down and see what I could do with it.

I filed a complaint with the human rights department over the fact
that men's toilets at the airport were free and women's toilets were pay.
Of course, I had to haul my husband all over town to check out the

men's bathrooms. *Now* I have him going in there to make sure there are condoms in the men's bathrooms. *(Laughs.)*

The bill turned out to be easy. There was a woman television reporter, and this was her favorite topic. She would ask me where I was going to be next, she was right on top of it all the time. We got lots of coverage.

I had buttons made up saying "Stamp Out Pay Toilets." The medical association lobbyist thought this was hilarious, so he wore a button. All the women in the capitol, the secretaries and so on, they said, "This is not foolish, this is dead serious." All the legislators' wives were saying, "This is dead serious, you have to do this." The company that makes the locks on toilet doors had a bunch of lawyers running around saying this was going to cost them money. It was fun. I think of it as a feminist victory. *(Laughs some more.)* Then I came back to abortion politics.

I still get angry. Was angry, am angry, will be angry. Sometimes it's all brought into focus by a picture in the newspaper or something. Last year, it was the picture of the man who came in last in a race. A woman won that race, but they didn't have a photographer there because after all, it was just some woman coming in. I can get absolutely outraged about that. It's so dumb.

Another thing that makes me angry is the constant emphasis on body parts of women in advertising. Even the whole body doesn't bother me as much as the body parts. Women have been identified as two classes for all these years, the classy woman and the slut. And now, the advertisers have divided women into parts to admire. You just see legs or you just see breasts or you just see something else.

If you're a feminist, the world is always clicking. Sometimes you get angry at women who don't see it at all. I'm angry that the women in Kuwait don't vote. I can't do anything about that, and I'm not wasting energy, but women in Kuwait *should* be allowed to vote. The next generation can take that on.

The young women coming up don't understand how close it has been. They don't know that 10 years ago, your husband was allowed to rape you. I mean 10 years, it's an eyelash of time.

I'm really glad I was there for all these changes. Those of us who lived through these years made a difference, instead of coasting on someone else's work. I really think our presence here, at this time in the world, has made a difference.

Groves of Academe

College administrators, professors, and students provide insight into the impact of feminism on college and university education. Anne Truax points out that it was students eager for knowledge—not professors with a political agenda—who started women's studies programs. As a recent women's studies graduate, Julie Dolan traces her own evolving perceptions and ponders the future.

Feminist professors have often been branded troublemakers, and Vivian Jenkins Nelson comments on the experience of being shunned on campus. Toni McNaron remembers how feminism changed the way teachers taught as well as the content of what they taught.

Anne T. Truax

Anne Truax, 64, was raised in a conservative Scandinavian family. She was the director of the Women's Center at the University of Minnesota for 20 years. During those years she saw the establishment of the women's studies program in 1972 and the Center for Advanced Feminist Studies in 1982.

Like any good '50s person, I got married and had five children. I had dropped out of college with one quarter to go. In 1961, I came back to the university to finish my degree—and never left. I was asked to be a candidate for director of the Women's Center in 1968, just when the women's movement came along. That made the center more important than it had ever been before.

The Women's Center here was the first one in the country, and as far as I know, in the world. It came out of a grant from the Carnegie Corporation called "The Minnesota Plan" for continuing education for women. It started in 1960 and provided a series of seminars and career counseling. There's no doubt in my mind that those early programs were forerunners of the women's movement gearing up again.

I think what they were picking up on was the dissatisfaction of college-educated, middle-class women—with having been at home, with having been pretty well confined to domestic kinds of things. I don't think women have ever been pushed into such a narrow funnel, in terms of their expectations, as they were at that time.

The first course I taught was called something like "Life Styles of the Educated American Woman." *(Laughs.)* That gives you the flavor. And they used to call our program the "Rusty Ladies." I think it was a long time before we realized what a sexist term that was, although of course at the time we weren't talking about sexism. We weren't even talking about feminism.

I remember being enormously grateful that I myself had the opportunity to return to college. I remember coming up the steps to register. The president of the university came out of the building as I came in and, before I knew what I was doing, I rushed over to him and shook his hand and said I wanted to thank him for the opportunity to come back to school. I told him I was so excited about the fact that they believed people like me could do the kind of work we were doing, and be able to function again as intellectual people, not just domestic people.

It was strange being a student again, because older women were ... well, I wasn't all that much older, but I had very different responsibilities from the other students. They still thought of us as a special category. They still worried about how we were going to behave in the classroom, as if our wits had deserted us somewhere along the line.

There was a great deal of paternalism that showed up, wanting to pat you on the head and treat you like a kid again. But knowing they couldn't do that, they would do you a favor by ignoring you. A lot of us had the experience of being allowed into a program without jumping the usual hurdles of admissions committees or other procedures. In a way you were invisible. They didn't expect that you were ever going to *do* anything. They just didn't know quite how to respond to your presence in the classroom.

After I became an employee of the university, I used to go through role changes, almost from minute to minute. My kids were at University High, and I remember one day being an administrator in the Women's Center and finishing a long-distance call about some national conference, coming out of the building and running into one of my kids who needed money or something—you know, instant mother—walking across the mall and seeing my adviser, who wanted to know something about a paper I was writing, and then going on to teach a class myself. You had to transform yourself, almost from second to second.

The kind of student who came to the center was primarily a self-selected kind of person. Somebody who had dropped out of school or had finished a bachelor's degree, who had done her stint at having

kids—because women were, overwhelmingly, married in that era—and
had realized somewhere along the line that what they were doing at
home wasn't enough. Or they were getting a divorce. There were a lot
of divorces, particularly in the late '60s, and women needed to support
themselves.

Regardless of their original motivation, they were normally very
bright. They had made up their minds what they needed and were entirely capable of doing it. They went through maybe one quarter
when they were nervous about whether they could compete again.
What was it going to be like? Could they fit in studying with all the
other stuff? But once they got through that first quarter, they were off
and sailing. Very interesting and dynamic women.

Much of what I read at the time made me angry. Much of the argument was over what women were intended to be. Were they the
culture-bearers, who were supposed to pass things on to children? And
therefore their best education would be liberal arts so they could answer their kids' questions? Or was it okay if they wanted to specialize
in something, become mathematicians, for godsakes?

Almost everything I read was so far removed from a woman's real
life, it was just astounding to me. The impetus of the women's movement hadn't hit yet, and there was just an enormous mass of real
junk—about how women can only be happy sexually if there's per-
fume and soft lights and all that kind of thing. You'd think women
were some other form of being.

The students started women's studies, to a great degree. There was
a bunch of students—many of them from a women's liberation group,
from the other radical groups on campus—who wanted to have a
women's studies program. They started coming in to talk about how
we could work together. They knew they needed faculty support.

The first proposal the students wrote was something like 52 pages
long, and was full of the most godawful liberation rhetoric. We could
just see some of the conservatives on campus reading this and having
hysterics. So they called a meeting of interested faculty, and we got 75
people at that first meeting. This was probably the spring of '71. By
then they had gone to a second draft of their proposal, and were in
pretty good shape.

The first course was offered in the spring of '72, under the American studies rubric. We had a course which brought in lecturers from out of state. We had people like Robin Morgan and, I'm pretty sure, Gloria Steinem. It was a wonderful success. In the fall, we started the women's studies program under its own rubric. The first instructor was not radical enough for the students, and they fought every day. But the program has done well. It's one of the few in the country that is now a full department, and enrollment is still holding up.

One of the results of all that success was that those of us on the faculty were getting many, many requests from women graduate students who wanted to do dissertations or master's papers on feminist subjects but couldn't find anybody to be their advisers. It got to be a real burden. People were doing overtime work helping women who wanted to get through.

We started the Center for Advanced Feminist Studies partly to make official the fact that there should be feminist studies available at the graduate level, and partly so that the faculty women who were doing that work could get official recognition. Then it would be part of their load.

The Center for Advanced Feminist Studies has a graduate program that offers a supporting minor for either a master's degree or the Ph.D. We have about 150 graduate students, which makes us a big department for that. We have some of the most exciting scholars on campus. Without a doubt, the good scholars in the liberal arts must know about feminist theory. You have to know about it so you can rebut it *(laughs)*, or you have to know about it because it's a vital theory in any of today's disciplines. We now have feminists in every single major department on campus . . . except economics. *(Laughs again.)*

When we started women's studies, just the label "women" was considered radical. I think we did briefly consider some kind of title with the word "feminist" in it, but decided there was no point in fighting that fight. When we started the Center for Advanced Feminist Studies, we wanted to differentiate it from women's studies—because it was going to be the graduate program and research arm—and we were feeling very feisty and put in the word "feminist." We have since gotten a lot of response from across the country about how come they haven't told us we have to remove that word? There have been other places that have tried to use it and have not been allowed to.

We started the center in '82. In 1985, one of the vice presidents seriously proposed that we change the name because we were going to get into trouble, that it was aggravating, and it made people angry, and it made us look ideological. We sat down and had a serious discussion, but decided, "Dammit, we're not going to change the name. We're going to stick with 'feminist' because that's the theory on which our whole study is based." We said, "No, we're not going to change it." We don't have any trouble anymore. *(Laughs.)*

Vivian Jenkins Nelson

Born in the segregated South in Selma, Alabama, Vivian Jenkins Nelson later moved to Minnesota and became an active member of the Women's Equity Action League (WEAL). In 1971 she filed one of the early employment discrimination suits at the small liberal-arts college where she worked. At 47, she is now the director of INTER-RACE, the International Institute for Interracial Interaction.

My family was a combination of white people, Indians, and black people. Both my parents were teachers, and my dad was also a Lutheran pastor. We lived in my grandmother's house. She was the dean of women at the college where my dad worked. Two women started the college, so strong educated women are part of my background.

Even when people weren't educated, they pushed their children to be. We have a wonderful picture of one of my Indian great-grandmothers who is sitting there, holding this book so proudly and looking like she's reading. But it's upside down. *(Laughs.)* It took me, three generations later, to say, "Mom, it's upside down!"

My mother, although she was a southerner, had lived in New York. She had worked as a governess and had interaction with well-to-do, well-placed people. They traveled all over the world, so she had a much broader world view of what was possible. When she married my dad she went back south, to the rural South, to the poorest county in the nation. She had three schools, my dad had five. He rode a mule between his schools, and she was rowed across the river to her schools. As kids, we were raised in high chairs in the back of classrooms. One-room schools, pot-bellied stoves . . .

But she had this burning desire—she was of that generation who were related to slaves, and she had these great notions. In fact, she said to me the other day, she said, "You know, you could have been president. That could have been you instead of Clinton." She raised us with the notion that we were going to break all the barriers. Their generation was just too close to slavery. They were involved in knocking the barriers down so that we could move ahead.

I didn't know Dick and Jane were white until I moved north. She colored them black in the flip charts. She would tell us on spelling bees—I would never forget her favorite phrase, "You'll have to know how to spell if you want to be president." So we were raised with this notion of equality. And there was to be equality between black men and women. I think it was that beginning . . . I mean, she allowed you no weakness, she took no prisoners.

I came to this college in 1969. I was the first black faculty here. They had started an outreach program to try to get kids of color, particularly black kids, into the collegiate system. We used to literally drive up and down Plymouth Avenue, and say, "Hey kid, you want to go to school?"

When I first came here, we set up a tutorial center. We got them literacy training. We did a lot of experimenting, anything we heard of, we were making it up as we went along. We started with kids who were reading at the fifth-grade level, and they were making A's by their second or third year. It was such a heady period. I was working my tail off. I did everything. I did academic counseling, I did personal counseling, recruiting, taught night school. I don't know how I did it, running groups, putting out fires. Some days I was here from seven o'clock in the morning to nine o'clock at night.

My colleagues and I were the first wave of baby-boomer women who were coming through in big numbers, right? This was the first group of women who didn't go to school to get married, and a lot of us weren't married. The college didn't know what to do about that. We were struggling with them over stuff like head-of-household insurance. I led the fight around here on that one. We came out of the generation where women were speaking up.

One day the phone rang at the college and it was one of the banks. It was a woman who said she was checking on a credit application for "Bill"—that wasn't his name, but we'll call him that. She named the date he was hired, and I said yes, because that was the same day I was hired. Then she said, "And I want to verify his salary. He's making $12,000?" I said, "I hope to God not," and hung up the phone.

When I was hired, they'd promised me $10,000—but another woman and I ended up taking $9,000. And this jerk, with the same rank, hired the same day, was making $3,000 more! We were so mad. I went in and grabbed our boss, who was actually a sweetheart, and said, "Tom! What do you mean?" He said, "But he's head of household." "It isn't fair," we said, "we're heads of households too," but we were told it was just the way it had always been.

Anyway, when we raised the issue later, the men just slapped us like you wouldn't believe. There was another woman in the psych department, same deal. She was the department chair, but guys with lower rank were making more. The long and the short of it was that we complained, but were told to sit down. We were told by the college president that we had to make sacrifices because the college was short of funds. Well, of course, the college is *always* short of funds. I said, "What kind of sacrifice is that, if the men don't have to sacrifice, and we do?"

So I went to the local newspaper, the *North Country News.* I talked to them, which was unheard of. I mean, you don't talk to the press. So they wrote an article, and the title was, "Christian Sacrifice: Male Christians 50, Females 0." *(Laughs.)* It was just a riot, even though it was only a neighborhood newspaper, a weekly.

The college went crazy. They went nuts. Then the university paper got hold of it. They came over to interview me and some of the other women. By that time, the Women's Equity Action League had gotten going. When the story hit the university, I got a call one night from a black woman on the university faculty. She said, "We hear you're having trouble over there." I said, "Oh, no," because I was burned by that time. I said, "I . . . Oh . . . Nope . . ." and gulped. "Well yeah, except we can't talk about it." And she said, "Well, we're here, and we'll back you up if you need help."

We didn't know what that meant. We hadn't done any suits. We figured, because it was a religious college, we couldn't do anything anyway. People weren't inclined, nobody had ever done that. Not even men sued, you know. And Lutherans don't sue, period. *(Laughs.)*

That was in October. Then in April, one of my students who was the editor of the college paper, and the first black editor, called me up and said, "Viv, is it true that you guys are going to have to go to part-time because the college is up against it?" I said, "What 'you guys'?" He said, "There's eight of you—women." I asked who, and he named them. I said, "Give me a break." He said, "Yeah, I'm going to put your pictures on the front page."

It took a black male student to make me understand that this was really a female thing. Before that, I had never known which they were after with me, whether female or black, or what they were up to. Sometimes it was a horrible mixture of both. I couldn't separate out, and didn't.

The men went into all this defensive posture, explaining why, trying to rationalize why it was us and not them. When that didn't stick, four of us decided to file a complaint with EEOC.* We knew we weren't covered, and EEOC knew we weren't covered, but they came anyway.

And, boy, then it hit home . . . This was not only happening to us now, but it had always been a pattern. The president called me and railed at us. You know, campuses are very closed places. You didn't talk about salaries and things like that. You were considered a troublemaker if you went around asking stuff.

It was rough. People wouldn't talk to us. They would ignore us. And this is a very small place to be shunned. It's pretty terrible when people shun you. I think it was all the accompanying punishment, the retribution and retaliation . . . I think we would have given up if they hadn't punished us so.

So we filed suit. EEOC represented us in hearings, and the whole notion of federal investigators on this campus just sent a chill through the place. Some of us had private suits, and we were also in a class-action thing together. This went on for just years. It took forever. But eventually they settled out with us. But the support we got from the

---

* The Equal Employment Opportunity Commission. Laws that prohibit discrimination exempt religious institutions.

Women's Equity Action League—the emotional support we got—
kept us from going really nuts.

In WEAL, we brought some important suits at that time. And I'll
tell you, any time I did it, the black leadership here would slap down on
me. "Oh man," they'd say. "What you doing with those women? Don't
you understand those white women are out to get our jobs?"

Oh Lord, I'll tell you, I was getting whipped regular. "What's the
problem with you?" You know. People would say things like, "You
have a wonderful position, you have everything. I mean, what's wrong
with you?" It wasn't like the civil rights movement, people could get
their heads around that. But women who had access, or had wealthy
husbands, or—what was the point? The need was not compelling.
They couldn't relate to it. If you could see someone being beat up, or
having a dog set on him, you could relate to that.

And you see, in the black community, women *had* power. They
had a lot of power. Black women thought they didn't need the
women's movement. They were strong, they could fight for what they
needed. Feminism came out of a different tradition, and it wasn't ours.
People said, we don't need that, and it doesn't fit us, it belongs to
somebody else.

When I first was active in women's groups, people were curious,
critical . . . and saying, "Girl, I don't know why you put up with that."
We'd heard from our mothers that the system had weakened men, had
not allowed them access. Black women had better access, so it was our
responsibility. We were raised with sacrifice and service. You learn that
before you learn anything else. We have a religious tradition, we're
more churched than white people are. So it was our job to help them.
Black women were supposed to line up behind black men.

The women's movement got the biggest shot in the arm with
Anita Hill. And yet, there's that race thing, still messy, still causing real
confusion and pain. That's really never gone away. That's been a constant. It's not that the movement hasn't worked well for black women,
but the Anita Hill event . . . it's caused a lot of pain and humiliation in
the black community. Part of what's always been difficult for us to deal
with is that messy intersection of race and sex.

Toni A. H. McNaron

Toni McNaron, 56, is a scholar of literature and a teacher at the University of Minnesota. A lesbian feminist, she was the first director of both the women's studies program and the Center for Advanced Feminist Studies. Her autobiography, I Dwell in Possibility, *was published in 1992.*

My response to the women's movement was instant delight. I gravitated to it like a moth to a flame. There was a time when I was going to something almost every night: the Twin Cities Women's Union, the Emma Willard thing.* There was a writing group that was forming. The more I could find other women I could talk to about things that we could agree on . . . and to learn . . . The Twin Cities Women's Union really taught me a lot. Even though it was almost a socialist-feminist group, it still taught me to analyze the system, as a woman, looking at it in terms of gender. And that was very exciting.

The Women's Union was set up to "educate and agitate," those were the two things. They ran teaching groups and they taught you process. It was grassroots organizing on behalf of children and women. Rape crisis centers. Press the medical establishment. It was really a wonderful bunch of people. You'd do consciousness-raising when you first came in, and then you moved into organizational strategies or political strategies or governmental strategies.

The women's movement on the campus and in the community gave me self-respect and let me understand that not only was I a woman, but I liked being it, and other people liked being it, that I could spend time with other women, and that we could do things together. That was just invaluable to me personally.

In terms of the academy as a whole, I think there's no way to min-

* The Emma Willard Task Force on Education advocated for equal educational opportunities for girls.

imize the effect of feminism. The first level of change was mostly in content. People realized that in their courses or in their studies or in their research or in whatever it was they did that the overwhelming data—whether it was books or "data" data—were all focused on male subjects. So I read all these books by and about men. Or by men about women—which were very confused. *(Laughs.)*

So the first things we did were to redress that. In literature, for instance, you had all those courses that were called, "Images of Woman in . . ." And then you'd have the sixteenth century, the seventeenth century, American literature, the twentieth century. Drama. Poetry. That was all content-based. That was simply saying, there are works by women from the eighteenth century that need to be read. There are works by women—everywhere. Put them in. In history, the same sort of thing happened. We asked, if men were building railroads, what were women doing?

What's happened in the second generation of academic feminism, and I find it much more exciting, is that we've begun to attack—and I think that's the right word—certainly to critique heavily the modality of learning, not just the outcome of it. So we ask different questions of male writers and male studies. I teach Milton now from a feminist and a lesbian-feminist perspective. Sometimes I think my colleagues who are nervous would rather have me teach Adrienne Rich or Toni Morrison. Because the encroachment on their territory, as it were, from a different perspective creates an entirely different text, one which students find very exciting. So, different questions.

And then, even different ideas about knowledge formation. Feminism is one of the groups, along with some of the cultural-studies and ethnic-studies programs in the country, that have said that the idea of monolithic departments—the Department of History, the Department of French, the Department of English—is not necessarily the most sophisticated way to group intellectuals. Wouldn't it be more interesting to have an interdisciplinary, a multidisciplinary, a cross-disciplinary world?

There's been a real push to de-center the kind of "disciplinary-ness" of higher education. It's those things, I think, that cause more trouble at universities than the earlier work did. Because it's easy enough for a colleague who doesn't want to pay attention to ghettoize it and say, "Well, that's women's studies, and I don't have to deal with that." Or they can have a day when they tell what women did in American history. Or they have a week on women writers. Otherwise they can leave everything else intact. It's this new thing that really un-dermines the whole enterprise.

In terms of pedagogy, feminist pedagogy has really altered higher education. There's all this hue and cry now, all through the country, about cooperative learning. Students working in groups, getting one grade for the whole group. The brighter students teaching the less bright students. All of that was prototyped in feminism. There's a wonderful Native American man who says it's no accident that there's all this emphasis on collaborative learning at the same time that more women are being admitted as job candidates and as professors.

I don't think most men understand all this. I think they do under-stand that we're attacking their way, but they don't understand what we're doing. That's why they're scared, and then hostile. We're in the middle of a terrible backlash in higher education. Just as we are in . . . it just plays out here in a different way. I mean, it's not physical vio-lence, but it never was physical violence.

There's a big difference in the older and the younger generations of male faculty. Well, some of it's just behavioral. No younger faculty would crack a sexist joke. I don't know whether he thinks it or not, but he wouldn't say it. I think about the faculty that I admire the most . . . *(Pauses.)* Maybe it's just intimacy. A lot of men change because the women they love have changed. The women have either tacitly or overtly said, "I need you to change, or I may have to go. Painful as that may be, I may not stay here." That's a good incentive for men, I think, unless they're just klutzes and don't believe it. Then they are in trouble, because they *are* left.

I'm not a skeptic. I'm a great believer that we can change. I mean, that's what I have to believe. It makes me different from my dog. My dog, every time you put her out, she cries. She's never learned not to do that, in 14 years. I hope I can do something different. Maybe it's the only difference between her and me. *(Laughs.)* I can learn something from past mistakes.

I get uneasy when I hear people talk about the "post-feminist" era because I'm sure that's a scrim to . . . that that's a wish they have. If men say it, they wish it would go away. If women say it—and they also say it—they are desperately hoping that they won't ever have to fight battle X ever again.

What's dangerous about it to me is that it breeds an ahistorical approach. It's not just people saying, "I don't like that history." It's saying there *isn't* one. That's how patriarchy won all the times it won, through that kind of amnesia.

I get concerned that not enough emphasis is placed on history. People who are now members of organizations for women don't necessarily know the history. Certainly students here don't know the history of women's studies, and how hard it was, or of feminism in America. They just don't know. And I get very concerned about it, so I keep saying, "Let's have a history of this," or "Let's have a history of that."

On the good side of what's happened, we've stopped believing there's any such thing as one kind of woman, one kind of feminism, one kind of anything. I find the plurality and the arguments and the disagreements and the difficulties—I find all that to the good. I really do. I think the diversifying of the women's organizations is what keeps it going.

We need some consciousness-raising, because what's required as we diversify is lots and lots of patience. I have to be willing to sit and really listen to what your life is like. And not just say, "Oh, you're a woman, I'm a woman, let's go do such and such." I really have to hear what is the nature of your daily life. And you have to listen to what is the nature of my daily life. And we both have to listen to this black woman over here, who will be very different from both of us. And then we have to listen to somebody in a wheelchair, who has a son, or a daughter, and a job. We *have* to do that, and still get the tasks done that have to get done.

Julie Dolan

Growing up, I was never aware of any difference in what my brother could do and what I could do. I was encouraged to do the best I could, whether it was sports, helping my dad, or being encouraged at school.

Julie Dolan recently graduated from a small liberal-arts college and has worked as a waitress for the past three years while doing volunteer work with the Minnesota Women's Consortium. She is 22.

I didn't start defining myself as a feminist until I was a junior in college. I took a class called "Philosophy of Feminism," because I had to take a philosophy course, and I didn't want to take a philosophy course, so I thought this would be more interesting than the other ones. I remember thinking, "I don't think I'm a feminist, I don't think women have been that discriminated against." In my own family, I had never felt discrimination. I didn't think men were terrible ogres or that they would do awful things to women. It just never occurred to me to think that I was a feminist.

I took the course, and we read Mary Wollstonecraft's *A Vindication of the Rights of Woman*. In part of the book she attacks Rousseau and what he thinks about the proper role of women. Then she compares her ideas about how a woman should have her own identity, her own personality, and not be reliant upon a male, or not live her life to please a male. It hit me! I thought, "This is *right*." I looked at fashion, I looked at the roles women are supposed to have, I looked at the situation of the women I knew. I thought, what she was writing two centuries ago still holds true today. Women are supposed to be for men's pleasure, they are supposed to cultivate their charms for men.

It started to occur to me that this wasn't right. Throughout the class we read more and more. My professor was a real go-getter. She was full of fire, and she would have us discuss. We sat around a couple of big tables, and we would talk all hour long. People would bounce their ideas off each other, and it seemed that the more we talked about it, the more radical everyone got. We said, "Wait a minute, this isn't *right*—how women are, how this is their role." Or we talked about whether men and women think differently.

That class shaped me more than anything. It taught me to think about how women have been systematically discriminated against, and have been told over and over again that these are their roles . . . that they shouldn't break out of these roles, that it's dangerous to do so.

I think I look at the world in a whole different light now. I see things—like the media, like everyday relationships between men and women—that I didn't see before. I have decided that being a feminist is one of the most important things in my life. I'm not going to tolerate . . . I have too much self-respect to tolerate sexism. I choose not to tolerate it, so I don't.

If people insult me, or people offend me, I tell them so. I say, "I don't appreciate your using that kind of language." I feel that I have more self-esteem because I know more about myself and more about other women. Knowing that there are a whole lot of other women out there who feel the same way I do makes me think, "Yeah, this is *right*. Women don't have to stand for the things they think are wrong." It's real empowering to think that.

Is there a down side?

The only thing I can think of is that I may not be willing to compromise. Yet I don't think women should have to compromise anymore. On the one hand, if you're going to get something done, you have to play by the rules. But if you don't like the rules, or you think the rules are unjust, it can get you between a rock and a hard place. You want to change things, but you don't want to buy into the system. Every now and then I think I shouldn't be so radical or so hardheaded. But then I wonder, "If I were a man, would I think that?"

I get angry at the way women have been treated, that women don't get the same respect no matter what they do. If a woman does something special, then she must be some extraordinary individual because she beat the system to get that far. It makes me angry that people aren't impressed by the things women do. They don't give them recognition.

In the civil rights movement, Martin Luther King gets all the credit, Malcolm X, Ralph Abernathy. These are the people they talk about. And Rosa Parks is not mentioned, and all the women who organized the bus boycott, who did all the behind-the-scenes work that made the whole movement function—nobody even knows who they are. That happens to women all the time.

I also get angry about the images of women, about women's fashions. The restaurant where I work, we have completely different uniforms for the men and the women. The women's uniforms are supposed to be off-the-shoulder, and then long skirts. The cocktail waitresses have short skirts. It's obvious to me why they do this: "Well, women are going to be an attraction for people to come into our restaurant." It's okay for the men to look uninteresting. It just infuriates me that we are on display, and that we're making money for the restaurant doing that. But at the same time I have to pay my bills.

What's ahead for you?

I don't know what I want to do yet. I'll probably go back to school again sometime, but not now. I want to have children, but I don't want to get married. I think marriage as an institution has been terrible for women. I don't think the *institution,* ideally, is sexist. But I think what men think they'll get out of marriage and what women think they'll get out of marriage are so completely different that I just don't have any desire to get married.

It doesn't mean I can't have meaningful relationships with men, but I don't think anything would change if I married one. What difference is it going to make if we have a piece of paper that says this is a legal contract now? I see no need to get married, absolutely none.

I would like to have kids. I love little kids, and I think they're great. A lot of people disagree with me when I say I don't think you need both a man and a woman to raise children. I think my friend Jane and I could do a great job, raising great feminist kids.

Seeking Justice

The path to justice is far from smooth, acknowledge women such as attorney Loretta Frederick. Practicing law on behalf of poor women turned her into a feminist. Judges do not necessarily understand women's issues, despite what the law says, but Ellen Dresselhuis found that losing cases in the early years was often a necessary step in the process of educating judges about discrimination.

Working in other parts of the justice system, probation officer Lurline Baker-Kent found that women offenders have fewer rehabilitation programs and job opportunities than male offenders. Going to jail for her beliefs offered Polly Mann a new perspective on the criminal justice system. Katherine Weesner discovered that climbing a fence can be an effective way to change a newspaper's policy, and Margaret Holden was near retirement when she filed a class-action discrimination suit against her employer of 35 years.

Ellen Dresselhuis

Ellen Dresselhuis is tall and rangy, with an informal manner. Throughout the 1970s she was a highly visible lawyer representing women in sex-discrimination cases. She founded the Women's Equity Action League chapter in Minnesota, and it was her clients who started the advocacy and support group known as Les Soeurs. She grew up in a small town in Iowa, where her father still is a practicing lawyer. She is 54.

When I decided to be a lawyer, my father just burst with pride. There was never any pressure that my brother should be those things and not me. It was never like that. It always was that the doors are open, you can be anything you want to be.

I went to law school because I wanted to be in a profession where I could do something concrete to help people. And while psychology and the social sciences help people, they don't seem to have any structure. You can't say you've done something when you get done. With the law, you take people's problems and you can go and find some kind of resolution for them.

The other reason was that my father was the person in our small town in Iowa that people called first. They knew he'd know how to take care of things. They relied on him. And I wanted to be that kind of person, I wanted to give the world something for what I'd gotten. That's why I became a lawyer.

I wasn't a feminist in law school. Rosalie Wahl* and I were in the

* First woman on the Minnesota Supreme Court. Her story begins on page 176.

same class, and she was a feminist back then. I'd say to her, "But Rosalie, there won't be many jobs for women and we shouldn't encourage too many women in this." I'm ashamed of myself now. She'd say, "We *must* get more women in law school." But I was hoping that I could slip in there someplace as a lawyer, although I don't think I gave a lot of thought about where I'd work.

While I was in law school, I had a job at a non-profit research outfit. I was the business manager, secretary. It was a new company, and I did all the purchasing, I did all the repair of the machinery, I did all the secretarial work, I did all the hiring. I did all these jobs. Then we got a contract that involved a lot of purchasing, so we hired a young man fresh out of college to do the purchasing.

I hired him, I found him. They were paying him more to start with than they were paying me to do purchasing plus everything else. I trained him in. When I went in for a raise, I said I thought I would get more of a raise. I was told, "Well, that may be true, but you know you're a woman and you could always get married and leave us." I thought, "You sonofabitch. I *am* a woman and I could always get another job and leave you," and that's exactly what I did.

After law school, I worked at Legal Aid for about four and a half years. Those were the golden years, at the end of the '60s. We were crusading for civil rights. I found I could get into crusading for civil rights because I could identify with what was happening, that things happened to people simply because they were black or because they were Indian. Just like things happened and people made assumptions simply because we were women. I had always understood that people needed to be treated with dignity, with fairness. We were working on civil rights issues, and they were extendable to women's issues. It just seemed logical to me.

I left Legal Aid in 1972 to start my own practice. Well, I was out to save the world. I was going to take these cases . . . *(her voice takes on a slow and heavy emphasis)* . . . those laws came down and I read those laws and I knew what they meant. You weren't supposed to do these things to women any more.

Of course, when those laws were first passed, we knew what they said. *We* knew what they meant because they affected us. But the judicial system did not know what they meant. They found excuses. Even one judge who was wonderful on welfare cases when we were at Legal Aid, he just snubbed his nose at us.

One of my cases, it was one of those "We picked a man for the job, but we'll have her do it for a year while we get him the credentials." So he was in North Dakota getting the credentials and she did the job for a year. Then they brought him back and paid him lots of money to take over the job. So we had a suit on it. Their argument was that she wasn't qualified for the job. Well, we got all through and the judge said, "Well, I'm convinced she is as well qualified as he is, but I believe a corporation should be able to hire anyone they want."

I had *Ridgeway v. United Hospitals.* We won. It was an equal-pay case, and we won. They appealed one of the points to the court of appeals. The court of appeals gratuitously puts a little footnote in there saying, " . . . and we're troubled by the size of the award for attorney's fees." In this footnote, he asked the trial court to reduce the attorney's fees. I mean, God forbid that you should pay an attorney to bring discrimination suits.

And there was the case of the mortician. She was working for a funeral home, she was a qualified mortician, she had her degree. They hired her when they took their secretary out to work at another location. Then the secretary was moved back, so they told my client, "You've got to go now. We don't need two women." That's exactly what they said, we don't need two women here now. And she said, "But I'm not a secretary, I'm a mortician." Well, of course she'd been asked to be secretary as well as mortician because she was a woman. She was allowed to do the mortician work when no one was watching.

You hear those stories and you say, "Well, no wonder you didn't . . ." *(Long pause.)* I became physiologically depressed. I was on medication for four and a half years. It's only recently that I can even talk about some of the cases without getting teary-eyed. I was doing this by myself. I was putting in 14-hour days. I would work 14 hours straight, and I would go home at three or four in the morning. You know, you can't do that for a long time.

I stopped doing discrimination cases in about 1985. At that point I was becoming totally ineffective. I would have a client come in and tell me her employment problem, and I would start crying. Now that's not something a client needs. They need their lawyer to be sympathetic, but they don't need to have their lawyer cry with them. You're spending all your time trying to keep from crying, trying to keep the world in perspective.

It was brought on by a number of things. One was the terribly discouraging situation of the kind of practice I was doing. These employment cases—I'd go in there and I'd crusade, but I began to feel that I was just not competent. I could never win, and even if I did win, then you'd get this crap that the attorney shouldn't get paid. I was struggling financially just trying to keep afloat. One year my tax return showed I made just $700. My father had to support me.

It makes a tremendous difference now to have women on the bench. It means that when we go in the courtroom, when my partners or I go into the courtroom, we're not in a foreign world. Cases are dealt with differently now, even by the male judges. We have precedents, legal precedents. The courts have made decisions on these cases, and the judges are bound by them. They make rulings because the law has been defined, and they now know what it means. They didn't know at that time.

I look back, and I have to say to myself it wasn't a waste of time that you did these things. Regardless of the fact that you seemed to lose one right after another. It wasn't a reflection on you. What had to be done was, those cases had to be lost in order for the education process to begin. In order for the things that have happened since to have happened at all. Because you can't win them in the beginning.

It was a new thing. The racial standard came first. They could see what was not right on race. It took longer for them to see that it wasn't right on women. And they still don't always. We're not there yet. But there's been a big change, a lot of change.

Katherine Weesner

Kathy Weesner is 48. She filed the first sex-discrimination lawsuit in Minnesota after state law allowed such suits. A friend describes her as "the first person to go over and educate the human rights department." Kathy became the first president of Twin Cities NOW in 1970.

I was a computer programmer. My boss didn't like women doing that job because the pay was too good, and he made that known. I got fired. Somebody said to me, "That's against the law." I said, "It is?" That was 1966 or '67. I took it to court, and I remember my attorney saying, "If only we had gotten the liberal judge, we would have won it." I remember being so surprised that it was against the law. Later I learned it doesn't matter what the law says, they can do whatever they want.

I was a good computer programmer. I deserved to make as much money as I was making. After I lost, I got madder. Then a bunch of us got together and formed WAMS, Women Against Male Supremacy.

WAMS went for quite a while. We picketed the newspaper. That was fun. The Help Wanted ads was essentially what we did, and it took a long time. We did it for months and months and months and months and months. Picketing certain days of the week, simply because we didn't have enough people to do it every day. I said, "You wouldn't have a newspaper ad that said 'Help Wanted—Black,' and 'Help Wanted—White.' Why do you have 'Help Wanted—Male' and 'Help Wanted—Female'? That's dumb."

We had lots and lots of meetings with the newspaper management. I remember one of the guys, very fatherly, concerned, said—like he was some type of a clergy concerned about our souls—said "What do your *mothers* think of this?"

We made stickers that said "Stop Sexigated Want Ads." They were sticky stickers. So we went one night and climbed over the—is the statute of limitations gone? *(laughs)*—over the fence of the newspaper and pasted these stickers on the windshields of their trucks, at one o'clock in the morning. So when the papers were ready to load onto the trucks, they had to delay it to get the stickers off.

Of course there weren't any stories about any of this in the newspaper. But we had another meeting after that. Finally the manager of the classified ads said, "We're going to change it. But we're not doing this because of your picketing, we're just doing this because it's a sign of the times," de-dah, de-dah. But before they got it completed, the man died of cancer. His death put a stop to it, yes. And I said, "They'd rather die than change." *(Laughs.)*

So we tried the human rights department, tried to file a complaint. The commissioner said, as I remember, that he would no more accept a complaint from WAMS than he would from the Black Panthers. Someone from the attorney general's office was there. So I wrote a letter to the editor of the paper, indicating that this statement was made, and the chief law-enforcement officer for the state was present and said nothing, and evidently selective law enforcement is okay.

After they printed my letter, the guy from the attorney general's office wanted to see us. I brought a copy of the law and started to read it to him. He said, "I have a copy, thank you." *(Laughs.)* Shortly thereafter, the paper again decided to change. There was a little teeny tiny paragraph back by the TV section saying they were changing their want ads to "Help Wanted" and that there had been some picketing, but that had nothing to do with it.

Some people reacted after it was changed. Some women were angry, because now they didn't know which jobs they could apply for. They said, "It's a waste of our time applying for jobs we're not going to get"—which was true.

Margaret Holden

Margaret Holden, 68, makes a small space on the end of her dining-room table for the tape recorder. The rest of her table, the whole room, the whole house, are full of papers from her numerous women's groups and her collection of railroad memorabilia. She recently retired from her job at the Burlington Northern railroad after 35 years.

I had started with the railroad in 1950, as a clerk calculator. Eventually I was transferred into a management position, and I spent the rest of my time there. I finished a degree in business administration while I was there. The last 17 years, I was an assistant director of my department. Many of the fellows that either started with me or started later got promoted to director. One of them became a vice president.

When I started, the only entry jobs for females were telephone operator, keypunch operator, typist, or calculator operator. The messengers who took the mail from one office to another were office boys. Many of the fellows who were hired as office boys ended up heading departments. In fact the assistant vice president who headed our department had been an office boy.

I never expected to file a suit against my employer. I had given advice to lots of women as a result of my work with WEAL, the Women's Equity Action League, but I never expected to file a suit on my own behalf. Then in 1980 we merged with the St. Louis–San Francisco Railway.

According to the merger plan, the department management in Missouri weren't supposed to be transferred up here. Well, lo and behold, a man from the 'Frisco railroad was promoted to be a director of my department. He knew nothing about the systems we were going to be using. I knew I was better qualified for that position. It was the straw that broke the camel's back.

When I didn't get that promotion, I knew I had six months to make a decision before the time limit for a lawsuit ran out. So I put it out of my mind for six months, I didn't want any emotion to enter into my decision. Then I looked at the facts and was appalled to see how many promotions had happened before. I was better qualified than any of those men. So I saw an attorney.

The suit was filed originally in June of 1981, and came to trial in November 1984. That was fast, compared to some. The final settlement was in June of 1987. It was a class action. My name headed the list of plaintiffs. I had the highest job for a female at the railroad up until then. After the suit was filed, it was amazing the number of women that were brought in from outside for high-ranking jobs. *(Laughs.)*

Some of them recognized why, and later thanked me for it. Also, people within the company got promoted after we filed, and these were women who had been there for years. It was interesting that their experience and education were so suddenly recognized. *(Laughs again.)*

I was in court every day. I made arrangements that I would use my vacation and be over there. If court let out early, I'd come back to the office and put in part of a day, so my vacation stretched out nicely.

I sat there in court in the front row. After the railroad started putting on their people, it was almost as if I intimidated some of them by sitting there. I knew most of these men who were coming in. When the president of the company came to testify, we had a real nice conversation out in the hall before we went into the courtroom and sat on our respective sides of the aisle. The women who came in to testify, they knew that there was a friend in the courtroom as well as their attorneys. I've been told that helped them.

When I sat there and heard some of the stories that these women told, it made me ashamed to be part of the company that would permit that kind of treatment. There was one woman, for example, she was on a track gang down in Nebraska. One summer day, she apparently was wearing a shirt that was buttoned down the front. The foreman took out his knife and cut the buttons off of her shirt and proceeded to cut the brassiere, and forced her to work like that the rest of the day. She was the only female in that gang, but that was the way he took care of things. She would have to go into town, the small town where she lived—the people of course would know about the treatment she received. It was just a bad-news situation.

We ended up with an out-of-court settlement, which I was glad to have. The important thing with a settlement is that it is settled, there is no appeal. Otherwise there would have been appeals for the next one-hundred years. This way we were able to turn the page and get on with our lives.

The settlement included money, but there were also jobs. Promotions from union jobs to management jobs. Also jobs where women were accepted into locomotive-engineer training, dispatcher training, other kinds of training. At one time, the number of women locomotive engineers was zero.

I'm satisfied with the settlement, but I wish I could have had the promotion. By the time the case went to trial I was retired, so I was out of it as far as a promotion was concerned. But the settlement has helped other women. At Burlington Northern, at other railroads, and at other companies.

I have no hard feelings towards Burlington Northern. I'm a stockholder. I love the pension check I get from them, I love the dividend checks I get from them, I'm very interested in their solvency and their profitability, and I have many friends who are still on the payroll. I have good feelings towards them. Burlington Northern provided a very interesting job for a great number of years.

Loretta Frederick

Loretta Frederick is a Legal-Aid attorney in Winona, a small city along the Mississippi River. She has been active in family-law issues, and in the founding of the Women's Resource Center there. Loretta, 40, has an infectious laugh.

I did family law as part of my poverty-law practice. I started in 1978, right after law school. And I was blown away by what was happening in my clients' lives, by the connections between them. It was as if their husbands had all gone to the same school, to learn to say exactly the same things. You know *(her voice becomes sing-song)*, "You're ugly, you're a bitch, you're stupid, you're no good. No one else would want you." All the same things.

It turned out most of these women were battered. Initially I thought "My god, this is awful. This guy, he's bizarre, he needs help." And then I realized that it was a political problem. It wasn't just about individual women with individual bizarre husbands.

You couldn't, unless you were really dense, practice poverty law on behalf of women for more than 10 minutes and not turn into a feminist. I was seeing these women getting jacked around, over and over and over again, and ending up poor with no rights. It's so clearly related to membership in a class of people that the culture doesn't consider worthy of shit.

We went around to other towns and talked about what we were learning about battering and about rape. Everywhere we went, people said, "This isn't going on here. Maybe Chicago or someplace like that. Some place without strong family values." We figured out after a while that we had to go to a group that was already meeting, a church group, or an extension homemakers' group. Then there would invariably be women coming up afterwards and saying, "This is happening to me. What can I do? Where can I go?"

I realized more and more how horrifying was the prospect of being battered and living in the middle of nowhere. On a farm, completely at the whim of the man who controlled you. Couldn't drive anywhere if he didn't give you the car keys. Couldn't walk anywhere, it was too far.

When we first started in 1978, we called ourselves the Battered Women's Task Force. Later we joined hands with the sexual-assault service and others and formed the Women's Resource Center. I remember early days, when we first applied for county money. We made a presentation to the county board. There were members of the county board who thought it was hilarious. They were cracking jokes. One of them said, "Well, all I know is, I smack my wife around once a week, whether she needs it or not." And they all snickered. That's not so long ago. These were public policy makers, government people, who were doling out hundreds of thousands of county dollars.

In 1983, my office decided to try an experimental project. For three months, we tried to fix just three problems. One was providing divorces for low-income people by designing a do-it-yourself book and teaching classes. The second was to fix all the bugs in the order-for-protection system. The third was, I was going to ensure that the child-support enforcement agencies responded to women's needs.

Do-it-yourself child support, do-it-yourself OFPs,* and do-it-yourself divorce. Self-help city. Well, joke, joke, joke, we didn't get done in three months. What a dope. Here I still am—10 years later.

My sister Emily was killed when she was 26. She had a friend named Bill who lived with his mother on a lake. My sister would often go up and spend the weekend there, floating around on the water. They were just friends, they'd never been lovers. Then she fell in love with a man she met at work. She went up one weekend to explain to Bill that she wasn't going to be coming up to the lake again. And she never came back.

At some point the mother had come home. The doors were all locked. And as she walked around to the patio door, she heard this loud boom. When she finally got into the house, she found he had shot himself in the head. Emily's body was lying on the couch. He had shot her in the head with a handgun, and he had been with her body for probably two or three days. It was a classic "If I can't have you, nobody will."

I'd been doing battered women's stuff for five years by then. And it was hard for me to do battered women's work for some time after that. Because I wanted to take women and shake them and say, "Run for your lives, you're going to be dead." I was incredibly overprotective, I couldn't let women make their own decisions at their own speed because I was too panicked.

After her death, I went through the rage that was partly associated with grieving, and part of it was giving up all vestiges of delusion I might have had about safety for women. You realize deep down in your soul how absolutely incapable any one of us is from escaping. And it will happen to you because of your gender and for no other reason. It doesn't matter how much money you've got. Although whether the cops come when you call has something to do with that, what color your skin is, where you live. But in terms of whether or not you're a target, it's something women just live with.

---

* Orders for protection, or restraining orders.

There needs to be more women who go to law school who want to work on battered women's issues. I want there to be seven people doing my job. There needs to be much, much, much more money spent on this. It's really clear that the systems just don't work.

And I want men in the community to start standing up and saying, "This is an epidemic. We need to stop doing this." Did you see that *Women's Press* story last summer? Some reporter went around and interviewed a bunch of prominent men, asking about violence against women and how big an issue this is to them. "Have you ever done anything about this? If someone else did, would you help?" The silence was just deafening.

In the early stage of the Women's Resource Center we did a lot of consciousness-raising as an organization. I remember these godawful weekend retreats where we would do long-term planning, like for six months. *(Laughs.)* We'd go out in the woods to some cabin, 20 women sit around, candlelight, eat organic food, process everything, oh lord, lord. It was so painful. It was also very exciting and intense. That is, in fact, where I learned a lot.

When we first applied for United Way money, what we were doing was perceived as "anti-male." So of course the closest thing that they could figure is that we were lesbians. Our response was, "We are not lesbians!" I am stunned in retrospect that we were that far off. It wasn't even true that none of us were lesbians. Then we went through a period of saying, "It's irrelevant, why are you asking that?" Which was better, but it wasn't near as good as what we ended up with. Now we say, "Fighting homophobia and racism is a necessary part of the work we do to stop violence against women." And when you talk to people like that, they don't know what to say!

We wondered if all our community support would dry up, and it hasn't. We've had some rough times, there's been times when the media coverage has been really negative. But mostly people have grown to respect our willingness to challenge the community's perceptions.

One of the most wonderful things about the center is that college students can go there for internships. In the door walks a 19- or 20-year old, with not a feminist notion in her head. They come in to get some experience to put on their resume, or because they have to do a practicum or something. And they are invariably just thrown into the work because there's so much to do. "Here, take this woman over and get an order for protection." Or, "Here, go to social services and get her AFDC* application right now." "Here, go over to her landlord's and tell him he can't kick her out of there just because her boyfriend came and blew the door down." Boom, boom, boom. And three months, six months, a year later, these kids walk out of there changed women.

This happens over and over and over again. There have been times when it seemed like nothing was going right, when the only thing that sustained many of us was the knowledge that we were churning out feminists, like a little feminist school. *(Laughs.)* Just watching those little clicks going on all the time—it's such a kick.

There's a real advantage to being in a small town, in a community where you know who's making what shake. You can identify where the problems are, what a fix might be. The numbers of people that you have to get to in positions of power are generally manageable. And everyone knows your gig, you know? They already know where you are coming from, whether they like it or not.

And you can have measurable impact on things. If you have dinner with somebody and get them to change their mind, and the next day they do it different, you can see it. It's obvious. It's different from big-city politics where you're a year away from any small change.

I really like the closeness of the feminist community here. In a small town, you know who your sisters are.

Lurline J. Baker-Kent

Lurline Baker-Kent is an assistant commissioner for the state corrections department, where she has served under both Democratic and Republican administrations. She has been an Army wife, a single mother on welfare with four boys, a probation officer, the director of a large YWCA, and a member of Minnesota's Commission on the Economic Status of Women. She is 45.

* Aid to Families with Dependent Children.

I used to be ashamed to be a woman, I used to just hate being black. Why would I want to be something that everybody disliked? Now I like being a woman, I like being black. I had to really understand who I was.

I was born in a rural part of Mississippi. My dad was a minister. My grandfather was also a minister in Mississippi—he got killed by whites for speaking out for equality and fairness. My *dad* got accused of eye-rape, and the Masons shipped him out to Chicago to save his life. Then he went to California, and later my mom and then my brother and I went.

My mother is a green-eyed, very fair woman, and she had relatives that "passed." Our heritage is African American, Choctaw, Chickasaw, and Irish. With that combination we came out very differently in the family. My brother looks more Indian than I do. He has more white features, and I was the darker of the two.

I had cousins that lived in Berkeley, and they could pass. We could not go visit them, particularly me, because I would show we were black. But they could come to the projects where we lived. When the cousins came to visit us, we would take them back home. When my brother and I got to a certain block in Berkeley, my brother would say, "Okay, Lurline, it's time for you to get down in the back seat." So I'd lay down until they dropped Maxine off. And then they'd say, "Okay, Lurline, you can get up now."

I used to be so insecure. I always thought I was the ugliest person in the world, because I had to lay down in the back seat of the car.

I was a rebellious kid. When I was growing up I could always outfight my brother, I could out-wrestle all the boys. My mom wanted me to be the frilly little girl, but every time she'd send me out with dresses they would be torn off. I would just beat up anybody. My dad would let me go anyplace, except I always had to go with my brother. And I rebelled against that. My brother was no protector of me.

I thought I didn't have any skills at all because I couldn't knit, I couldn't crochet. The yarn would get so wet, so balled up, because I was holding it so tight. I just couldn't. I didn't like to cook, I didn't like to sew, I didn't like dolls.

My mom said the time I hurt her feelings the most, she went out and did some day-work, because everybody had a Shirley Temple doll and she couldn't afford to buy me one. So she worked all day, and then when she got off work, she went downtown and searched for this doll, and they didn't have it. So she went across the San Francisco Bay, she took the bus, and she walked all over San Francisco until she found that doll. And when she brought that doll back, on Christmas I opened it up and I just broke down and cried, "Oh Mom, why did you buy me this doll? I wanted guns and holsters."

I had a strong role model, a female principal. If it hadn't been for her, I wouldn't have survived the way that I have. She came to me and said, "Lurline, you're smart, you're good-hearted, and I don't understand why you fight." I grew up to do some things like her.

That's where my spirituality comes in, too. That's what kept me balanced. For myself personally, I had to understand that I was a child of God and I was put here on earth for a purpose. To understand that Afro-Americans were not what I was taught in history.

In history, the only time they would show you an Indian or an African, they would show you an African with bones through his nose, refer to them as savages. You would just sit there in class and go down in your seat, because you knew that your heritage was Indian and African. I had double, triple whammy.

When I was 12, I wanted to be a probation officer. I think because if I hadn't been helped, I probably would have been in the criminal justice system. It was inevitable. I was really a tough kid.

During that time women weren't probation officers, and no blacks. The teachers used to give me wholesaling and retailing and consumer-training classes to take. Never college-preparation classes. My mom only finished the sixth grade; my dad, third. When they would go to school open houses, they never knew what the teachers were gearing me to. Then I went on to junior college, and I said again I wanted to be a probation officer. There, too, they gave me the runaround.

During junior college I got pregnant with my oldest son. So I have had the experience of being a single parent, the welfare system, trying to make it off of that. Then later on I got married and had three more boys. I finished a year of college and then I was doing janitorial work.

Eventually, I fulfilled my childhood dream by becoming a probation officer. I developed a program for women offenders because I was looking at our system. I was finding jobs for men, good jobs, like welding. But they were sending all the women to welfare. I said, "Don't we have any women who need jobs around here?" *(Laughs.)*

When I tried to find jobs for the women, it was a lot harder than for the men. The employers would say, "I don't want any woman with disorderly conduct." But it was okay for a man to have disorderly conduct. And women and girls coming through the system were not getting chemical-dependency treatment like the men were.

The majority of women in the criminal justice system are sexually abused, abused by men. Most of them are in prison because of their male counterparts, pleasing them. They never stole for themselves or their kids, always for the male. That's sad.

I went to the administrator of corrections and I said, "You know, we're going to have to do something for women." And he nodded, he said, "There's no money available . . ." So I called a group of women together and we applied for a federal grant to develop a program. After we developed it, the male probation officers wanted to apply for the director position. But I competed for the job and got it.

The women's movement gave me the freedom to know I was a normal human being. And it's given me the opportunity to be in touch with other feminists, to educate other feminists about the plight of poor women, black women.

You know, I was 35 before I first felt whole. I didn't get my self-esteem until I started working with women, doing some group dynamics. Support groups, starting in college. We'd sit around and talk about the ills of the world and ourselves and our pain and our blackness. Then there were other groups I was mixed in, all white women, talking about the women's side. Being a woman and black, you don't know if you're discriminated against because you're a woman or because you're black or because of both.

I don't get angry anymore, I get more hurt that things don't change. Even with my feminist friends, to get them to understand that black women are women. People always distinguish the two, but women is women.

Women have the power to change the world. Women are the gateway to the world, a child can't even enter the world except by a woman. A woman is a powerful creature. That's where my passion is.

To get women to understand the power of our birth, our gift of entrance to this world. Men don't have that. They want to keep it under control.

White women can try to understand, but they can't feel it, the depths of it. And we have some black women who don't understand or even know that they themselves have been discriminated against. It comes from a denial factor. Back to my cousins passing for white.

Polly Mann

Polly Mann, 66, grew up in the South and came to Minnesota after World War II with her lawyer husband. For many years they lived in small towns near the Iowa border. Known as a peace activist, she was a founding member of Women Against Military Madness (WAMM). Strong traces of the South remain in her voice.

I think my mother was a feminist of sorts. She was divorced, a single parent. She was a very liberated woman. By that I mean she smoked when it was not considered "nice." *(Laughs.)* And she liked to drink, and she played the piano. She was a social worker, but she also played the piano in a jazz combo. She did what she wanted to do, and the heck with what people thought.

I grew up in a household of women. My grandfather died when I was about 10. There were nine of us in that house: my mother and her younger sisters, my great aunt, my grandmother. There was never any question about the importance of women or girls. They were more important than men. Men weren't really quite so nice as women—that was the unsaid message I got.

The feminist part for me has been a gradual process. It's taken me years to put that all together. Just years and years of seeing, and thinking, and reflecting on what's around me. I believe a feminist wants equality, absolute equality. A feminist could be a man or woman who believes in that. But equality does not mean your share of a rotten pie. You've got to want to make a new pie. I'm really not concerned about women who want a piece of a rotten pie, who want to get to the top of the corporation, to exploit others.

For that reason, I have difficulty when people say, "We've got to have a woman in that job." I say, "No, I don't agree with that. It's got to be a woman who has a concern for other women, who is concerned about society, concerned about children, and concerned about the economics of this country."

When my husband was appointed judge, I knew who I was. I didn't care whether I fit the stereotype of the judge's wife. It was never my intention to fit that stereotype. I knew I wasn't going to play bridge, because I'd done my share of that before, and it didn't make me happy. After I got there, I was very discouraged with what I found in the church I belonged to, so I dropped out. That didn't make people happy with me.

And then my involvement about the Vietnam War . . . that was the last straw in that small town. I was very, very visible, and very vocal, and very active in protesting the war. I participated with the student peace group, and I walked in marches with the students. I took a carload of students to the Moratorium in Washington, D.C., I was in Chicago in 1968 during the Democratic convention, I was out in the streets and got gassed. When I got back, there was an article in the newspaper and then there were letters to the editor about my calling it a police riot. And really personal attacks on me.

That was difficult, but it was probably more difficult for my children. They had to suffer through some of this stuff. Even to mention my name in the classroom . . . children don't want their mothers to be different. It was terribly embarrassing for my children. My one daughter dropped out of school, and I know that was part of it. We had several incidents with my kids. I think they suffered during that period.

Women Against Military Madness was started in 1982, after I'd moved to the Cities. An antiwar friend and I were talking about the great incongruities in our society, about how the military runs everything. We got a small group together and we started meeting. We met for probably six months, once a month or so. Then we asked the group to bring their Christmas-card lists so we could send a letter out asking for $100 contributions. We wanted a visible organization. We wanted one that would be active. We wanted an office and we wanted staff.

I think the feminist aspect of WAMM developed over time. We

didn't start off thinking about feminism. Using "women" in the name was all instinctive. I've learned that instinct is really good. We've been programmed to believe that instinct is something to be wary of, like emotions. But I prefer organizing that way rather than white male organizing, drawing a chart.

Do you ever worry about your activism? About cops beating you up, or something like that?

No, not really. At the Seneca army base in New York, we chained ourselves to the fence up there. Then the soldiers came and fingerprinted us, and everything else. No, and I guess the reason I don't worry is because the police are aware of who you are. I'm not going to be treated the same in a jail . . . not anywhere near the same as a young woman, or a poor, black woman.

That's why I believe in going just as far as I can. Using everything I've got to challenge the system. Because I can get by with it. Not always. There have been times when it hasn't worked. I've never been physically mistreated, although there is a form of psychological mistreatment. You get sneered at, and ridiculed. But I accept this, it doesn't really bother me.

I've been arrested, and I've spent time in jail. I spent time in the workhouse here in St. Paul, about six days. That was for sitting in at a senator's office. The judge sent me to jail, but I didn't care—I wanted to see what it was like. The women who worked there, they knew who I was, they knew about WAMM, and I was not treated badly.

I've been arrested four or five times, at least. Usually you're taken into a jail cell, and then you're fingerprinted. And they take your picture. So many times I've been in there with a bunch of WAMM women, and we laugh and talk, and they tell us to shut up. The police are irritated with us because we're taking up their time. They don't think we should be doing what we're doing, that it trivializes their authority or something.

They will tighten handcuffs, and they will be brutal . . . if they're outside the cameras and so forth. But at my age that's never been my experience. One of my younger friends was hit in the chest with a billy club about six months ago, and she has a suit against the city of Minneapolis because she was really hurt. They don't brutalize me, because they're afraid to.

I do what I do because I have to do it. I feel better about myself because I do some of these things. I'm thinking about getting a letter from WAMM to every member of Congress, about Iraq and all that's going on there. It's terrible, and I'm not sure that letter will do a darn thing, but I want to write a letter that says, "How would you feel if your children went to the hospital and there was no money? And no drugs, and they were going to die? Or you didn't have enough food to eat? How would you feel?"

I wouldn't change anything, even the stuff that went on with my kids. That was the saddest part, living in a small town and having your mother held up to ridicule. But I've said this many times, the greatest thing is the wonderful people you meet. When I go to something like the WAMM meeting the other day, and there are so many wonderful women there . . . women I've learned to know and admire. It's moving, I could cry almost. I'm so touched by them and their caring. The opportunity to talk to people at a level that's real. That's important to me.

Most people don't get to that level. When I go to Florida and meet with my sister and her friends, we don't have one real conversation. I smile, and we have a good time . . . but I wouldn't trade that for anything about my life here. And I have so much fun doing what I do. I would probably do it even if I didn't believe in it. *(Laughs.)*

Something I've felt all my life is that I've been so fortunate. I've never in my life been hungry, even during the years of the Depression. I've been pretty healthy. I love to read, and I love to learn. My children have all been bright, although with the usual difficulties. One child died when she was 25. That was terribly tough to go through . . .

But even with that, if I matched my life up with most other lives, I've been so fortunate. In a sense, if I give anything back, it's nothing in comparison with what I've been given. That's what keeps me going.

Witches, Nuns
& Presbyterians

While some women work to change secular systems, others focus on chang-
ing religious institutions. They ask what spirituality would be like if it were
based on women's experiences and what role churches have played in women's
lives. Their answers vary widely.

Drawn to female images of spiritual power, Terri Hawthorne and Antiga
rediscover the Earth Goddess, while Sister Eileen O'Hea embraces the Mother
Church. Kristine Holmgren and Joy Bussert left the church altogether before re-
turning to pastoral positions. Holmgren remembers her childhood attraction to
the church as a place of stability and privacy, while Bussert is inspired by the sol-
idarity of church tradition. Whether reformers or separatists, these women find
ways to incorporate reverence for women into their spiritual lives.

Terri Berthiaume Hawthorne

I don't think there is enough honoring of the time and energy it
takes women to get traditional women's skills—parenting skills and
homemaker skills. I'm one of those feminists who love to cook, and I
still maintain a huge garden. I loved homemaking. I was the mom who
had the Halloween parties and the birthday parties and the neighborhood kids for backyard ball games.

*In the early 1970s, Terri Hawthorne was a Catholic and living in the sub-
urbs with her husband and four small sons. She is now a teacher and author and
offers workshops on ritual, art, spirituality, celebrations, and women's studies.
She is 50.*

During those early years in the 1960s, my church was one of the
few places that was interested in me. I was in a sort of cocoon out in
the suburbs. I didn't have a car, so I really was isolated. Like many
women, I found a great deal of help in the church. They would provide free child care, and there were seminars, and there were ideas that
were intellectually stimulating. They wanted my services to teach religious education. There were book groups and discussion groups—it
was a "home place" for me.

In 1972, our women's group at St. Thomas started this six-week series called, "Women: Who Are We?" The group still meets, although
now it's only a birthday group. *(Laughs.)* In the beginning, we were
looking for a place, I think a personal place, for us to talk about ourselves and about ideas and about our lives. In this group, our kids went

to school together, we had joint baby-sitting, we went to lunches together. We helped each other when we had new babies. Our lives were
intertwined in many, many different ways.

Our group differed from the traditional altar societies. We were the
study group, the self-focused ones, doing personal-growth things—and
social actions on women's issues. Later we were known as the real liberal far-out feminists. Then, some of the other women got afraid to
join us.

In the beginning, the word "feminist" wasn't so much what we
were worried about, but . . . one of the big problems for me is how
being pro-woman is interpreted as being anti-men. That was seen real
early in the group. Because we were pro-woman, we were seen as anti-
men. We were all married, living traditional lives, and raising sons and
daughters and living with men. Almost all these women are still in first
marriages. I've been married for 31 years—to the same person.
(Laughs.)

I got angry being the token feminist at parties, where the men
would say certain buzzwords to set me off, and then would think it was
funny. Fairly early I learned I wasn't going to fall for that. But I don't
identify with anger real strongly. I don't think there is enough written
up about long-term marriages, and how feminist marriages survived.
In my suburban circle we were all living in long-term relationships
with men, and we weren't anti-male at all. We simply wanted a more
equal partnership, both in personal relationships and in our relationship
within our church.

At about the same time, I became interested in the Equal Rights
Amendment, and my group decided to investigate that. So I started
calling my church and asking questions. I knew my church was not in
favor of it, but I couldn't figure out why. I went to the legislative hearings, and then I called the diocese to see if they could give me some
literature, or some information on why this was a problem. And they
told me, basically, "Drop it." They said there was no literature and it
was enough that the bishops were saying it was not appropriate. I was
supposed to just believe them.

At this point, probably with the media and the focus on women's
issues and on women's rights, I began to be aware that the church that
had provided me a home was also the place that taught the sexist codes.
The church passed them from generation to generation, and did it

mostly through women. Women are responsible for teaching those codes to both boys and girls. There was that incongruity between the "home place" for women and the place where the sexist messages were passed.

A few years later, we started doing innovative women's rituals. Our women's group at St. Thomas wanted to bring the sense of community and warmth and camaraderie we were feeling together into our spiritual place. A ritual is not much different from a birthday party or a Halloween party, that kind of thing. I think most people have a lot more creativity than they know. Ritual is really a lot about art. You have prayer, but then you put it into art forms. You can use music and dance and visual images.

It all coincided with the "home" masses and the other things that were happening in the early '70s, with the opening up in the Catholic Church. The effects of Vatican II were really being felt, and our priest was very open and creative in his worship. We would find poems and prayers and write songs, and then he would add wonderful little things to what we were doing. He would let us have almost complete control.

We were having a wonderful time and, because we were all mothers, we started doing things like Mother's Day masses at the church. Then when our kids were fussing about going to church and so on, we started having a series of children's masses. In one of those we did a "velveteen rabbit" mass. We had this little home mass in the summer, with all our kids in shorts, and with real rabbits there, and had this wonderful, wonderful service.

Our women's rituals were . . . in the beginning, we were just combing the scriptures for things that were relevant to women. Positive images. And then we would maybe put an Adrienne Rich poem into the mass instead of the traditional reading. Like on Mother's Day, we might pick honoring of women, but we wouldn't do just the sentimentalized version. We might pick a poem that talked about how hard it was, and how you were sometimes frustrated and angry at your children.

Women in my art circle found the Goddess in '75. I ended up studying creation-goddess myths from all over the world. I mean, this information is pretty commonly known today, even among people who aren't doing a lot of spirituality. But back then it was all brand-new. There might be one woman artist's name in an art book but no pictures. So we'd have to take this tiny fragment, and track it back in multiple ways. It wouldn't be in the textbooks, but if we went back to the archaeological finds, then it would be just everywhere.

Most of the early Goddess scholarship was done by art historians, not by regular historians. That's not accidental, because the texts, the words, the interpretations are from a male perspective. But the images alone allow multiple interpretations. I studied creation myths, another friend would be doing Egyptian goddesses, another one would be doing African, and somebody else would be . . . we were all pooling this stuff. It was collective in a way that was really unusual, and very exciting.

We started to do more earth-based traditions somewhere out of this growing Goddess awareness. We started, well, passing babies in a circle and blessing them, and a lot of things that were old ways of doing home-based rituals. We began to celebrate the earth—to ritualize our beliefs about ecology and ecofeminism. At some point, some of us found that there was a European history of earth-based traditions called witchcraft or wicca. Some people began actively researching and reclaiming that. It's very closely connected to Native American spirituality. Wicca can mean willingness to bend or it can mean wise woman.

One of the exciting things that's happening now is that I get asked to go out all the time and do these one-time evening presentations. And there are *hundreds* of little grassroots women's spirituality groups, all over the city, and all over the country. This is where women are getting together, becoming more earth-based. Spirituality has always been—has always asked—the same questions as science. Where do we come from? And how do we get here? What are we? And what are we about? Looking at beliefs from many cultures and times challenges the "one right way" of monotheism.

These small groups are happening all over, in surprising places. Most of the groups are between 10 and 20 people. I think they've replaced the consciousness-raising groups, but there hasn't been much written about them. I had a small group at my house the other night— a cross-section, some of them are homemakers and witches and some of them are Catholic nuns and Protestant ministers. A wide spectrum of people—and most of them have background in ritual.

Ritual is a way to use your creativity. It makes people feel good to

use their creativity. Singing and drumming and dancing and playing together is fun. It's more a celebration of that life force—that life force is
in you and in me and in the rocks and in the flowers and in all of
what's around us. A lot of what we're doing is going back and taking
from that tribal period when we were more connected to the earth. To
take some time out and just sing and play and celebrate renews me for
more political kinds of work.

There's an openness and a freedom there. Most of why we're doing
it is because we have so much fun. Have you ever sat in a drumming
circle and just drummed, even though you thought you couldn't drum,
and danced and moved? You probably haven't done that since you were
about five years old!

Because I'm around feminists so much, I'm often struck that—
when I move into non-feminist worlds, I'm struck by how differently
I see the world. I'm struck by how often we're taught to see the world
from a male perspective, and how radical it is to see the world from a
woman's perspective. I think the people who are involved in both spirituality and politics have run up against a wall, the patriarchal wall, that
has forced them to either open their eyes or to go way backwards.

Now when I go back to the Catholic Church, the male God-
language is just so overwhelming to me. Feminists started by objecting
to not being part of "all men," and by the time that changed, we were
objecting to all-male God-language. Now we object to hierarchical
terms, like "Lord" and "King." Once you start seeing in a new way,
everything begins to change. And the more you think about it, the
deeper it goes.

Many women today still don't have a forum, a place in the world.
Every once in a while I think, "How have women survived?" There's
so much oppression of women, and we're taught to pretend it isn't
there. It's been said that we're taught to wear blinders, like horse blinders. We go through life stuffing the things that hurt women, and not
looking at them. Then one day the door flies open. I think that's
maybe why more women aren't feminists, because it's so painful to
look at the misogyny and the hatred of women. The un-love, the hate
in the culture. So for me, feminism isn't about hating men—it's about
loving each other.

Kristine M. Holmgren

Kris Holmgren, 43, is a Presbyterian minister with a small, rural congregation. A graduate of an Ivy League seminary, she also writes short stories. Kris is a born mimic, changing her voice and body language for each person she quotes.

Everybody has to have a place where they can be private and have it be okay. I see the church as a place like that. I decided when I was about seven years old that I was going to be a minister. My mother said, "You mean you want to be a Sunday-school teacher." I said, "Absolutely not."

Usually I only went to Sunday school and then went home. But once when I was about 10, I went to worship. There was this man leading the service, and I thought he was wearing a dress. I remember looking at him and thinking, "He looks funny!" because my dad was this big macho guy with dirty hands who barked at everybody, slammed things around the house, slapped people around. He was a "real man." This guy standing up front, he sang songs, he dressed like a woman. I thought, "This isn't right."

The ushers were men, too. I came home and said to my mother, "They had *men* doing these things." I was baffled by it from the very beginning. I thought it was a female thing, it really should be women doing it.

Recently, my daughter went with her friend to a different church. She came home and said, "Mom, you never told me they let *men* be ministers!" She had the same attitude about it, I love it.

When I was 16, my father decided my mother was mentally ill and tried to have her committed. She was 11 years older than him. I think he was tired of her. One day I came home from school and my mother was in a straitjacket in the living room. They carried her off to the hospital. My mother passed all the sanity tests and was released from the hospital, but my father refused to live with her. So for a while, I lived with my father and an older sister, while my mother lived with a grown brother.

That was the beginning of the destruction of my family. My mother came home when the divorce was filed, and my father and my sister moved out. My mother said, "Who are you going to live with?" And I said, "I go with the house." Because the only stability I saw was real estate.

The first night she was back, I went up to the bathroom and closed the door and looked in the mirror. I said, *"They* are crazy. *You* are just fine. You are going to be okay, everything's going to be okay."

My father started drinking again after that, then married a much younger woman. He died four years later. A lot of my stories have these gentle fathers who take little girls by the hand and walk them out to the end of the sidewalk on Christmas Eve and look up at the stars. That guy was never there for me.

My mother was the classic displaced homemaker. She had no train-ing, so she worked as a maid. And I started working full time when I was 16, eight hours a night any place I could get a job, to help pay the mortgage because we didn't have any money.

During that time I had some good friends in my youth group at church. These kids knew nothing about my family. They only knew what I presented on Sundays, which was always this fun-loving, hap-py, everything's-fine-thank-you-very-much kid. All the kids in high school knew what was happening, all about my family, but people at church did not. So church was a nice place to be.

I got married after my sophomore year of college, quit school and moved to California with him. Eventually I found out from other men that he was gay, and I divorced him. When I saved enough money, I came back and finished college.

I saw him five years later, and then I realized, this guy is dead inside. He was like hamburger meat where there should have been a soul. He was a cold-blooded man, and I never knew that. I thought he was funny and sweet. But *I* was the one who was sweet and funny, and I just projected all that on him because he was a blank slate.

It was after that second betrayal that I started to think about some of the things that were in the air then. This was 1970 or 1971. I started to think about males and females and privilege and poverty and all the things that happened to the women in my family. I thought, "What is this? We follow these people, we trust them, and when they drop us— they drop us in the middle of nowhere." I was in the middle of California, I had very few friends there.

I started speaking the language of feminism about that time, though I didn't know it until men started calling me a "women's libber." I still didn't really consider myself a feminist until I got to seminary, in 1975. That's when the pie broke right open in the middle and all the blackbirds flew away.

When I was in seminary, less than a third of the students were women. About half of the women were in the education program, only a few were looking for degrees in the ministry. And of that group, I'm not sure how many are still in the ministry. I can probably name about five women I know now who are still in the church.

At seminary, there was something called "sherry hour," afternoons from three o'clock to five o'clock. It was in a men's dorm. At first I thought, I don't want to go drink sherry, it's nothing to me. But then they started bringing in these heavy-duty Presbyterians, like this famous guy who graded the ordination exams. Well, I wanted him to know my name, so I went to sherry hour.

I walked into the room where he was, poured myself a glass of sherry and sat down. A senior came up to me and said, "I'm sorry, Kristine, you'll have to leave. Women aren't allowed here unless they're escorted by a man." I was just amazed. So I went outside the building. I went up to this man and asked him to escort me in. So he walked me in. Because I was walked into the hall with a man, I could stay—even though the man left. Bizarre.

I took a course on liberation theology. The male professor was really into Jungian psychology. This whole concept of the animus and anima, male and female within each person. It still to me smacks of the individual and the "other." And the other is always the female: the passive, the receptive, the emotional. It aggravated me, these men telling me what it was to be female. This was all woven into theology.

Part of this professor's "liberation theology" was the idea that to begin the journey to wholeness you must break from the mother. I would say, "Why should I break from the mother when I'm female?

I should break from the father." "Well, you have to come to the Father." "No, I'm *not* going to the Father." We'd go around and around. At the end of the term, I wrote this massive paper, completely destroying his idea that religious reality comes when we find the Father God. Well, I got "B+ . . . See me."

I met with him. He said, "I enjoyed your paper, it was brilliant, you documented your sources, we just need to spend more time together. I feel if we spend more time together you can understand what I'm trying to bring to you when I talk about the Father God." It finally hit me. I said, "You're a married man." He said, "My wife and I have an understanding." I said, "I'm not interested." He said, "Then you're getting a B+."

I had no vocabulary to describe that. This stuff made me crazy. These things happened to me in seminary over and over again. I took them to the appropriate people and nothing was ever done. So finally I went to the president of the seminary and said, "I'm going crazy, I need to get out of here."

I finished seminary through independent study back in the Midwest, where I set up a job as college chaplain. Later I spent three years as an assistant pastor at a suburban church, but again I ran up against male expectations. I left the church and worked in nonprofit organizations for a number of years.

Then I returned to the ministry at my present church. In this setting, I'm the only minister. There's nobody looking over my shoulder except the people in the church. When they criticize me I listen, because I figure they have something I should listen to.

Every Sunday I'm in the pulpit interpreting things for people. They can choose to accept or reject my ideas, but they have to hear them if they come to my church on Sunday. There's a little glamour, ego, theater . . . that I really like.

Eileen P. O'Hea

Eileen O'Hea, 56, is a Sister of St. Joseph of Brentwood, New York. During the 1980s she served the priests and seminarians at Maryknoll Seminary as spiritual director—the first woman in that role. A family therapist and psychologist, she is the author of Woman: Her Intuition for Otherness, *a book on Christian meditation.*

During my early days, the structure of religious life was very tight, very strict. We were bound by rules and regulations. The habit we wore goes back to the 1600s in France. It was the dress of the widows. With all the devastation of the wars, groups of women gathered together to do what needed to be done. A lot of the ministry started with prison work, and with the sick and dying. Groups of women gathered together, and then they became more formal groups with names, like the Sisters of St. Joseph.

I'd never wanted to be a nun. I had never thought about it as a child or teenager. I was all set to go to college, but I had a friend who was thinking about entering the convent. One day I began thinking, "Do *I* have a call to this?" I went to one of the high-school sisters and explained my dilemma, and she had me pray for a period of time. It was a confusing time. And one morning—I woke up one morning and had this clear understanding that that's what I was meant to do. The confusion left and didn't return. I entered the convent in 1954, two months after my high-school graduation.

The habit, when you are young, wearing it, you know . . . I remember when I first received the habit, it was such a nice feeling. You felt whole. You felt like you were good. You had all these images of other people who had worn the habit, how you had looked up to them, and how they were so good. But it separated you from people. Even when you went home to visit your mother and father. They treated you differently. In some ways you probably liked that when you were young, but as you got a little more mature, you could see . . . There was always a fuss, you were always treated with too much deference at home.

In the '60s, everything changed. Everything was up for grabs. We had many friends who decided to leave the convent and get married. And every time one of them left, you'd question your own vocation. What am I doing here? If they're not staying, why am I staying here? Did I enter for the right reason? With all the turmoil, with Vatican II, everything was being seen differently.

Before this time, we weren't encouraged to question. We believed, because of the faith of our parents. Now, everything was up for question. The way you prayed. What religious life was. And what it should be. Change in the habit wasn't just changing the way you dressed, it was changing the way of being with people.

Then you questioned who God was. Everything you believed. Was God a judge? Was God a father? This was a big switch, because the image of God as handed down to us was always God as Father. For me, a relationship model of life began to emerge. It was no longer just keeping right rules and doing good things. What became central to my life was how I related to people, and if I really cared about people. It became a model for prayer as well.

During this time, I'd say I was an observer of the women's movement. Subliminally conscious of it and maybe living it out, but not claiming it for myself. Gradually, more and more, the women I was living with were discussing it. We weren't owning it, but we were discussing it. But within the larger community, there were people who were pushing. They saw and they knew that a male model was being perpetuated in the church. It wasn't something I owned immediately or easily, but as I got older I began to see the injustice.

It seemed to me that there was so much happening within the church that was political. We began to take some stands on issues, some groups of religious women began to act together against injustice. This was new for us, we even had members of our congregation arrested. We were trying to find our way, to find out what we could do to influence the structures which were oppressive. But we operated with consensus and it wasn't always easy to have everybody agree on what should be done, to have the whole group agree so you could say, "The Sisters of St. Joseph of Brentwood . . ."

Did the women's movement cause the changes in religious communities? No, I don't think so. I think there was movement within the religious communities, and it paralleled what was happening outside. I think it was happening simultaneously. And it just couldn't be stopped.

The way I remember it, there was never any sense of separation, because we *were* the women's movement. We were women who were experiencing the same things. It was never, "This is what is happening to *us,* and that is what is happening to *them.*" We were the women's movement. We just happened to be women in the church.

For a while I was even suspicious of saying I was a feminist, because I didn't want to be labelled with some of the anger I saw in the feminist movement. So I held back on that. I had all the same beliefs, but I didn't put that label on myself. Then I worked in a seminary, and in the beginning I was the only woman there who was doing spiritual direction and therapy. Everything was male, and I became very conscious of the differences in how we saw and experienced things. I also became conscious of the old-boys' club, and how it worked behind the scenes.

At that point it was unusual to have a woman in the role of spiritual director for priests. In the beginning it was very difficult for me, not because they were male, but because nobody knew me. I was in this office with nothing to do because I wasn't a teacher, and therefore I wasn't meeting the men who were students. Then finally I was invited to take someone's place in giving a lecture. I lectured on "Guilt"—and then I had all the business I could use. *(Laughs.)*

Maryknollers were a good group of people to be with, and they were probably one of the most liberal groups. I worked with them from about 1979 until 1988. It was a great learning experience. I was a woman working with all males, although later they had more women there. They opened their programs to lay missionaries, both men and women, so they were continually dealing with . . . The women's movement kept rising up to confront these very male structures. The men were constantly being confronted by women there in the seminary about the male ways of perceiving things.

Over time I began to claim myself as a feminist. I began to see the oppression that existed in the church as well as in society. Even though the church has said that sexism is a sin, it continues to be sexist in many areas with little consciousness that it's doing so. To this day, to try to get to a liturgy where you sense that women are not being excluded is very difficult. Changing to inclusive language, which would be a very simple thing to do, is still not happening to the extent it should. To say "All people" instead of "All men," or to use inclusive language, is important to me.

When I was at Maryknoll, during the last two years I was there, the pope was tightening things up. He thought things had become too liberal since Vatican II, so there was an investigation of seminaries to see if they were measuring up to Vatican standards. Three representatives of the Vatican were sent. Two bishops and a priest came to study the seminary. During their week's stay, they never interviewed me. They interviewed the faculty, but they deliberately didn't interview me. I felt dismissed and discounted.

What came out of their report was that women should not be in the role of spiritual directors to priests. When I questioned this, I was told that only a priest could understand the spiritual journey of another priest. So I said, "Then no priest should ever counsel a couple who are married?" *(Laughs.)* But I didn't get a clear response to my question.

As a child I was always taught—and I never realized how deep this was within me—we were taught and we saw the church as Mother Church. It wasn't a very conscious thought, it was just a way of referring to the church. As I sat and listened to the bishop's report, and heard my role dismissed, I felt like a child being slapped in the face. It touched such deep levels in me. It was like a trauma had happened on some level of my identity. I don't ever remember anything touching me the way that did. And this from the church I called Mother.

For the next three days I was just stunned. I remember being down, very down. And then I remember thinking, "How can the church truly be Mother unless I am part of what the church should be?" That was a moment of great freedom for me because—I *am* the church. It was the first time I claimed that. The church is not the structure, or these rules, or the hierarchy. The church is this group of believing people, and I am that church.

This church is very dear to me. It has, for me, the greatest of resources. What happened over the years is that it took on sets of decrees and moral codes and ways of worshipping that in many ways, and over the years, no longer represent the initial experience—that is, the experience of Christ's presence among us. I think this is what many women are calling the church back to—an experience of human liberation and celebration.

The older I get, the more I see the real truth and wisdom within the church. This deposit of faith is a real treasure to me. It gives hope and meaning to life. It invites us to be truly human . . . and I'm not going to give that up.

Joy K. Bussert

Joy Bussert, 40, is a Lutheran pastor. She comes from a long line of clergy— her great-grandmother had a theological degree, her great-grandfather and grandfather were both prairie preachers, and her father was a Lutheran minister. Her mother died when Joy was eight, and her father raised five daughters and a son as a single parent. She says the one thing most valued in her household was the right to be a nonconformist, the right to think independently.

When I was in college, I threw out my childhood. Everything I had grown up with as a clergy daughter was thrown into question. When I became a feminist, and studied feminism, I threw out religion for a couple of years. I didn't go. I didn't care. I saw religion primarily as a problem for women, not part of the solution.

I just chucked it. But there was always this interest in the question of God, and the question of ethics, in questions of justice. I knew that somehow the politics of the women's movement were related to questions of values and of ethics. Not just what you do politically, but also why. Why are women to be valued? Why care about the quality of life for women? Why care about justice and equality and mutuality? I knew I was articulating ethical categories, not just political categories—although the language is very much the same.

I wanted to study theology and I went off to Yale Divinity School. There I was introduced to feminist theology. Until that time I'd only read feminist literature. This was in 1974. It was the era of William

Sloane Coffin, and Mary Daly, and Rosemary Radford Reuther. There were a number of feminist thinkers who were surfacing at the time. I became coordinator of the women's center there at Yale, and that took me even further into the feminist movement.

Yale was very much a male institution. I mean, we just knew that when we got there. You could feel it, you could see it. All the pictures on the wall were men. The faculty were all male except for two women.

At that time, there was a shift in theological thinking. From thinking from the tradition to thinking from the experience of a people. So African-American theologians said when you begin to do theology, you don't start from what the tradition has said about theology, about the nature of God. You begin with your experience as an African-American people in this culture. It's a different direction. You move from the experience of a people to questions about God, the nature of people, the nature of the human community.

Then feminists came along and said, "Here's a model for doing theology for us." And they began asking questions out of the experience of being female in this culture. That meant they questioned the maleness of God, they questioned what theologians had said about women, about men, about the family. They went back to the scriptures and said, "We're going to take our own questions to it and reinterpret it according to our questions." That's a whole different way of doing theology.

So I went to Yale in 1974 looking for ways to ask the questions I wanted to ask. I didn't plan to be a pastor. I wanted to go off and study theology and literature—feminist theology and feminist literature.

At that time, I didn't know any ordained women. I didn't think of being ordained until I got there. But there was this one woman who was on the faculty who was an ordained woman—Joan Forsberg. It was in October of my first year there that she preached, and presided in chapel. I saw this woman in clergy vestment, standing in front of the church, articulating . . . It was just . . . I can still remember, my knuckles, my hands on the pew in the chapel at Yale . . . just shaking.

It was something I'd never seen. It flipped something in my unconscious. At some kind of visual level, symbolic level. 1974. Joan Forsberg. And I remember the other women in the chapel at the time.

Afterwards we all sat down off to the side of this big huge pulpit—and just started to cry.

It had to do with having a model, having a visual model, that none of us had ever had. There she was. There she was. I know that so much of this is symbolic. I know that there's something powerful in the ritual and the symbolism that alters and changes things. But why, I don't know. I don't know how these things happen. But that's why I say my understanding of God includes the feminine, and She is at work.

When I was in seminary, of the other women who were there, I would say that about a third of them were post-Jewish and post-Christian. They had thrown that out and had moved into more alternative kinds of spirituality. They were looking at Goddess traditions. They were saying that the traditional Jewish and Christian—the mainline—traditions were just not salvageable for women. And they threw it all out and they went into the more alternative women's spirituality.

And then another third of us said no. We were not so much spiritual feminists, we were more social-political feminists. We said we are social and political people, and we are part of a history. There were women like Elizabeth Cady Stanton, there were women way back in the early whatever, who were writing about theological questions. We wanted to stand in some sort of historical solidarity with them. Therefore we would stay within the tradition because our grandmothers and mothers were all part of that tradition. We want to look for ways to reform it, find ways to change it.

And then there was the other third who said, "What problem?"

So we were all there together, in this male-dominated institution. Three different camps. And when we come back for reunions, we've all stayed about the same. I don't know why that is. Perhaps some people think more historically and politically, and others think more about spirituality. I don't know. But the divisions are still there. You read feminist theology today—and now 50 percent of the books being sold in theology are feminist theology—and the divisions among women are still there. Those three divisions: those who want to reform it, those who are more separatist, and those who still don't get it.

I think, in the '70s, I felt more hope than I do now. We were caught up in the momentum of the times, and there was so much more visibility. Back then, the women students were raising these issues, doing our own thing, meeting in clusters with the two feminist faculty we had. It was like a little pocket of something, in the midst of this big institution. A little alternative pocket. But there was so much hope back then. We thought it was just a matter of time. It was the liberal mythology that you get out and you educate and you work hard. You just point out the injustice and something will happen.

I was a parish pastor for two years. At that time, the whole battered women's movement was really at its height, in the late 1970s. They'd gotten shelters, they'd gotten funding for data collection, and they'd been doing training with lawyers, with doctors, with police, with nurses, and county attorneys—but they kept running up against clergy out there. They knew that somehow they had to get to the religious community.

In 1978—no, 1979—they convinced the governor to hold a statewide conference on religion and domestic violence. I went to that. I got myself invited somehow. And thought the kingdom had come on earth—that it's really going to happen, in the religious community. From that there was funding to do training of the clergy on violence, and I got the job.

I don't think any of us knew what we were doing at the time, except we knew something had to be done. I really took my cues from the movement, from the women who were running programs for battered women and sexual assault. They knew they were running up against something out there when they hit the churches, but they didn't know exactly what it was.

. We devised this plan—it was interfaith, ecumenical—we'd bring the Protestant clergy, the Catholic priests and sisters, and the rabbis together, and form committees to develop an event for their particular location. We had 26 conferences all over the state. Also in the African-American community, the Hispanic community, and the Native American community.

But first I spent nine months sitting in the shelters and the rape crisis centers listening to the women. I went out with my journal and said these are the people who know best what the religious issues are. I interviewed women in shelters and centers, and said, "What theological issues, what spiritual issues, came up for you? Or are relevant for you? What experience have you had with your churches?"

Back then, you know, the clergy thought the women's movement was breaking up the family. And the women's movement thought the clergy were the patriarchal problem. And my goal was to get them to talk to each other. If you could find a handful of clergy out there, in towns all over the state, who caught on, then you had something to work with. And if there were one or two women who worked in the shelters who would be willing to talk to the clergy, you'd try to get them to talk to each other.

The clergy were often resistant, very much so. The rabbis were always supportive, so we had the Jewish community with us. But the Catholic community was just an incredible bastion. They didn't know what we were talking about. So I worked a lot with Catholic sisters. There were key Catholic sisters all across the state. And there were some Catholic priests—not the hierarchy, not the bishops—although the monsignor who headed up the Catholic conference was very supportive. But he had trouble working with me, a woman who was ordained. I think the ordination issue was always in the way. And the pro-choice issue was always standing in the way. There was resistance because they saw the whole violence issue as somehow contributing to divorce and breaking up the family. They wanted to hold the family together.

With the Protestant community, often the debates got around to the Bible. You would run up against the conservative fundamentalists, the Jerry Falwell types out there, and they're all over the place. They'd be upholding these traditional Biblical notions about the family. They were the real far-right, conservative fundamentalists. I ran into them all the time. They were quoting scripture, but I just took them on. I knew the Bible as well as they did, so I'd just take them on.

Mainline Protestants, the mainline Presbyterians, Methodists, Lutherans, Congregationalists—they were more supportive. Where we got into things with them was more around alternative images of God. They were a little looser about divorce and separation, and they said if there was violence in the family, we need to address this. They were a little easier to deal with than either the Catholics or the far-right fundamentalists. It was the Jewish community and some of the mainline Protestants who were the most receptive.

I was kind of a bridge person. The women's movement saw the church as the problem, and the churches saw the feminists as the prob-

lem. I wanted to get a conversation going between them. That was the
only way I saw. Let them fight, get them to debate, get it out in the
open. At the time, I thought we'd go through this for a couple of
decades, and then we'd be through with it.

I had a grandfather and a great-grandfather who were circuit rider
preachers on the prairies, and a great-grandmother who finished a theological degree. She came back to Minnesota and started schools,
which was probably the only thing a woman could do back then. She
was a scandal in the family, although I always knew about her.

My feminism is rooted in that history. I have a whole sense of
being rooted in a history which started long before me, and which is
going to go on long after me. My task is to figure out what to do right
here and now. You can't just ignore what our grandmothers and great-
grandmothers did. Nor all those women who never had an opportunity to do anything, because of the culture or because of the society. I
think they're still working, they're still alive.

In theological terms, we talk about the communion of saints; we
talk about the great crowd of witnesses. I believe they are out there.
Like muses. I've often had the experience when I'm writing that there
are muses with me, and I know there are women from history who are
orchestrating this still. I really believe that.

And now—although I don't see the same kind of hope that I saw
back then and I struggle more with periods of despair—I now have
much more of a sense that what we do now is going to pay off in the
future. Probably long after our lifetimes. There's something theological—we call it eschatological hope—that what we do now will make a
difference for generations to come. Long after we are dead. There's a
dimension of faith to it, or I wouldn't be able to keep going.

Antiga

I wanted clergy credentials as a witch, and I got them through a national group called Covenant of the Goddess. So I'm now registered clergy in Minneapolis, I'm quite official. There are some women in town who practice the craft and don't want to call it that. There's a big discussion about whether to use the word "witch," because it has a lot of negative associations purposefully put there by the oppressor. I have chosen to use the word "witch" because nothing says "powerful woman" quite the way the word "witch" says "powerful woman."

Antiga is a 61-year-old witch. Her front porch smells like the sea, with baskets of seashells everywhere and a sign: "This home is protected by the Goddess." She was raised Presbyterian and then converted to Judaism before coming to the craft.

In 1963, I had a husband who was doing what he was supposed to do, which was make money. That was his contribution to the family. Here I was with four children, I had four children within six years. The one thing I had in the way of contact with adults was a book group. I looked forward to it all month. We were doing Simone de Beauvoir, *The Second Sex,* and he didn't want me to go. He tried his very best to keep me home. Also, I had almost a master's degree in psychology, and I wanted to go back to school and finish it. That was not permitted, he said absolutely no.

Finally I went back to graduate school in linguistics. It was the only department that they would allow people to go part time. I had to go part time because I had four kids, and I had a huge amount of entertaining to do for my husband, for his career.

At one point I made a very important decision: I decided to have my own friends. Up until this time, my friends had been wives of my husband's colleagues. I got divorced in 1977, a few years later.

Around then, I went to the Arts Core at St. Catherine. It was a program in feminist art, with some dynamic teachers. Sister Judith Stoughton— she's dead now and I really miss her. She was such a guiding light . . . This was a turning point in my life. I'd been in feminism and I'd done a lot of public speaking and I was incredibly articulate *(laughs),* but the Arts Core was more about my personal life.

We met from 8:30 to noon every day. We would do consciousness raising on Monday on a topic like "mother," or "father," or "me" . . . you name it. Then we would make what we called "quick art." We did all sorts of things: wrote songs, sculpture, drawing, painting, we did collage, performance, everything we could think of. A lot of what came out when we did our stuff on "mother" was incredible fury at our mothers. Several other women and I, we did a whole week on being a mother and what that was like. We wrote a mother's bill of rights.

Then Sister Judith set us this task: study any culture all over the world that you choose, but go to the time before patriarchy was entrenched. There was very little published on this in 1975, 1976. We would read a whole book just to get a footnote. A couple of people studied Africa, I did the Mediterranean, somebody did Chinese footbinding, Celtic Isles . . . We had women studying all over the world and everywhere—before patriarchy—there was the Goddess. Even though I knew something about the Goddess before then, to see that it had been worldwide and totally eliminated by patriarchy with brutal force . . . The brutal suppression of Goddess reverence was hard to take.

I did not expect the force of the backlash against this program at the college. There were some male faculty people who were resentful of the space, the money that was coming in for this—and we were doing raw work. We were just putting our pain out there. One woman did a thing on rape. This huge big roll of butcher paper, it was as big as the wall of this room. It was her experience of rape: words, images. It was too much for the college. The program was scheduled to be two years, but at the end of the first year it was eliminated and never spoken of again.

Out of the Arts Core came a group celebrating the new moon. The new moon is an ancient, ancient women's festival. Because in the days when we were tribal, women in a tribe would bleed together on the new moon. That's when you don't see the moon, the dark of the moon. The new moon festival had been incorporated into the Jewish tradition. Two Jewish women got it started here, and I knew from the moment I got involved that this was for me. This was so important to me that I kept that group going for six years.

Underlying everything we did in the new-moon group was, "What would spirituality be if it was based on women's experience?" We would tell our stories, and support each other when painful things came up, like divorce. And of course we all sat around in a circle.

The circle form is very important in feminism and in women's spirituality, because it reflects the reality that nobody is above some-body. In patriarchal religion you always have the preacher standing up on a platform higher than everybody else. But we'd sit around in some-body's living room just like this. We'd do an altar, we'd have flowers, we would sing.

For me, divination—which is very much a part of witchcraft—is the process of listening to my own inner voice. Feminism for me is helping women get to our authentic true self. Helping create the setting in which that can happen. When we plan a ritual, it may be very loose. Our last solstice, we didn't have any plan. We just got there and asked everybody, "What do you want to do?" It can be quite planned, with a story and a drama and so on. But what the ritual is about is creating this circle. We cast a circle and we are creating—hopefully, because it doesn't always happen—a safer place where you can be yourself.

That's what led me into the craft, the new-moon group and this. In 1981, I went to a gathering called Pagan Spirit Gathering. This is out-and-out witchcraft. I looked around and I thought, "These people are doing just about what we did in the new-moon group—I must be a witch." I came back home and decided to use that name. This was not necessarily a popular move. *(Laughs.)* I met Starhawk, who had pub-lished a book called *The Spiral Dance* about how to be a witch. I started learning from her.

I did that until I lost my vision. I've had diabetes for 25 years now, and it can wreak havoc with your vision. I had this year in which I was blind. I was having a lot of eye surgeries, and I didn't have any energy to do anything. That year I had three surgeries. They did help, my vi-sion is restored to usable. But of course it could happen again any minute, any time.

So that was a very intense time of personal transformation, and I was so happy that I managed to get my divorce before I lost my vision. Because if I had still been in that marriage, I would have been taking care of him emotionally around *his* not being able to have any feelings about *my* losing my vision. So thank you, thank you for taking me out of that marriage. My kids were grown, so all I had to focus on was myself. That's what I needed.

There's a Quaker woman who does past-life regression. She did this one, and I found myself on Crete as a priestess—that was no surprise, of course. She said, "What is your name?" And I said, "Antiga." It was not a name I'd ever heard anybody use. I thought to myself, "This is a name I want to hold onto," so I just kept it there. When I was initiated into my first coven, I decided to take this name. A lot of people have a craft name that they use only in circle, but I decided to have it be my name. Antiga seemed to be the more powerful incarnation of Mary Lee.

After I was initiated, one of the other women was studying Greek and she said, "Do you know what that means in Greek?" I said no. She said it means "Next to the earth." So I thought, "Of course, so that's what my name means." A lot of people get my name mixed up with "Antigua," which is a Spanish word meaning old, and as I go into my crone years I'm claiming that as another meaning too. I'm claiming the richness of being old.

In the craft, the Goddess has three aspects: maiden, mother and crone. The first two are self-explanatory, but the crone is the aspect of the Goddess that patriarchy is most frightened of because the crone is the midwife to death. The concept of the crone is a different way of viewing life, where death is a transition to the next, a rebirth into something else. I think this year I'm going to do a crone celebration. *(Laughs.)*

Here's a good example of why I don't think politics and spirituality are separate. At the last solstice we had two covens together. We were talking about rape, and about how our city has the second-highest incidence of rape in the country. We needed to do something that made us feel empowered. So we got together and did this action on Valentine's Day downtown at midnight, a stop-rape action. That came totally out of my spirituality.

It was a good action, the media covered it really well. I did a little magic so that no other news was going on that day. *(Laughs.)* A friend had reminded me of the South American women with their pots and pans, so we asked everybody to come and bring their pots and pans and make noise. It was entitled "Our Silence Breaks at Midnight." The idea was to make a lot of noise, and we did. This was outdoors at midnight in the middle of the winter—can you imagine? And then we had a speakout. Anybody could say anything they wanted to. I said something that was very hard for me to say about something that happened in my marriage, that I could never say before because nobody would believe me. For me, I can't separate politics from spirituality at all.

Feminism certainly cost me my marriage, no question about that. It has cost me connections with my sons—neither one of them want to be in touch with me. It cost me separation from society, not agreeing with the way society is.

The cost of feminism . . . though it has been incredibly high in my life, it was worth the whole cost that I paid. I've gotten to do what I want to do. Every once in a while it gets rough when my food stamps get reduced, you know, but I have a good support group—and if I don't have enough food, somebody brings me some. I've gotten to live the life I wanted to live.

Our Bodies, Our Selves

In 1973 the book Our Bodies, Ourselves, *published by the Boston Women's Health Book Collective, quickly attracted the attention of other feminists. It discussed topics that had previously been ignored or glossed over by standard health texts—rape, assault, drug addiction, teen pregnancy, venereal disease, pornography, prostitution, thalidomide, breast cancer, abortion, forced sterilization. Feminists believe health care is a core issue because, as activist Jeri Rasmussen says, controlling your body is crucial for being in control of your life.*

Many women have found personal satisfaction working in medicine and health. Betty Jerome enjoyed dashing around on streetcars and delivering babies in Chicago tenement houses. Evelina Giobbe credits the women's movement with saving her life: it helped her out of prostitution and gave her a sense of purpose. Elaine Smith grins as she flexes her biceps in the mirror. Judy Mahle Lutter began distance-running to get out of the house, and outdoorswoman Judith Niemi loves helping women gain personal strength through whitewater canoeing.

Elizabeth K. Jerome

When she was a child, Betty Jerome was sent to kindergarten early because she was "small and feisty and into everything." At 70, she still is. A blunt and outspoken pediatrician, she was the medical director of Teen Age Medical Service in Minneapolis from 1970 to 1991. The clinic serves troubled adolescents, primarily girls, who need confidential care for such problems as unintended pregnancy, venereal disease, drug abuse, birth control, and family violence.

I knew when I was five what I wanted to do. I never deviated. There were no doctors in the family, but I just wanted to be a doctor. All my dolls were bandaged up. Every time my father would take a snooze on the couch, I'd bandage him. Or he would sit in a chair, and I'd have him all bandaged up—I'd have bandages on his shoulders, on his legs, on his knees.

There weren't any women doctors at that time, at least none that I knew of. But that didn't make any difference to me. When they said women weren't doctors, I just said, "Well, I'm going to be one," and that was it.

When I went to medical school, I had to go up and be interviewed by the heads of the departments. I later found out that none of the males had to be interviewed by department heads. They always said, "What are you going to do if you get married and have children?" I said, "Well, you just have them." My mother had always worked, as a school teacher, so what was the difference?

I lost a good position at the Cook County Hospital in Chicago by saying I didn't think women were at a disadvantage in medicine. I mean, the powers that be sat there and said to me, "Do you think a woman in medicine can do as good a job as a man?" and I said, "Certainly." They all looked at each other and their eyebrows went up and they said, "Well, we'll take her off the list." And they did.

It was tough. Not only that, they let us know that our grades would be watched carefully and that any girl that dropped below average would be out. There were only 10 of us in a class of 168. I said, "You let me in, and I'll practice." They were afraid that I wouldn't practice when I got through.

When it came time to pick a specialty, I wanted to train for something besides family practice. They said they wouldn't write letters for me unless I'd be a pediatrician. I didn't want to be a pediatrician. I wanted to be a plastic surgeon. *(Laughs.)* I could have been anything.

Then it came time for me to have letters written to get a residency in pediatrics. The head of the department hated women. I knew if I went in and asked him, he would refuse. So I decided that the secretary and I would write the letter. We put it in a whole pile of letters for him to sign, and he signed it and it was sent off. It was right after one of the women physicians had attempted suicide by taking an overdose of pills. He showed up in her hospital room, and told her what a horrible person she was. He walked up to the foot of her bed and said, "You know, you're not only a lousy doctor, you don't even know the fatal dose of sleeping pills." Then he walked off.

There was a maternity hospital in Chicago that did home deliveries. There'd been a big epidemic of diarrhea in Cook County Hospital, so they closed the nursery, took everybody out, and yelled for help. They said, "You people are going to have to do the deliveries at homes."

We'd go out on the streetcar, with our little packs, these two medical students, and we'd deliver a baby. Then we'd call back in, and they'd say in such-and-such a section you've got another baby coming, she's in labor, and we'd run over there on another streetcar. I didn't get back sometimes for 24 hours. I delivered four babies in 24 hours one day.

Always on a streetcar, because no one had an automobile. We didn't have enough money even for food, let alone that. We had a great time. I delivered one baby that was eleven and a half pounds, the biggest kid

I ever saw! I had to call for help. I had to call the resident and he came tearing out and he helped me deliver it.

Some of the places we had to deliver babies were terrible. Down in the basement of buildings, back through dripping hallways. You'd think this was the setting for a horror movie. Water dripping down the walls. It would be cold, and there'd be one spigot of cold water for everybody who lived in the basement to use. There was no place to wash clothes, you couldn't take a bath, and they all lived in one room. I'd have two students with me, and one of them would sit on a chair, the other one sat on a trunk, and I got in bed with the mother. I learned a lot about OB, and I kind of liked it.

I came up to Minnesota to do a rotating internship in 1950. I liked Minneapolis. I liked the people—they were friendly and helpful and warm. The physicians made me feel like I was really something. There were some marvelous women practicing in this town. The doctors liked them, and they were good physicians. This town was really open to women, not like Chicago.

I met my husband here. He was a doctor, and he was 12 years older than I was. He was a sort of staid, proper character and lived with his mother. I told him I would not stop practicing medicine, the only reason I'd consider marrying him was if I could continue practicing. I told him I wasn't going to be a loving, waiting wife, and do a lot of fancy cooking or anything. That was perfectly agreeable to him.

Since he was older, we decided we'd have our kids, just bing, bing, bing. I got pregnant on my honeymoon. I didn't menstruate for three years. *(Laughs.)* At one point I had four children under the age of 5. I had two boys and circumcised them both. Got up out of bed and walked down the hall and did them. I practiced medicine every day, I rarely skipped anything. And the babies were big—the last one weighed ten and a quarter pounds. These were big kids, but I was strong as an ox, you know.

I was in private practice about 27 years. The last few years of that, I began to realize . . . One of my little pediatric patients grew up and was murdered. She was a prostitute, but I kept seeing her as a darling little girl. I couldn't figure out how I had missed it. I mean, what had happened? How could this happen to this girl?

Then I started looking around. A lot of my patients had gotten pregnant, they had screwed up their lives. I paid more attention to the young women in my practice than I did the men. The little girls were so disadvantaged. There was so little expected of them. They had to cook, and reproduce—and that was about it. And I had a lot of mothers who were battered.

I was one of several pediatricians who got together and rented a house to see adolescents. A lot of pediatricians are uncomfortable with teenagers. They don't like people with pubic hair. They're scared to death of them, because that's a grownup. They hadn't had any training for it, I can't blame them. But I just took to it like a duck to water. I liked it so much that I began to spend more time there than I did in my practice.

The first month Teen Age Medical opened, not many people went. We got listed in Youth Emergency Services and got referrals from there. Then there was a girl at the Bridge for Runaway Youth who was a Catholic sister. She was a rebel. She wore slacks and a red turtleneck sweater. I got in touch with her, and she referred to us. Then I'd go downtown to Dayton's* and into the women's room and put, "Need medical help? Call Teen Age Medical Service" on the toilet-stall door. And we spread it by word of mouth. Once word of mouth got going, we had no trouble.

I had to go back and retrain myself for a lot of things. I had to learn about early pregnancy and about doing pelvics. I'd had a pretty good background in that. You just pick it up again. You know, it's just like washing dishes—you never forget. (Laughs.)

There wasn't much then for women. The boys could go somewhere and get care. Almost every teenage clinic in the United States was male, very few females. The girls really needed a place where we weren't going to squeal on them. They were runaways, they were into drugs, they were doing things they had no business doing. Some of them had gotten arrested and they didn't want to be found or known. They didn't give us their right names.

We got younger and younger girls who came in pregnant. By the time I left, I was heartsick. It was so discouraging. I mean, this girl is just 14, she's barely 14, and pregnant. I couldn't believe it. We worked

* A large department store.

on sexually transmitted diseases, we worked on sexual and child abuse. That was a big sleeper, we'd missed most of that. There were so many girls who'd been abused.

Most of the girls who were prostitutes . . . almost every girl who was a prostitute that came in had been sexually abused. There's a tie-up there. Girls don't turn to prostitution because it's a way to make money. That's where they turn because they're desperate and they're already ruined, already soiled. And used. That was such a typical picture, and I kept thinking, "Why don't I know more about this?"

Nobody knows about prostitutes. They don't know what they do. They don't know what their day is like. They don't know how they solicit. We'd get one in, and we'd treat her, and she'd have terrible gonorrhea, just awful pains—and we'd have to take her home. I really felt the women had been short-shrifted all the way around, and we'd better do this job as best we can.

I've never done abortions. I actually wouldn't know how. But we did have to make sure the girls got safe abortions. I remember in 1973 when *Roe v. Wade* came down, I went into the waiting room and just let out a big scream. I was so excited, because we'd been sending kids all over. We were sending them to Japan. I think there was a time when a third of all the planes to Japan were to see a sick grandmother. *(Laughs.)*

There was a criminal abortionist on the North Side, and there was another one down on Lake Street. There were people selling pills to girls. If they'd leave $100 in a brown paper bag . . . there were several girls caught in this one. They'd get the medication left in a pay telephone down in a hotel. Somebody was working it for all it was worth, and girls would leave their $100 in this paper bag. Somebody would come by and leave some aspirin or something. It was amazing the things that happened, but women were desperate.

My mother died of cancer. When she was dying of cancer, she said, "Do you think the Lord is punishing me for having a criminal abortion?" And I got her to tell me a little of what that was like. It must have been terrible, with two kids that were half starving. My mom and dad just trying to squeak by. She was pregnant, and they couldn't afford anything. They couldn't afford a damn thing—and she thought she was being punished.

I think women are better off today than they were. When I heard this week that they finally found some bones they think belong to

Amelia Earhart, I can remember how I cried. That was 1937. And I cried and cried and cried over her. She was such a great figure, standing up there with her scarf loose and her hair in the wind—what a magnificent picture. And then all of a sudden she was gone.

Evelina Giobbe

Evelina Giobbe ran away from home at 13 and became a prostitute in New York City. In 1985 she founded WHISPER—Women Hurt In Systems of Prostitution Engaged in Revolt. She has since moved to the Twin Cities where she operates her counseling and advocacy program in a large, nondescript office building. A gifted speaker, she talks openly about her years in "the life." She is 43.

I don't think I thought it out, I don't think kids do. They run away from their problems. The first night I was away from home, I was raped. The second night I was away from home, I was down in Greenwich Village, where I stayed at a hippie commune, and got gang-raped. So much for free love. The third night I was away from home, kind of wandering around, I met a man. He was very kind to me and befriended me. He saw I was a vulnerable, runaway, dirty little kid. He gave me a place to stay, and I stayed with him probably a couple of weeks.

One day he brought me to another man's house. He said, "Wait for me here, I'll be right back," or something. I had no reason not to believe him, he hadn't done anything. When he left, the other man said he had bought me, that I was to work as a prostitute and turn a profit for him. I said, "You're crazy," and he proceeded to show me just how crazy he was.

He battered me, he sexually assaulted me, he threatened me, he intimidated me—this in a period anywhere from, I don't know, a few days? A week or two? I agreed to be a prostitute. It was horrible, it was really horrible. I didn't know anything about sex, about this. The man who bought me was old enough to be my father, my grandfather.

My life kind of went on like that. When I was about 16, the juve-

nile authorities caught up with me. The best they could do for me was
incarcerate me for being incorrigible. My parents couldn't have me,
even though they wanted me. And I wanted to go home. But the state
didn't want to do anything except punish me. In any event, I was put in
a secure juvenile facility. It was really scary. They put me in Spofford in
the Bronx. The ever-notorious Spofford, and from there moved me to
"kid hell"—the little island across from 59th Street. It's condos now. It
was a juvenile facility then, a little-kid jail.

While I was there, I don't know if they still do this now, but at that
time they had males who were working in the facility. Guards, you
know. And myself along with many of the other girls were sexually
abused by them. The girls weren't all prostitutes—they were deserted
kids, shoplifters, truants, anything. All kind of thrown in there.

In the end they sent me to a girls' home. Like a reform school they
called it then, this home for bad girls, run by the nuns. They had nuns
and psychiatrists, a fate worse than death. The name of the game was,
they were going to lock me up until I was 21. So the first opportunity
I had, I ran away.

I had nowhere to go to, so I went back to New York City, and back
to prostitution again. Had a pimp almost immediately. Essentially that
was my life, that's who I was. I knew that everything my pimp told me
would happen if I tried to get away from him was true. They would
lock me up, they would put me in prison, they would never let me out
again. But it never occurred to anybody to do that to him, or any of
the men who abused me. I was in prostitution until I was in my early
twenties, and became completely addicted to drugs.

Eventually I wasn't worth any money to the pimp, the madams
didn't want me, or the out-call or the brothels in New York. My body
was pretty destroyed—from drugs, from beatings. One day I ran away
from my pimp for the ninety-ninth time, and he didn't bother to come
after me. I ended up being a drug-addict homeless kid. I would do anything not to do prostitution, so I was this street-criminal kid—petty
crimes, stuff like that. Eventually I just kind of burnt out on heroin. I
was really lucky, I ended up in a drug program in California and stayed
there for two years.

When I came out I tried to put my life together. I had no education, I was severely traumatized, I had no socialization skills. I didn't

know how to do anything. I'd never had a job. So I started from zero, literally, at about age 23.

What made you decide to get out of drugs?

I was dying. And I knew it. I was about 90 pounds, about 70 pounds less than I am now. Yeah, I was dying. I mean, the drugs were the only thing that kept me sane. Doing drugs, when you're in prostitution, is just a survival skill. I mean, I never wanted to be a prostitute. It had been like being incarcerated since I was 13 years old. The prostitution was a form of incarceration. The drugs were a form of incarceration—like everything stopped, everything that would make a life for somebody stopped.

Somewhere along the way I got my GED,* and spent the next years just trying to put my life together. Some kind of normal life. I started to work. I didn't know anything about getting a job, but I remember the first job I had. A woman I'd been in a drug program with got me a job as a secretary-receptionist. I knew nothing, nothing. We bluffed my way in. My boss would leave dictation—I didn't even know how to turn on the damn machine—but my friend would come on her lunch break and type these letters for me.

Eventually I got fired, and I would go from job to job, each time getting a little more experience. By the time I was 30 years old I was a production manager, making about as much money as I'm making now. I had a marriage, I lived in Queens, but I was still a mess.

It was different then. At that time I thought prostitution was something I did because there was something wrong with me. Because I was bad, or neurotic. I don't know what I thought, I was filled with guilt about it. Everywhere I looked, the media myths said, "This is a great deal, women make lots of money, they have lots of fun, the sex is good . . ." But that wasn't true for me, and there was nobody to talk to about it.

When I was about 30, a friend of mine was back in school, back in college, and she was taking a women's studies class. She had to go to some women's group and find out what they were doing, so she picked out Women Against Pornography** because she thought it would be kind of like a hoot. She said, "Come on, Evelina, come with me. I'm

* A degree equivalent to a high-school diploma.
** A New York organization founded in the late 1970s.

afraid to go, who knows what these crazy ladies are like." And so we went.

We went. And suddenly, I finally heard somebody talking about the sex industry the way I had experienced it—as abusive, as exploitative, as degrading, and as women being victimized. It was like, I don't believe this, I've found a home here. I was like one of the people you want to have come to your volunteer meetings. "Yes, this is it!" and they volunteer every minute of their lives, for the rest of their lives. And so I did. I immediately started volunteering for them.

Because of that, because of the kind of mentoring I got from women . . . I mean, forget it, I learned from the best. All these women I met were just incredibly wonderful to me. I was amazed that anybody, much less these women who were writers and lawyers and activists and had nice lives—that they knew about what happened to women like me. They validated all my feelings.

While this is happening, and I'm becoming kind of radicalized, my marriage was falling apart. I'm not this insecure, going-to-therapy, guilt-ridden, ex-prostitute wife any more. I'm getting empowered, and I say things like, "No, I don't want to have sex with you, I don't have to, it's my body." *(Laughs.)* Those things start coming out of my mouth. The first year I was pretty obnoxious to everybody, my family, my mom, everybody. I see the young women do it now. Suddenly everything is offensive, everything is sexist, I cannot live in this world any more, nobody understands it. It was heady.

Everyone thought I was wacky. I'd gotten involved with these wacky women who were putting ideas into my head and ruining my marriage. The real deal was, my husband didn't have this guilt-ridden wife trying to be normal any more. I stopped going to therapy, and he started going. I would say things like, "My mother didn't raise me to do your laundry." All that stuff is pretty old-hat now. It's not a bad thing, it's just a funny thing to me, now.

I started doing some speaking on behalf of Women Against Pornography and tore myself into it. I started working full time for them at something like $100 a week. It was hard at the time because I didn't have a lot of support—except from these "crazy" women. But I didn't think of them as crazy, I thought they were wonderful. I thought they could do anything. And *I* got less crazy. I was less fearful. I had less anxiety. The trauma would subside a little.

Women who leave prostitution—it's like coming out of a war. I've talked to grown men who sleep with the lights on, or who don't sleep at all. Who still take drugs to medicate the pain. Prostitution is like this, okay? When your job is to get fucked, that's what you get. Fucked. Literally and metaphorically. You can't fix that. That *is* the job description. How can we say, it's your body, your *self*—and suddenly it's for sale? We take women who have no choices, who sadly may have adapted to this system of abuse . . . and say, "You can choose, you can choose to be a prostitute."

Did you at the time connect pornography and prostitution?

Yeah. Well, yes and no, I take that back. When I was speaking on pornography, very few people knew I'd been a prostitute. Maybe one or two women in the group. But today I'd tell you pornography is the ultimate technological recycling bin of prostitution. That's all it is. Somebody gets to sell you over and over again.

In 1985, there was the U.S. attorney general's Commission on Pornography, and by then I was a real little activist. Had a little bit of a reputation. I'd debated a couple of people. The right people hated me. The pornographers and their attorneys, the American Civil Liberties Union—they all knew me. I'd been out there in the fray and debated them. And I was good, because I was a fighter.

After that, the big turning point was a Women and the Law conference in New York City. There was this big debate, there was all this buzzing about the antipornography feminists and the anticensorship feminists, that was when it was all in its heyday. So we went to this conference, that's when I looked like your generic feminist, buzzed all my hair off, had jeans on. Well, I walk in late, and I walk in on this panel on pornography—and it's the same eight people all over again. Having the same damn debate all over again.

At some point a woman gets up—a woman of color—and she says, "That's a lie, you're just a bunch of middle-class white girls. Prostitutes are free agents, and prostitutes make a lot of money . . ." Well, everybody stops dead. I'm listening to her going on and on. So I raised my hand, and started to say, "You claim to be a prostitute . . ." And then right in my face, she says, "I never claimed to be a prostitute." I took a step toward her and said, "Thank you very much, we can speak for ourselves." And that's how WHISPER started.

The women's press picked up my story and published it in New

York. I started getting letters. Letters saying, "I was a prostitute, and I hated it, too." So I had all these letters, and I said to myself, being naïve, "You know, I have all these letters, and they're sitting there in my drawer. Everybody's got a newsletter—the incest people, women who got raped, the women who have abortions—but nobody ever hears from us. We should have a newsletter." I'm kind of thinking out loud, not having any idea how to do this at all.

So I made up flyers, for this newsletter that didn't exist. And I made up this name WHISPER—Women Hurt In Systems of Prostitution Engaged in Revolt. I was going to take all these letters that everybody wrote to me and paste them up. I typed them up, I laid them out. My original purpose was to educate people about prostitution as a system of violence and abuse.

WHISPER was founded to unmask the lies and the myths about prostitution, we were modelled after Women Against Pornography. We were this feminist organization, and we were going to expose the truth, and we would do it by telling our stories, and collecting women's stories. The time was right.

Were people receptive? Not always. Sometimes. Sometimes not. People would argue with me about it. They would argue with me about my victimization. Let me tell you, do something for me before you do something about your freedom of speech. I was the woman on the other end of the camera. If you understand that prostitution is violence against women, then pornography, taking a picture of a prostitute, does not suddenly become her liberation.

I've worked with Women Against Pornography in New York, and WHISPER here in Minnesota, and we work with the women that nobody cares about. We work with the non-deserving victims. There's a class difference. I see it in terms of the women we serve, women who are seen as a problem. We see it in the battered women's movement, it's not only prostitutes. You're a "good" battered woman if you're middle class and white and your doctor husband beats you up. We want "good" victims to be put forward, so "good" county attorneys will bring cases against "bad" batterers. I mean, that's a reality.

And then there are all the women off Lake Street, who drink too much, and take too many drugs, and are strippers. Women who are prostitutes, women who are problems. Not that the things that happen to them are problems, *they* are problems. It's hard to serve them, they don't get well quick. They're not grateful. They're not clean. They spank their children.

Maybe part of it is that my naïveté is gone. That if you just go out and say this is bad and tell people why, then they'll hurry up and do something. Well, they won't. We have everything in this culture working against us. Every part of this project is working against the culture. You can't do the work we're doing without looking at the interconnections between racism, classism, sexism, sexual violence, battering, male privilege.

For me, the women's movement saved my life. It really did. Everything that I am, and what I've been able to accomplish, I owe to women in the women's movement, I owe to women who've made really big sacrifices, during the second wave of feminism. It's not just what we've accomplished together, but personally—my sanity, my purpose. What makes life worth living.

Jeri Rasmussen

Jeri Rasmussen, 57, lives on a cul-de-sac in a quiet suburban neighborhood, but protesters often surround her house and she has to call the police. She has worked on women's health issues for over 25 years and is a target for the Lambs of Christ, a radical anti-abortion group. She first became involved in the Abortion Rights Council as a volunteer and later became their first staff lobbyist. Since 1988 she has been the director of the Midwest Health Center for Women.

I think my first stirrings on health issues were in 1960. We were in Europe and thalidomide* was being widely dispensed, basically as a sleeping pill. Then in 1962, I became pregnant. It was shortly after the whole thalidomide episode had exploded on the American scene. I was keenly aware of what I could face. I became very curious about what happened to me as a female. I guess that was really the advent of my desire to control my own life.

---

* A drug found to cause severe birth defects when taken by pregnant women.

After my first child was born, I became very active in the natural childbirth association, which was just forming. I was a charter member of La Leche League in Minnesota. I think it's the only meeting where I've ever seen my husband blanch . . . when I had 16 breast-feeding women in our living room. He didn't know if he should avert his eyes, or what.

About half the women who were part of that group became very active in choice and in politics. And maybe a quarter became actively anti-choice. La Leche League was not considered conservative at that time. No one was being encouraged to breast-feed. That was the all-time "no-no." The league was really radical in terms of helping women, it was really a self-help group.

If you go back to the early aspects of women's health, you read about women, midwives, and gypsies being outlawed as criminals for having anything to do with women's health. Midwifery almost disappeared in this country. Childbirth was taken over by male physicians. Not only that, you were usually anesthetized to within an inch of your life.

That's one reason why I got involved in the natural childbirth movement and La Leche League. That was self-determination for what I wanted to do. If I look back on peak experiences, I would always count the birth of my second child. I was totally in control, and I birthed that kid myself. You used to be strapped down, you know. If you tell that to young women now, they can't believe it, that it was quite so primitive. It was primitive then, and it's primitive now when you say it out loud.

I read a lot. I read Dr. Grantley Dick Read from England, his book on natural childbirth. I became really fascinated by it. I read some other articles about childbirth and hypnosis. My first labor had lasted 36 hours, and delivery was only after I was given drugs. I was determined that the second time around wasn't going to be like the first one.

I think seizing control over my own life in that sense . . . *(She trails off.)* I don't think I was ever the same after that. It was in the mid-'60s, but those were very formative years for me. If you don't control your own body, then everything that ever happens to you just happens. You might get lucky or you might get unlucky. But this determines whether or not you're going to live in poverty, what your life is going to be. I felt that very strongly, but at the time I was really bucking the tide.

I'll tell you my ultimate outrage now. I suppose it's a very personal one, because I'm a survivor of breast cancer. My sister-in-law didn't survive. I'm outraged that the rates of survival are no different from what they were 50 years ago. That the rate is now one in nine women who will experience breast cancer. The fact that there's no research, no fundamental research done for breast cancer. That women are left out of the studies. That RU-486* can't get into the country, even though it has the potential to have an impact on other health issues. Yet we spend enormous sums of money on AIDS research.

That says something about our condition as women. Something that has the potential of affecting every one of us nobody pays any attention to, simply because we're female. The first menopause center was opened by a male. A part of me rages against that. I mean, I'm glad he's doing it, and he's a good person. But this one part of me says, "What the hell does he know about a hot flash?"

In 1970, I ran for the state senate. That was at a time when only one woman was in the legislature. So of course there were all these jokes when I ran for office. "Oh my God, they don't have bathrooms," or "They're going to plant some memorial gardens." It was really gross stuff.

Then there was a conference in the spring of '71 where the document, "DFL Women: Present but Powerless," was being presented. Three of us who'd run for office were asked to be part of a panel and speak of our experiences. The keynote speaker was the first woman who'd been elected as mayor of her city, someone from New Jersey. It was really an exciting event.

Our conclusion was that we had to form a woman's caucus and develop our own strength in the party. We began setting up meetings, going out and training women. We went throughout the entire state. And those trips were exciting. They were heady. In some ways it was easy, because it was all so new. And it was so obvious. The enemy was so identifiable: we slept with the enemy, we worked with the enemy, the enemy was in the legislature. It was white males, and they were everywhere.

Those words like "sexual assault" and "battered women," all those words that came into the lexicon later, we thought were just "life."

---

* A drug that induces abortion.

That was the way life was. And then we identified them, named them. Of course the irony is that once we identified them, and were able to get funding for some programs, then they became male issues. Like "family violence" instead of just "battering."

In 1973, we were seeking the ratification of the Equal Rights Amendment, although those of us who were working to decriminalize abortion couldn't work on the ERA. Somehow we would "taint" it. We were kept in closets, it was really bizarre.

Do you sometimes feel like throwing it all over?

Yes. Yes, one does. Especially since I wouldn't identify myself as a true believer. I am only a true believer in the sense that I believe fervently that I could never make a decision for another human being. I believe that people have to have that as a guarantee, as free citizens— the right to make their own determinations about their lives. That's what keeps me going. There are a lot of ups and downs, a lot of disappointments, as well as successes. There's a lot of anger. Sometimes I think, "Oh God, has anything moved along in all this time?" But a lot has. A lot has.

For me personally, the good things have come from within. The struggle I've been engaged in has been a lonely one in lots of ways. I've never been appointed to anything by any governor. I've never really had any kind of acknowledgment. I'm almost a pariah because of my involvement with abortion. In fact, there *are* days when I say, "Oh poor me, woe is me."

But it's also strengthening. You have to look into yourself, your strength—and your spirit becomes really strong. You have to believe you're right in what you're doing or you wouldn't survive it. I know who I am. I know what I'm about. I know what I want to do. I'd like to be 35 again, but I'd like to have the knowledge I have now. Some of the things I'm doing now I couldn't have done without the steps along the way.

Feminism is so much at my core of being. It's nothing I separate out. Everything I see, I see through that prism.

Judy Mahle Lutter

Judy Mahle Lutter is 54. She is president of the Melpomene Institute, a nonprofit national agency for women's health research and education. She ran her first marathon at age 36. As we talk, Judy glances out the window frequently, explaining that the volunteer party is being held in her yard this afternoon, but if it rains she will have to go home and clean house.

I was a fat kid and that has had an influence on some of the things I've done later. I was also a bookworm and that served me well in later life, but was sometimes painful in early life.

I started distance-running—it must have been about 1974—by running around the block. It was entirely to get out of the house. Running was not to lose weight, it was not connected with body at all. It was just feeling confined with three little kids and a husband who worked very long hours. Then I gradually extended my one-block run, and later began to do some racing.

Prior to that I really was solely the wife and mother. That was not a negative, but it wasn't enough. Very quickly after I started running, I started making new demands on my husband. I had been doing all my studying at night or when the kids were in bed, and I never expected him to take any of those responsibilities. So I started saying that on his half-day off he should take the kids. I would study and go to class and be home at noon so he could go in to the office. He said it was pretty amazing, everyone thought he was a divorced dad. *(Laughs.)* There weren't dads taking care of children then.

I also made other suggestions in terms of the way he might relate to the kids and give me some more free time. He went with the three kids to his family in Illinois for the entire weekend so I could finish my master's thesis. I needed the house and I didn't need them, and his parents thought I was absolutely horrible. Anyway, running was definitely the wedge that said I'm an important person, too, and I need time for myself.

I think it was when we left our oldest daughter at college that he thanked me, in a formal way, for the fact that he knew his kids. He said, "An awful lot of my colleagues, especially physicians my age, they don't know who their kids are, and they're dropping them off at school, and that's it." He was never resentful, never pissed about being asked to do things . . . but he never thought of doing things, either, until I brought it up.

When I ran my first marathon in 1975, I was one of only three women. Not too long afterward, I began to get calls from women, hesitantly asking if I'd experienced changes in my menstrual cycle as a result of running. I had not, but I began to wonder if my situation was unusual. My research position at the university made it easy to check on available information. To my surprise, I discovered there was little published on the subject.

A friend and I prepared a questionnaire to see whether women runners were experiencing changes in their menstrual cycles. All of the questions fit nicely on one page. But then we realized we hadn't asked about oral contraceptives. Since this was a critical question, we decided to put it on the top of a second page. Then, so it wouldn't look as though the question was an afterthought, we asked for questions and comments.

Our questionnaire was published in a local running newsletter and then by two national publications. We were astounded to receive over 400 replies. The most amazing thing was that almost everyone filled that nearly empty second page with paragraphs of questions and comments. And lots of them added extra pages expressing frustration that no one seemed to know much about women's health and physical activity.

As we worked on the data, we talked about creating an organization that could help answer the questions women were asking. We thought and talked about these ideas while running together. In 1983, after four years of talking, one of my friends said, "Let's just find out what it takes to incorporate." It was her pushing that got the thing started.

A man we knew mentioned that he had just run across the name "Melpomene" in his research. He told us that she had asked permission to run in the first modern Olympic marathon, held in 1896 in Greece. She was denied official sanction, but she ran anyway. We liked the name. Melpomene was an ordinary person, a runner, who had dared to do something out of the ordinary. Her example had helped other women. Melpomene Institute wanted to achieve the same goals. We settled on the name without thinking of the problems pronunciation or meaning might cause. *(Laughs.)*

The first focus was more on research than it is today. We were lucky early on because Tampax—I knew someone who was a senior vice president. He actually requested that we submit a grant to do amenorrhea research, and we got $45,000 over a three-year period that we had to match. That allowed us to jump into the research arena. We got about 100 members immediately, mostly friends of ours. We produced a newsletter and that quickly became the journal. Many of them were academics or physicians or nurses, and they passed the info along.

In 1984, I appeared on the *Donahue* show with Billie Jean King* and Sister Marion Irvine. Sister Marion Irvine had qualified for the Olympic marathon trials at age 54. The response to that show was amazing, even though I embarrassed my children by saying that running did not cause breasts to sag. Responding to those who wrote became a full-time job for a volunteer for the next two months.

We were in my attic for the first four years. By the second year I wanted to give Melpomene full time, and fortunately didn't need the income. This is something that somebody without a working spouse couldn't do. Then, as more and more people volunteered, that little office was not workable. We moved from one attic room to a second attic room to the hall. At the time we left, we had seven people working, and my attic was about to burst with desks that bumped into each other.

One of our first research projects was exercise and pregnancy. That opened some of the first doors to the medical community. I recall getting phone calls from physicians who needed information quickly. "I'm giving a talk next week" was a typical comment. "I'm not an expert on this subject and am having trouble finding information. Can you help?"

We also did early projects looking at osteoporosis. With the menopause project, later, we were lucky and smart—we did it just before everyone decided they had to talk about the menopause. One of the

---

* A well-known tennis player.

best projects we've done is on girls, which is kind of ongoing, looking at the role of physical activity in their lives.

There are still a lot of times when I think things are unfair. That Melpomene struggles the way it does, that this work is undervalued. We do holistic research. We don't just look at your hormone level, we look at what else is going on in your life. NIH* certainly . . . anyone who's going to have big research bucks looks at us and almost gets hysterical laughing.

Now we have a staff of eight people. And last year there were 7,000-plus hours donated by volunteers and about 6,000 staff hours. We've been concerned about diversity from the beginning. We got into the issue of women with disabilities, because in terms of physical activity and sport they have not been given the kind of attention they deserve. We try to broaden people's perspective of what it is to be physically active. Whenever I organize a panel that deals with the marathon or something, I always include a wheelchair athlete. And last year we got some fellowships. Three individuals came up with $5,000 each and then we got a match from our members, and we specifically designated one fellowship to be for a woman of color.

Initially we were about 70 percent research and 30 percent education. It's flipped now. We did conferences from the very beginning. From those conferences we developed materials and then realized that could also be beneficial in terms of our bottom line, so we've sold packets on specific topics. Our book, *The Bodywise Woman,* came out in 1990, and our breast-cancer handbook came out in 1992.

Survival continues to be a problem. That's the hardest thing for me personally and for the other people who work here. They work really hard, and the pay is decent—$18 to $20 an hour—but they've been here a long time. I see a lot of people on my staff, myself included, being a little bit overwhelmed too much of the time, sometimes feeling like you're not doing a good job because there is absolutely too much to do. That frustrates me. I think we're thriving most of the time, but . . . we had this mini-meeting yesterday to look at the damn bottom line. We've never not paid salaries, that won't be an issue here, but how many paper clips you can buy is.

* National Institutes of Health.

Elaine Smith*

Elaine is in her thirties. She became disabled as the result of a childhood farm accident, and she gets around in a wheelchair. She has been involved with several women's groups, including an organization for women with disabilities.

The first years of my life were spent on a farm. To my brothers and sisters, my disability was natural, normal. They didn't make any excuses for me, they didn't have double standards. I was always a bit of a tomboy. If they went out to the rockpile, I went out to the rockpile. If they climbed in the hayloft, I'd climb in the hayloft. If it was up a flight of stairs, we all did it together. It was no big thing.

But after we moved to town ... The first couple of hours I was out playing, I remember a woman coming out of her house with a little blanket, because she thought I should cover myself up. I remember people pointing, staring. I was becoming a spectacle, and I had never been a spectacle before.

I remember trying to climb a tree in my front yard. All the other kids were climbing, and I have a very strong upper body. A couple of days later, my mom said, "You can't go outside the house anymore if I'm not home." She said the neighbor lady had reported her to the county social worker for neglect. The neighbor thought it was horrible that I was outside trying to do something.

Mom got paranoid, so she put restrictions on me. I rebelled. I remember once screaming, "Why? Why?" It wasn't the disability that was causing my anger and frustration, because up to that point it was no issue. It was when I started to be treated differently. It was a hard time in my life, staying in my house when everyone else was outside.

My dad was killed in another farm accident when I was young. My

* Not her real name.

mom is a wonderful woman, but she had eight kids. She worked real hard bringing in the money. She was too tired to deal with some things, so my brothers ruled the roost.

It was such an injustice, even to a little kid of 12 and 13. The boys would sit and watch television and we girls would have to fix them something to eat. Or they would walk through the room and throw a shirt at us and say, "Go iron this, I need it for tonight." That kind of crap.

I remember thinking, "I swear to God, I'm never going to put up with this when I grow up, never again. If I have to be single for the rest of my life, I will never put up with this stuff again." So far, I've not put up with it—but I'm single, too. None of the girls in my family married, I think we all made that same vow. There's a lot of anger there.

I went to the university and ended up in women's studies. I took women's studies because I needed to connect, I needed to make sense of what was going on. Why were women expected to do this or that? Why weren't people with disabilities employed? I knew there had to be some answers, and I found them in women's studies.

A lot of the discrimination women encounter is similar to the discrimination disabled people encounter. Unlike race discrimination, which can be hostile and violent, most of the discrimination women and disabled people encounter is overprotective. "Let me take care of you, let me make that decision for you, you should be grateful that I'm looking out for you." A lot of people who are disabled and being discriminated against, as well as a lot of women, don't even realize it.

Women's studies provided a lot of insight and direction for me. There were no disability studies, but I remember reading things and thinking, "That's true of disabled folks, too." That was probably 1977 or 1978.

Later on, I was in an organization for women with disabilities. A wonderful organization, I just loved it. We were in operation for several years, mid to late '80s. The organization isn't around anymore, but there's still an incredible need out there. Women with disabilities have a lot of the same issues that non-disabled women have, but we also have some issues that are specific to us.

It felt really empowering to be in that group. A lot of us lived next door to each other in what we call our "gimp ghettos," the housing complexes that were built for people with disabilities. But a lot of folks had never shared because there's so much shame with disability, so many bad feelings.

Even today, if you see a person with a disability in a movie, they're not strong, powerful decision-makers. They're not moms. They're the victim, and the entire plot is for some non-disabled white male to come in and save them from despair and suicidal tendencies. I'm waiting for that movie I want to direct, where the woman with the disability rides in on the horse and saves the day.

We were trained to be nice, pleasant, and grateful above all. So people didn't complain, share bad experiences. People didn't report people who abused them. People got left for hours on the toilet, and didn't say a word because they were to be grateful for what little they got. If that happened, well obviously it's because you're lesser of a person and should expect that.

A lot of women had never talked about their goals, or wanting to learn something, do something, be somebody. They were afraid that people would laugh at them, not take their ambitions seriously.

We also found a whole bunch of women who were violently assaulted and had never done anything about it. Never reported it. Women with disabilities who had been raped and who had had children. Women who had been raped and *had* reported it, and who had been told by the police to shut up and go home. It was incredible, the stories of women who'd gone through these experiences. Forced sterilization, or having their children taken away from them. And we're talking now . . . we're not talking 50 years ago.

Women with disabilities, we're still the lowest, way at the bottom, in the statistics. For people with disabilities, it's a hundred times—a hundred times!—more difficult for us to get employment. Yet we are one of the most highly educated protected-class groups in the country because of all the money that goes into rehabilitation.

There was a five-year study of voc rehab* conducted in the 1980s. The study demonstrated massive gender discrimination. Voc rehab has a "home-keeper" status which is considered a "successful closure." The study showed that a whole lot of women were being rehabilitated as homemakers. But there were never any disabled *men* being closed out as homemakers.

* Vocational rehabilitation.

In tenth grade I remember meeting my first voc-rehab counselor. He's going to come in and help me get through the rest of my life, right? Get me an education, some training. I go into this room, he looks at me and talks to me for a few minutes, and then he laughs and says, "You're going to make a dynamite secretary." He had no idea what I wanted to do with my life.

Women with disabilities, many people don't think of us as sexual. And we don't fit today's image of what a woman should be. I'll never achieve the Barbie-doll look . . . not that I have any desire to achieve Barbie status! But I know dynamite women with disabilities who don't date—because men aren't interested in women who don't match that standard.

Our bodies aren't made that way. My shoulders are broad, my biceps are large. I'm very strong. And I'm not ashamed of it, I'm proud of it. Sometimes I sit in front of a mirror and flex my muscles. *(Grins.)* But men don't find that appealing. It's like, hey, I'm not going to compromise my independence and my mobility because somebody doesn't think I'm cute in a T-shirt.

It's easier for disabled men to date. Many men with disabilities do okay because women are much more accepting. Many women I know who are married to disabled men, they're looking for a commitment, somebody to build their lives with. But most women I know with disabilities are not married, and many are not dating.

There's also the violence issue. We're perceived as vulnerable, even though many of us wouldn't describe ourselves that way. Rape, abuse —not only by family members but by attendants, people who are hired to take care of you, institutional abuse, it's very prevalent. That's clearly a problem which needs to be dealt with.

And as with women in the early days, society doesn't expect disabled people to make demands. They don't expect us to crawl up the capitol steps or tie ourselves to busses. They get mad at us when we do, because we're not being nice. Historically, they would send us a check every month, and we would go home and shut up and be grateful. But we're not grateful anymore, we don't want to be nice anymore.

After my women's studies course I joined women's groups, but I wasn't real comfortable there. When I'm in a women's group, I don't get recognized as a woman, I get recognized as a person with a disability. It's always, "Is this ramp okay?" or "Is that bathroom going to work for you?" or "Can I get you some coffee?"

That's another thing about women, caretaking. Once I had a job with a bunch of wonderful women. But they had such a double standard for me. I remember once I went to get a cup of coffee. I got back to my desk, and I practically got a standing ovation. Because I got my own coffee! It reminds me of when women first entered the workplace. Men had low standards for women, the slightest accomplishment was praised.

Then there's abortion. I'm 100 percent pro-choice, that's clearly not in question here. But sometimes it's hard for me. When a woman tells me she's going to have an abortion because the fetus might be disabled, I'm real torn. It's like, I know it has to be her decision. But as a person with a disability, I want to explain that it's not that horrible.

It's not horrible at all. I don't cry at night wishing I could walk. In fact when I was growing up, what I heard about walking was that it was painful. I remember my brothers and sisters crying because they had to walk to the store or walk to school, people constantly complaining about their backs or their feet or their knees . . . People didn't walk into a room saying "God, it's good to walk." People came in saying, "God, my feet hurt." So all these years I've felt, "Hey, I got around something!" *(Laughs.)*

I'm proud of having a disability, adjusting to a disability, learning from that disability. Without my disability, I wouldn't have the understanding of humanity, the perspective that I have. So it can be a real enlightening and positive experience, to acquire a disability. And it's part of me.

But I also get angry. And I get real pumped up. I sleep with a shotgun next to my bed because I'm not going to be anybody's victim. I live alone, and I want to feel comfortable living alone.

I get angry all the time. I figure that's why I've gotten as far as I have. Because anger is my fuel, my reason for getting up half an hour early in the morning so I can get that extra letter out. Many times, what drives me is my anger, my sense of justice, my need to fix things.

I have wonderful friends who know that their primary purpose in life is to listen to me yell and scream . . . and give me a beer.

Judith Niemi

My mother tells me that when I was seven, she'd always said she would never become a Girl Scout leader, never, because there were only two ways you could get out. Have a heart attack or have a baby. *(Laughs.)* She said, "I'm too old for one and too young for the other." But she got the Girl Scout magazine, and there was a picture of a little girl building a campfire in a little Brownie outfit, and I said, "That's me, Mommy, isn't it?" And she thought, "Oh Lord, okay," and she became a troop leader so I could become a Girl Scout.

Judith Niemi runs an outdoor business, Women in the Wilderness. Since the late 1970s, her career has been a balance between running a women's outdoor program, teaching outdoor skills, and writing. She says, "I try to spend more of my time writing, but that's much harder than portaging canoes." She is 51.

Some years ago I went on a canoe trip with men for the first time—a former student of mine and three teenage boys—just because I couldn't find any women friends who wanted to canoe this particular route. So this guy came up and said, "Do you think we can stand each other for a two-week canoe trip?" and I said, "Yeah, let's go."

But I was so bored. They could not have been nicer, but there was no one to talk to. That got me thinking, "Why aren't there other women here?" I can remember sitting on a rock saying, "I think I'm going to start some kind of program to teach women outdoor skills." One of the 16-year-old boys said, "Oh great, I'll come along and carry the old ladies' packs!" I said, "Oh no, Chuck, you've got it all wrong here. That is *not* what I had in mind."

There weren't any women's outdoor programs in the country at the time, but it seemed like a very natural idea. It sort of grew slowly.

We put out some flyers, and had just a few Boundary Waters* trips the first year.

I remember one of the early trips. Somebody called and asked, "Do you take moms? Do you take grandmothers?" I said, "We sure do." It was my first year of doing trips, and I can remember getting nervous because I realized we had one woman in her thirties whom I didn't know at all, a woman who saw a notice at her church and wanted to know if we took grandmothers, two young, radical, lesbian feminists who were traveling around the country together, and a couple of others. I thought, "Oh-oh, how's this mix going to work?"

It worked fine. The two young, radical, lesbian feminists turned out to be young Quakers, the sweetest people you could imagine. Early on, I got the women who I thought might be nervous about this to relax. I'd say, "The moose don't care who you are." I've always found that this is a non-issue. Everybody gets to be exactly who they want to be. You see people get off the plane, and they have their guarded city faces on, and you know that in a day or two everybody's going to be looking healthy and tanned and themselves. Their emotions will be there in their faces.

What I've found is that women are really cooperative, because they aren't competing with nature. "You think you can't keep up? Who's there to keep up with? It's just us." We try to arrange the trips so people who want to go fast can do it sometimes, and people who want to be laid back can do that sometimes. Nobody gets to do what they want all the time. But everyone's wishes get respected.

Some of the first women who came, their brothers got to go on trips but they didn't. It was something they'd been deprived of learning. And then there were all these women who'd gone when they were little Girl Scouts. Why is it people think 14-year-old girls can go camping and canoeing, but adult women aren't capable of doing it? On their own, as they say? You know, "Are you girls all alone?" *(Laughs.)*

You can have trips with both men and women in them, but they're men's trips with women along. The men define how it's going to be. Women's trips, if it's all women, are more playful. The conversation is more open and intimate. And they're much less goal-focused. I didn't start off saying, "We're a feminist group and we'll do it this way." But

* A wilderness area.

by following my intuition about what I wanted and what other women wanted, it all evolved naturally.

If you have a mixed-group outdoor trip, men define it and don't even know they're defining it. They think this is the norm. And certain of them are, in fact, American cultural norms. "What are we doing? We're challenging nature." The reason for doing an outdoor trip is to improve your character, build fiber and all that stuff, like Outward Bound programs designed to do certain things for teenagers—teenage males in fact. And then assuming that's the norm for the world.

There's nothing wrong for women wanting to do that, but it's not what the outdoors is about. We go there for its own sake. It's much harder for men to drop the competitiveness. My brother-in-law told me once—he'd gone on a trip—he said, "You know, the women had more fun." I asked why, and he said, "Well, when a woman learns something new, she can say, 'Wow! Look what I did!'" He told me, "We kind of feel the same way, but guys aren't supposed to say that. Having to be in charge, having to pretend you know everything . . ."

Women go on the trips not only for the physical activity. I think it's a combination of a draw to nature, wanting to get closer to the natural world, and feeling like they've lost some abilities. It's not the standard vacation of taking a break, but it's living out a part of themselves they don't get in the city—more adventurous, or silly and rowdy sometimes.

It's getting a chance to fulfill parts of yourself that you know are there, and then it becomes addictive. Once you know who you can be, a lot of women say they're happier, or they go back to feeling some way they did before they became adolescents and closed down. It's wanting to get to be who they know they can be, and that bond with other women, and that bond with nature—all those things.

Look at this as a metaphor: How many women come on trips and say, "But I've never been allowed to paddle stern"? It's this big mystique to steer a canoe. There are actually lots of reasons why women should be there paddling, but it's the "power" position, as men perceive it. So that's fun to do. How do you work together, particularly with mixed couples; how do you canoe together as equal partners? Not like, she sits in the bow and spaces out, and he does all the real work.

Generally we teach solo canoeing, little teeny boats, elegant, the dancing form of canoeing. And we teach whitewater. That's in some ways the most . . . you can't keep women down once they've learned to do whitewater! It brings out all the rowdiness, the total living in the moment. It doesn't have to be dangerous. Of course, you can make anything dangerous, but if you're careful, it's a big adrenaline rush with little risk.

It's rich in metaphor, because we always say the river is your third partner. You're not competing with the river. She's your third partner, and you've got to pay attention to her. All these old metaphors about going with the flow, and being in the moment. It's the dance, not the competition. It's not just shooting the rapids and toughing it out. It's the dance, and responding to nature and being respectful. It's something women really take to.

There's this perceived risk in outdoor things, but in fact it's a lot less risky than everyday life. What about driving the freeway? Or parking in ramps? When you're out in nature you're not in control, but at least nature is not out to *get* you. It's you and your judgment, a neutral sort of thing. The city is a hostile place, so the risks in fact are bigger. We've been taught to think it's risky for us to get out of line by going in the woods and doing things. It's risky because we don't have policemen around? 9-1-1 is the absence of risk? Come on! *(Laughs.)*

One of the things we say is, it's okay to be scared. Say it. People don't get laughed at to be scared. I remember one woman, she started to cry one day.

We'd been running rapids, and she said, "You're all having such a good time, and I'm scared shitless." So we stopped and talked about it. I can't say, "Don't be scared." All I can say is, "Here's the level of physical danger you're dealing with"—although that doesn't make her fear go away. But her talking about her fear was the important thing.

A week later, she was one of the boldest of anybody, just whooping it up in rapids, which were no more or less dangerous than they had been. Then she told me a fascinating thing later, some months later when I saw her. She came back from the trip and said it was like there was so much fear and peril going on in her life that she'd put it all on the water. She realized she'd been doing that. She'd brought the fear with her. And by overcoming the fear of the whitewater, she came back and changed a lot of things in her life. The fear was gone, she had worked it out.

I'm one of the lucky people because I get to work in one of the positive branches. I admire the people who are in there taping up the wounds, but I think it's also important to . . . What we're doing is not the remedial stuff. It's like validating the strength, and setting up the situation where women build their own strength, and get excitement, and take courage from each other. That's incredible luck. There aren't many parts of the women's movement that are not in there fighting the problems.

The women who come on our trips are not free of any of that. They've been through the same problems as anyone else. But the trip is also celebrating the strength. There's an incredible political power that comes out of joy, and strength. It's really a privilege to be around that.

GLOSSARY

AFDC—Aid to Families with Dependent Children, a government-assistance program.

BPW—National Federation of Business and Professional Women's Clubs. A membership organization formed in 1919 "to promote full participation in the workforce, equity, and economic self-sufficiency for working women."

Council on the Economic Status of Women—A Minnesota legislative committee, later a commission, created in 1976 to study and make recommendations to the full legislature.

DFL—Democratic-Farmer-Labor Party, Minnesota's Democratic Party, formed in 1944 by the merger of the Democratic and the Farmer-Labor Parties.

DFL Feminist Caucus—A political membership organization formed in 1972 to support women's issues and candidates who subscribe to feminist principles.

ERA—Equal Rights Amendment, a proposed amendment to the U.S. Constitution stating, "Equality of rights under the law shall not be denied nor abridged by the United States or by any State on account of sex." The amendment was never adopted.

Human Rights Commission/Department—Agencies charged with enforcing antidiscrimination laws in city and state government in Minnesota, similar to fair employment agencies in other states.

LWV—League of Women Voters, a nonpartisan political organization formed to encourage informed citizen participation in all levels of government.

Minnesota Women's Consortium—A coalition of organizations supporting women's rights, formed in 1980. In 1992 it had 175 member organizations representing 180,000 persons.

MWPC—Minnesota branch of the National Women's Political Caucus.

NOW—National Organization for Women, a membership organization formed in 1966 to "take action to bring women into full participation in society . . . in truly equal partnership with men."

NWPC—National Women's Political Caucus, a nonpartisan political organization formed in 1971 that supports women's issues and encourages women to run for political office.

SDS—Students for a Democratic Society, a radical organization of student activists in the 1960s.

Title IX—Federal law passed in 1972 prohibiting sex discrimination in any federally assisted educational program or activity, including athletics.

WEAL—Women's Equity Action League, a membership organization working to help women through "education, legislation, and litigation."

YWCA—Young Women's Christian Association, a nonsectarian organization established in the United States in 1866 that advances the physical, intellectual, and spiritual interests of young women.

INDEX OF NAMES

ACKNOWLEDGMENTS

Our deepest thanks go to the women who contributed to this book. They were generous both with their time and with their thoughts. Remembering times of change, and exposing private moments to public view, is not easy. We are grateful for their honesty and openness, as well as their unfailing good humor in describing themselves and their lives.

Those we interviewed but whose names do not appear on these pages also contributed to the book by expanding our understanding of feminism and enriching our lives. Only time and space constraints prevented us from including them by name, and we hope they will find echoes of their experiences here.

At early stages of this project, Mary Ziegenhagen gave us invaluable advice and encouragement. Other early readers also kept us going with their wise counsel: Ann Regan of the Minnesota Historical Society; Ann Ryan of The Loft; our sisters, Sally Nelson and Judy Greenberg; and Bonnie's parents, Peace and Miles Watkins.

Special support and encouragement came from our husbands, Ken Rothchild and John Zakelj. They read the stories in many variations, made helpful suggestions, gave pep talks when needed, and never lost faith in our ability to bring the project to completion. We are fortunate indeed to be married to men who "get it."

Heartfelt thanks also go to the Minnesota Historical Society Press for its willingness to put a human face on history. In particular, we are indebted to Jean Brookins, who provided enthusiastic support, Ann Regan, who helped shape the book, and to our editor, Marilyn Ziebarth, who skillfully shepherded the manuscript through the editing and production process.

Two organizations, the Minnesota Women's Consortium and the Commission on the Economic Status of Women, sustain the feminist spirit for us and many others. Our thanks go to Aviva Breen, Chris Halvorson, Cheryl Hoium (and her treasured Rolodex), Gloria Griffin, Grace Harkness, Dede Wolfson, Annie Lee—and, above all, Lorraine Hart—for cheerfully tracking down names, addresses, phone numbers, and stray historical facts. In addition, the Groupies—Cheryl, Charlotte, Carol, and Mary—cheered us on at many times of crisis, and Patty Balsimo of the White Hat restaurant laughed and kept the coffee coming.

We also acknowledge a debt to author Studs Terkel. His use of oral history to illuminate an era served as an inspiration and a model. We have shamelessly copied his format and hope he will forgive us, knowing that imitation is the sincerest form of flattery.

Last, but far from least, we are grateful to Senator Linda Berglin. Her moral integrity, her political skills, and her steadfast support for all women are a shining example of how one woman can make a difference in the lives of many. We dedicate this book to her.

Bonnie Watkins & Nina Rothchild

ABOUT THE AUTHORS

BONNIE WATKINS graduated from college in 1973 and became a hippie farmer, clerical worker, and co-founder of Women in State Employment. She staffed the Minnesota governor's Open Appointments Commission in 1976 and was assistant director of the legislature's Council on the Economic Status of Women from 1977 to 1984. She managed pay equity compliance for 1,600 local governments from 1984 to 1989, when she worked at the state Department of Employee Relations. She is now a freelance writer and a director of a neighborhood-nurse program. Among her writing projects have been *Pay Equity and Minnesota Public Libraries,* published by the American Library Association in 1993, and *Toward a Universal Family Allowance,* published by the Child Care Workers Alliance in 1994. Watkins, 46, lives with her husband and two children, Johnny and Cecelia, in St. Paul.

NINA ROTHCHILD describes herself as a "homemaker turned bureaucrat." A local school-board member in the early 1970s, she advocated for girls' athletics and wrote *Sexism in the Schools: A Handbook for Action* (1973). She was director of the Council on the Economic Status of Women from 1976 to 1983 and commissioner of the state Department of Employee Relations from 1983 to 1990, overseeing the nation's first comprehensive pay equity program. She has spoken on women's issues throughout the United States and Canada and has received awards from the National Governor's Association (1984), the National Committee on Pay Equity (1987), and the American Society for Public Administration (1990). Rothchild, 66, has three children and five grandchildren. She and her husband divide their time between Mahtomedi, Minnesota, and Fire Island, New York.